I0815284

# SUNSET LIMITED

# SUNSET LIMITED

## AN AUTOBIOGRAPHY OF CREOLE

WENDY A. GAUDIN

LOUISIANA STATE UNIVERSITY PRESS
BATON ROUGE

Published with the assistance of The Noland Fund

Published by Louisiana State University Press
lsupress.org



Manufactured in the United States of America
First printing

DESIGNER: Michelle A. Neustrom
TYPEFACES: Ten Oldstyle, text; Veneer Clean, display
PRINTER AND BINDER: Sheridan Books, Inc.

FRONT JACKET: Photograph of Marietta Roussel, the author's maternal grandmother, New Orleans, 1928, from the author's family collection. Map from the David Rumsey Map Collection, David Rumsey Map Center, Stanford Libraries.

Unless otherwise indicated, photographs are from the author's family collection.

Portions of this book first appeared, in somewhat different form, as follows: chapter 1 as "The Marian Apparition," *Indiana Review* 41, no. 2 (Winter 2019); chapter 4 as the preface to *Family Legacies: Our History Told through Stories and Tributes* (2020), published by the Louisiana Creole Research Association; chapter 6 as "Taxonomy," in *New South Journal* 14, no. 1 (2021); chapter 12 as "Topophilia" in *About Place Journal* 5, no. 1 (May 2018); portions of chapter 13 in "Day One in Nông Sơn," *Rappahannock Review* 5, no. 2.

Cataloging-in-Publication Data are available from the Library of Congress.

ISBN 978-0-8071-8365-6 (cloth: alk. paper) — ISBN 978-0-8071-8439-4 (pdf) —
ISBN 978-0-8071-8438-7 (epub)

*For my beloved ancestresses,*
*Marietta Roussel and Rita Roux,*
*Ida and Elizabeth, Aliska and Rosella,*
*and for my cherished grandfathers,*
*Augustus Lawrence Burns and John Norah Gaudin:*
*all of them forever tying me*
*to Louisiana*

We all need histories that no history book can tell.

—MICHEL-ROLPH TROUILLOT

# CONTENTS

List of Illustrations . . . . . . . . . . . . . . . . . . . xi
A Note on Language and Naming . . . . . xiii

Introduction . . . . . . . . . . . . . . . . . . . . . . . . . 1
1 The Marian Apparition . . . . . . . . . . . . . . . 18
2 A Blond Roux Is the Lightest One . . . . . . 35
3 Sun Fire Leo . . . . . . . . . . . . . . . . . . . . . . . . 51
4 Holy Name . . . . . . . . . . . . . . . . . . . . . . . . . 67
5 Sunset Limited . . . . . . . . . . . . . . . . . . . . . . 86
6 Taxonomy . . . . . . . . . . . . . . . . . . . . . . . . . 105
7 The Habit and the Ghost Shirt . . . . . . . . 121
8 A Work of Fiction . . . . . . . . . . . . . . . . . . 134
9 Mounds . . . . . . . . . . . . . . . . . . . . . . . . . . . 153
10 "My Father Was a French Doctor". . . . 166
11 Miss Audrey's World . . . . . . . . . . . . . . . 183
12 Topophilia . . . . . . . . . . . . . . . . . . . . . . . . 196
13 Another Country . . . . . . . . . . . . . . . . . . . 211
14 Time Is a Wheel . . . . . . . . . . . . . . . . . . . 227
Conclusion . . . . . . . . . . . . . . . . . . . . . . . . . 242

Acknowledgments . . . . . . . . . . . . . . . . . . 249
Notes . . . . . . . . . . . . . . . . . . . . . . . . . . . . . 253
Bibliography . . . . . . . . . . . . . . . . . . . . . . . 263

# ILLUSTRATIONS


Creole Wedding . . . . . . . . . . . . . . . . . . . . . . . . xvi
May Crowning . . . . . . . . . . . . . . . . . . . . . . . . . 17
Of the Singular Name . . . . . . . . . . . . . . . . . . . . 23
Sweet Little Mary . . . . . . . . . . . . . . . . . . . . . . 25
Look with Your Mouth . . . . . . . . . . . . . . . . . . . 33
Pale as Wax . . . . . . . . . . . . . . . . . . . . . . . . . . . 34
FMC . . . . . . . . . . . . . . . . . . . . . . . . . . . . . . . . 43
Of the Cathedral School . . . . . . . . . . . . . . . . . . 48
Sun Fire Leo . . . . . . . . . . . . . . . . . . . . . . . . . . 50
Two Pullman Porters . . . . . . . . . . . . . . . . . . . . 58
Venice, California, May 10, 1930 . . . . . . . . . . . 59
A Man . . . . . . . . . . . . . . . . . . . . . . . . . . . . . . . 66
College of Pharmacy Graduates from Xavier University of Louisiana . . . . . . . . . 83
California Creoles . . . . . . . . . . . . . . . . . . . . . . 85
Pioneers . . . . . . . . . . . . . . . . . . . . . . . . . . . . . 94
Professor . . . . . . . . . . . . . . . . . . . . . . . . . . . . 104
Fine, Nut-Colored Men . . . . . . . . . . . . . . . . . . 112
Speak With Your Eyes . . . . . . . . . . . . . . . . . . . 120
Braids . . . . . . . . . . . . . . . . . . . . . . . . . . . . . . 123
Superwoman and Child . . . . . . . . . . . . . . . . . . 127
Blood Math . . . . . . . . . . . . . . . . . . . . . . . . . . . 142
Foremothers . . . . . . . . . . . . . . . . . . . . . . . . . . 151
Can We Call Them Creoles? . . . . . . . . . . . . . 182
The Gaudin Girls in Easter Suits . . . . . . . . . 241
Past and Future Tense . . . . . . . . . . . . . . . . . . 243

Creole: a person of European or African descent
who is born in the colonial world

Creole: a person of French or Spanish descent
who is born in the colonial world

Creole: a person of blended Latinate, African, and/or Indigenous
descent who is a product of the colonial world

Creole: a person native to Louisiana whose race may vary

Creole: a Francophone, Catholic person raised in Louisiana

Creole: a Louisiana-born, light-skinned, mixed-race
person who easily passes as white

Creole: a Black person from Louisiana who has
negligible European or Indigenous ancestry

Creole: a person from Louisiana who has many ethnicities
represented in their ancestry, but whose blackness
is the primary source of pride

# A NOTE ON LANGUAGE AND NAMING

Throughout this text, there is language and there are terminologies that deserve a note.

Because some of the main subjects of this book are ethnicity, ancestry, race, and color, there are plentiful references to phenotype throughout. This is the hard work of the writer: describing the vast and subtle differences in skin color with words that do not do justice and leave us asking "light compared to what?" or "which shade of brown?" or "what is it to have fair or bright or dark skin?" Describing skin color by using other comparative references—such as food, or earth, or bark, or feathers—may be off-putting to some readers. "Nut-colored" is a description that I heard from more than one Creole elder to describe themselves and others. It also does not do justice, since nuts come in many shades of brown. So do soils, and seeds, and trees, and birds, and toads—and humans. A friend asked me, "Why not just say brown because it is melanin that you're writing about, not the bark of a tree?" This advice was taken in many revisions of this text. References to skin color abound not because of a personal obsession with the subject: these references reflect Creoles' concerns with skin color, as racialized people living in a society that was, in part, founded on race, racial difference, racial preference, and status. The subtle gradations located within the spectrum that we call "brown" could make a tangible difference in a person's life, their identity, and perhaps their racial categorization in historical records. Descriptive terms are part of the creative process.

Racial epithets appear in altered form several times in this text, as do the words "Colored," "Negro," "Negress," and "Negroes." These words are used when quoted by others, and I have left them unchanged as they are the words used to convey a specific and timely meaning. The word "Colored" appears in quotes to convey a specific social category or context in which "Black" would likely not have been used. For example, the "White" and "Colored" sections of a streetcar: those detestable signs did not typically say "Black passengers," because "Black" is a term of empowerment originating in African-descended populations, not in the lexicologies of the state.

In an effort to address a syncretic population that has been assigned different racial labels across time, I make several orthographic choices in this text. The terms "Black," "African American," "Afro-Creole," "Mulatto," "brown," "of color," "white," "mixed-race," "mixed-heritage," "mixed," "multiracial," "Métis," and "métis" are used throughout. Choosing terms that might (or might not) be better (or differently) suited to individuals, I grapple with race and racial language within this text.

*Creole* will appear as "Creole," "Afro-Creole," and "Creole of Color." This is an acknowledgment that *Creole* is an ethnic term that has historically been used by people who were assigned different racial labels or who chose different racial labels for themselves. "Afro-Creole" and "Creole of Color" are used to remind the reader that there are Creoles who center or highlight their African ancestry within their multifaceted Creole identity. There are others who do not. Why there is the need to make that known will be revealed in the following pages.

Finally, acknowledgment of speakers will appear differently throughout this text. Some individuals' names have been changed due to the sensitivity of the material. Some people were unreachable in the years since I originally interviewed them; some people have passed away since we spoke. Some agreed to share their memories with me only if I altered their names. Others were more than happy to be quoted. Some anecdotal material came from people whose names were not recorded. One person will never be named in my writing. The changing of names throughout is, in part, a reflection of the challenges of talking about race and personal history.

In one early interview from the years prior to Hurricane Katrina, the subject told me to "turn that thing off," in reference to the tape recorder, "so I can tell you a story." The need to alter some names will become apparent as the reader continues through this book.

# SUNSET LIMITED

Creole Wedding. My parents' wedding photo, Holy Name of Jesus Catholic Church.
Los Angeles, 1958.

# Introduction

We come from rivers and bayous, from marshes and deltas, from flowering okra gardens and sugarcane fields, from palmetto forests and coastal grasslands. We are the sharp edges of oyster-shell streets and the red dust of brick roads. We embody the threatened islands in the Gulf, our languages in need of rescue, and our bodies, the curving levees that follow the curls of the Lower Mississippi River. We are Louisiana: the neglected backwoods of France's western kingdom, the unwrapped gift to Imperial Spain, the cheap procurement by the expansive empire of the United States. As are we, Louisiana is a patchwork of territorial binaries: the north Anglo, English speaking, and Protestant; the south Latinate, French speaking, and Catholic; the north, hilly with piney woods, and the south, below sea level and sinking. We are the indeterminate waterways, the sedimented wetlands that produce our seafood-based diets, and the prairies where cows give towns their names and horses still convey trail rides. Louisiana the colony: stolen from the Houma, the Chitimacha, the Tensas, the Opelousa, the Pascagoula, the Tunica. Stolen from the Natchez and the Choctaw. Stolen from nations whose names melded into those of others, whose names were erased and later resurrected, re-formed in the mouths of the living. Louisiana, a stippled peninsula of the South, powerfully remade by Africans, Europeans, and Caribbean islanders, all of various extractions and class positionings, of various ethnicities, unified by their strangeness in this beautiful land.

As far as our stories go, and as clearly as the evidence points, my people were Mississippi Choctaw and Chitimacha and Eastern Cherokee, Fon and Yoruba, Amhara and Fula, Haitian, German, French, Francophone Cuban, and Scots Irish. They were laundresses and seamstresses; they were printers, tinsmiths, and carpenters; they were farmers and oystermen, day laborers and physicians, bricklayers and Pullman porters, cigar makers, plasterers, deacons, priests, and nuns. Shredding every line that time and space and sovereignty drew around their bodies, my ancestors—the named and the unnamed, the dominant and the disempowered, the vowed and the fecund, the invaders and the invaded, the Indigenous, enslaved, immigrant, and migrant—turned completely upside down what had been familiar in the world. They made something brand new: the first truly intercontinental tribe. They made the people who made me.

My mother and my father are both mixed-heritage Creoles who have experienced race in different ways; both are children of Louisiana people who left the Jim Crow South behind and remade their lives on the hopeful West Coast. All four of my grandparents were of mixed heritage, their embellished Louisiana accents and Deep South grammars holding on for decades after they migrated to Los Angeles, my grandmothers having different colors of skin than my grandfathers, who tanned beautifully in the sun. Of my eight great-grandparents, six were racially and ethnically mixed. Of my sixteen great-great-grandparents, ten were mixed. Of my great-great-great-grandparents and their grandparents before them, less is known, but this is where the originals appear—those who were mono-racial or pre-racial, or those whose identities were ethnic rather than racial, such as the man who arrived from Germany or the woman who was brought from Benin, or the person whose ancestors dwelled in this watery place for generations uncounted. Their presence was recalled in oral histories and imprinted on the land, in oyster beds and palmetto dwellings and ceremonial mounds and other landmasses large and small. However, scholars of the genome and of history alike would point out that these labels of nationality that we translate into identity today are not what they once were: that man from Germany likely called his homeland something else, and that woman from Benin likely named herself something that is absent from memory; certainly, she would not declare the "Slave Coast" to be her natal origin.

Although both my parents met their maternal grandmothers when they were children, grandfatherlessness punctuated both their childhoods. All my parents' grandfathers lived and died in Louisiana; never making the move to the West Coast, they took their final rest in the concrete tombs of Orleans and Ascension Parishes. Of them, three had been legally designated as "Colored" or "Negro" men—they were Francophone Afro-Creoles or Creoles of Color; these three were plasterer, printer, and farmer. The fourth was my mother's maternal grandfather, often storied as the "French doctor" in our family line. Unlike my parents, I was lucky to know one grandfather—my father's father, whose name Gaudin I carry and whose generously offered memories of Louisiana helped root me in my ancestral land.

In my Southern California youth, I craved connection with other mixed kids, but I found none. Regularly interrogated and challenged regarding my identity—"What are you?" a recurring refrain—I wanted to have a better answer than what I had: "*I'm mixed.*" Once, when I was a student at Alfred Nobel Junior High School, a Black classmate asked me, "If there was a race war, which side would you be on? Would you go with the Blacks or the whites?" I struggled to answer, guessing at what he wanted me to say, but feeling suddenly as if I'd been placed on the sharp edge of a knife: cut either way I slid. If I'd said the white side, I would be immediately rejected, called out as a traitor, a Black girl who "thinks she's white." Even though virtually all my childhood friends were white or Jewish, I knew that I was different from them and I never thought of myself as white. If I'd said the Black side, I would be claiming a belonging that I hadn't felt, that I hadn't been taught by my parents or other elders, but one that I knew I must not ever abandon nor deny. Either answer would have been a performance of allegiance. The question was a weapon aimed at my body, the mixed body: it is a perpetual question seeking to be answered, a site of historical debate, a problem that needed to be solved.

What would I have said if a white classmate asked me the same? Would it have still felt like a threat or a test?

I suppose I could have said, "*The Creole side,*" in answer to his question, since both of my parents were of the same heritage, but that hadn't occurred to a teenage me.

"Would you side with the Blacks or the whites?" There is the perpetual conflation of mixedness with biraciality, the either / or, half-and-half ideation of mixture. This imagining of mixed race presents a quandary to those of multigenerational admixture, like Louisiana Creoles. We are not half one thing and half another; we are the product of centuries of cultural syncretism. On the playground of that junior high school in the 1980s, in a suburb of Los Angeles where Creole had no meaning, I was imagined to have a mother who was one thing and a father who was something else. My blackness must have been the tangible gift of one parent in my skin, in my hair, in my perceived affinity; likewise, my whiteness must have been material, visible, the explanation for my yellow-brown skin, the reason for the ways that I presented myself, the way that I spoke, how I carried myself: Was it my mother who picked me up from school?

Even earlier in my life, I was confronted with a similar question. At Beckford Avenue Elementary School, which was in walking distance of my childhood home, a classmate asked me, "Were you adopted?" I remember her words: "Well, your mother is white and you're not, so you must be adopted." At eight years old, I had no idea how to answer the question. Was my mother white? Was my father Black?

These experiences are common among those of mixed heritage or those whose race is interpreted as ambiguous. Based on my appearance alone and with no actual knowledge of me, people have spoken to me in languages that they assumed I could speak; others have also presumed that I am familiar with cultural references that I often do not immediately understand. I see these as compliments, as assumptions of belonging. My mother is often mistaken for Eastern European; my father, East African or Middle Eastern. I have encountered a strange curiosity from white people, a correlation of mixture with exoticism, my features read as something special, my surname a curiosity, my speech pattern familiar. A woman therapist I once saw said to me, "Wendy, your Caucasian features, your dark, curly hair, and brown skin are such an interesting combination." I have also encountered an understandable hesitation from African Americans, an assumption that blackness is something I cower away from or something that I don't claim because of internalized anti-Black racism. More times than I can count, I've been referred to as a "light-skinned Black woman," which I perceive to be a specific kind of identity that I've never held for myself, especially given that I'm darker than my sisters, my mother, my child, and my father (at least above the line where his suntan ends), not to mention the personality traits that are perceived to accompany it. I've heard from Black people, like a student in my Creole Louisiana history course, "Of course, you're Creole, Dr. G., but what are you *really*?" This question suggests a common theme: Creole is perceived as a weak and ambiguous category of identity.

We Creoles are the result of generations of mixed-heritage people finding refuge in the middle ground that they shared. My ancestors and their peers met each other at dances and at novenas, they chose mates who shared their culture or who spoke the same idiom, or who practiced Roman Catholicism, or whose skin color matched their own, or who ate gumbo on Sundays and red beans and rice on Mondays. In this way, we Creoles are not unlike other people who spring from ethnic enclaves that exist in every region of the United States. We seek our own people and the perpetuation of our own culture; we search for safety in commonality, especially as people of color who are historically excluded and despised in the United States. Some of us are racially categorized as white, and some of us as Black; some of us are marked as Other or seen as racially ambiguous. Some of us emphasize our indigeneity, refusing to allow that important element to be erased or elided. Creole people and culture have generated dictionaries and art exhibits, have defined neighborhoods and wards and parishes, and have filled theses and dissertations with explanations of our foodways, our manipulations of the structures of white supremacy, our substantial generational differences, the effects of our migrations away from Louisiana, and our extravagant fixations on tones of skin.

Throughout my youth, I wanted to understand why my grandparents spoke the way they did, why they ate the foods they ate, why we carried French surnames, why we were Roman Catholics when nearly all my friends were Ashkenazic Jews. I wanted to know why my mother and my two grandmothers were often perceived as white women but weren't actually white, and why my elders so often spoke in the alchemies of skin tone—who was "dark" and who was "light," or "olive," or "yella," or "bright," or "red"; who was a "briqué" or a "nation"; who could "pass" and who could not. This obsession with skin color was grounded in history: it stretched back to the earliest years of French colonialism in Louisiana, and it survived through slavery and the Jim Crow period, when the ruling class of southern whites emphasized phenotype in every way imaginable, issuing punishments to those most approximating blackness and rewards to those who were seen as, and publicly considered to be, white. The meanings and interpretations of skin color held my elders together, but I knew that there was more to being Creole than that.

My childhood friends went to synagogue on Friday nights, their fathers wore yarmulkes, and mezuzahs hung at an angle next to their front doors. My two older sisters and I engaged in childhood Jewishness through them, and we understood that their religious and cultural Jewishness held them together. In junior and senior high school, I made African American friends. I listened as they put emphasis on the value of someone who "looked like them": actresses on TV shows or models on the covers of magazines or teachers at our schools. My Black friends' age-appropriate references to the importance of representation encouraged me to reflect on my own experience: I had no teachers who looked like me. I knew of no public figures who looked like me. My own mother, sisters, and grandmothers didn't look like me. Until the appearance of actress Lisa Bonet on the eminently popular *Cosby Show,* I didn't identify with anyone I saw on TV. In the 1970s and 1980s, there were few examples in the media of mixed couples, those who might very generally resemble my parents. I counted two friends, Donna Mecozzi and Leah Big-Lang-Awa, who were Catholic like me, but they didn't look like me—Donna had long, straight blonde hair, and Leah was Filipina with shoulder-length, straight black hair. On Sundays, we went to Mass at Our Lady of Lourdes, which was predominantly white, and sometimes we drove over the hill into Los Angeles to attend Holy Name of Jesus, my grandparents' church, which was predominantly Creole. There, where the people were of every hue, I often saw someone who looked like me.

Throughout my studies, I learned that our family was something much more than Catholic and "mixed." My history and my extended family's history, as Louisiana Creoles who migrated to Los Angeles, are a layering of many elements, many cultural influences, many imperial hegemonies, many practices of resistance, many experiences of race. When I refer to Louisiana Creoles as *hybrid people,* it is not an othering or an exoticization or a simplification—it is a description of the entirety of our existence as a people. We are a true American mosaic. Our language is creolized. The way that we worship is hybrid. Our history is one of syncretism. This text is also syncretic: it is simultaneously personal, scholarly, creative, and speculative. Here, the reader will find narrative history, poetry, family saga, and oral history. This book is a record of the past, rendered into a hybrid form that challenges the dominant understanding of history as a strict and linear record of agreed-on and proven facts.

Informed by both historical research and participatory observation, yet freed from the traditional confines of written history, this text embodies a creative, hybrid form. I will engage with eighteenth- and nineteenth-century lexicologies, with published histories and literature, with autoethnographies, and with emblematic stories from my own life and the lives of other Creoles of Color. This text is not a complete, chronological rendering of all Creole history, nor is it meant to be. Instead, it is a historical, personal, and creative ethnography. My mosaic approach connects the past with the present, connects what is ancestral to what is current, connects oral history with historiography, and, perhaps most importantly, connects the subjective self with the ethnic and historical context of that self. This is a collection of stories about a collective self that is my story, my immediate and extended family's story, my ancestors' story, my community's story, and the historical developments that provide a context for all of them.

*Sunset Limited: An Autobiography of Creole* grows out of two beds of soil. The first is my doctoral dissertation. After graduating with my bachelor's in history from California State University Northridge, and my master's in history from Louisiana State University, I made the seemingly dumbfounding decision to attend New York University to earn my doctoral degree. After all, I had left Southern California to attend LSU, the preeminent institution in the state where I yearned to be, where there were still family members whom I'd never met, where there were strangers on the street who looked profoundly like California kin. However, deeply moved by the works of historians Walter Johnson, Martha Hodes, and Robin D. G. Kelley—all southern historians who taught at NYU and who approach the South from quite different ideological and theoretical backgrounds—I moved to New York to study the South.

It was a wise decision: the history faculty at NYU sharpened my ability to think critically about race, about colonialism, about the body, and about memory. My doctoral dissertation remains a piece of research that is often quoted by younger historians. Its focus is on what I, at the time, called "separatist Creoles"; that is, Creoles who outright rejected the racial binary and persisted in another self-definition, thus othering themselves and deliberately separating themselves from both Black and white people. Their stories were not heroic. Indeed, in some ways, their stories were unflattering, and they lived in a kind of unsettling limbo. These were *my people,* my grandparents, their parents, their peers—essentially, the people who provided the seedbed for my sense of self, which was similarly unsettled as a result. In reflecting on my own self-definition as a Creole of Color, I respectfully contest many aspects of our collective history.

*Sunset Limited: An Autobiography of Creole* also begins in my own creative personhood, the side of me that hadn't yet fully formed when I was a doctoral student riding the subway to Greenwich Village to attend classes at NYU's downtown Manhattan campus. Most of my fellow students were, logically, focusing on histories of the Northeast, histories of urbanization, immigration, and Black and women's radical histories. I wanted to write about the Deep South, about people who didn't fit neatly into preset racial categories, people whose radicalization may have been more nuanced, more contestable than others. In some ways, I imagined myself allied more with my peers who were working on Caribbean Studies, as the New Orleans land- and humanscape reflect more closely those of Jacmel or Santiago de Cuba or San Juan than those of Boston, Newark, or Philadelphia.

I also struggled through the first draft of my doctoral dissertation. When I finally submitted it to my committee, they returned it to me, insisting that I entirely rewrite four of the five chapters. I cried and thought, "Why?" The work wasn't historical enough; it was too ethnographic. There were too many references to myself and my experience; history shouldn't have so many "I's" and "we's." With my son Aubry toddling at my feet, I revised and resubmitted my dissertation. Successfully defending my work, I finally graduated, earning the honor of being called Wendy A. Gaudin, Doctor of Philosophy. I grew immensely from the experience, and I also knew that what I wanted to do was to write more creatively about my family's history. I wanted to write about the aspects of my family's history that may not have been evidenced in the census record or documented in official historical texts. I wanted to write about my experience as a Creole of Color who was raised in our West Coast diaspora. I wanted to push beyond the confining racial binary in my writing, not to deny or to dismiss race but to render Creoles as people who grapple in particular ways with the paltry racial categories that have been offered to them, and to all of us, here in the United States.

Joining these two halves into a whole—my academic work and my personal, creative work—is not a practice original to me. This work is shaped by the works of others who mastered the grafting of the historical onto the personal or perhaps the sewing together of the personal with the historical, both being equally legitimate phenomena, both being able to occupy the same productive space. We are, after all, historical actors; we are immeasurably and intimately attached to history. And we historians sometimes choose research subjects based on our own history, the populations that we belong to, or the diasporas in which we were raised.

The most prominent scholarly work in my life as a historian is *Silencing the Past: Power and the Production of History* by the late Haitian anthropologist Michel-Rolph Trouillot. His articulation of how history and memory are produced out of power dynamics vibrated in my mind when I, as a doctoral student, first read this text. I've read it again and again over the years, the pages forever bent and annotated in pencil and in varying colors of ink, and I've taught the text to undergraduate students. I imagine *Silencing the Past* as a great literary and theoretical ancestor; I ponder the power dynamics ingrained in the telling of Creole history. In that slim but mighty book, Trouillot uses the Haitian Revolution and European colonization of the Americas to argue for a more inclusive and democratic telling of the past. Focusing on that revolution and the shifting waves of strife, ecstatic joy, radicalism, creativity, dictatorship, occupation, conjuring, devastation, migration, and resistance that followed it, Trouillot centers those whose stories are rarely told or those whose stories are told through filters that reduce them to mythology, to mystery, or to trope. Trouillot's voice, his sharp critique of how history is written, and his ability to fold personal stories into historical narratives electrify me as I humbly attempt to use my voice to accomplish the same.

Furthermore, as a Haitian scholar, Trouillot does not pretend that history exists in a vacuum or as some collection of events with no consciousness. He is the descendant of exploited people who empowered themselves through their own radical actions, who remade the landscape of their own humanity, and who were erased from history by those who rendered them somehow incapable of the very remarkable feats that they achieved. When Trouillot writes about Haiti, the French Caribbean, the Atlantic world, and the relationship between radical collective action and published recorded history, he is directly referring to himself, his family, and his ancestors. He is also referring to the culture to which he is deeply attached and the academic discipline that he practices. Likewise, when I write about Creole Louisiana, I am writing myself and my family; I am writing about history as a dynamic, living thing; and I am sometimes writing against the narrative of the discipline in which I am thoroughly trained. *Sunset Limited: An Autobiography of Creole* argues for a Creole narrative that centers plurality, hybridity, creativity, and fluidity. It makes no false promises of objective, personless fact. This book stretches its arms across spaces left unanswered by documented history; it is a text that is both historical and creative.

I introduce Trouillot here, at the beginning of *Sunset Limited,* because this text exists alongside others that make connections between the personal and the historical, between the individual and the collective. This text would not exist without *Silencing the Past.* It would not exist without other ancestor texts, or sibling texts, or aspiring-friend texts that have helped guide my process, sparked my imaginings, and given me permission to write and to continue writing. I am thankful for Ruth Behar's *An Island Called Home: Returning to Jewish Cuba,* which uses photographs, narrated memories, migration histories, kept objects, and the act of deliberate returning to recover Jewish life in prerevolutionary Cuba. I am also deeply thankful for Dao Strom's hybrid poetry text, *Mình sẽ luôn là người nọ đến từ nơi nọ,* translated from the Vietnamese as *You Will Always Be Someone from Somewhere Else.* Strom's work is a meditation on home, returning, and belonging for those of the Vietnamese diaspora. Behar and Strom inform my work as I too returned to the place that my family left behind, as I too consider my return, as I reflect on language, as I consider where I belong, and as I hold onto and preserve kept objects like my grandfather's pocket watch or my grandmother's crystal rosary.

This book was also profoundly inspired by Monique Verdin's gorgeous memorial, *Return to Yakni Chitto: Houma Migrations.* Verdin works in the overlapping fields of art, environmental justice, tribal governance, cultural preservation, and autoethnographic writing. As a citizen of the Houma Nation, Verdin has observed and recorded the devastating ecological collapse that we are experiencing here. Watching Houma and other surrounding communities sink and chip away—we seem either inundated with floodwaters or cracking under extreme heat and previously unheard-of drought—Verdin uses interdisciplinary work to bring critical attention to the environmental emergencies that we are all living with.

The expansive works of Christina Sharpe and Dionne Brand have deeply moved me. Sharpe's *In the Wake: On Blackness and Being* uses the tropes of the transatlantic slave trade—the ship, the wake, the hold—to reflect on the lasting representations, impressions, consequences, and survivals in the African diaspora. Tying together the horrific crossings of the Atlantic in centuries past and the heartrending crossings of the Caribbean Sea in times present, Sharpe gives me permission to see strands of my ancestors' movements, of their embodied fluidity, of their strategies of survival in my own grappling with movement, migration, and the persistent violence of Anglo-America. Brand's *A Map to the Door of No Return: Notes to Belonging* likewise wrestles with the idea of home and the destinies of those compelled to leave the place of their or their ancestors' birth. The forced migration across water carries fraught meaning that cannot be separated from the violence that compelled those leavings; nor can it be understood without considering Black people's consistent acts of resistance. In my work, I consider the twinned implications of leaving Jim Crow Louisiana: those Creoles who left were people of color who fled a brutally racist society, *and* those Creoles who left had the privilege and the resources to do so. The class element stretches our understanding of survival, and it arises time and time again as I interact with those who never boarded the Sunset Limited train for California, those who never left Louisiana behind.

Louisiana historiography today looks quite different than when I was a university student. I was fortunate to come of age in the time of Gwendolyn Midlo Hall, whose work on African populations in colonial Louisiana broke ground on how we define this region and those who built it. Hall centered African enslaved laborers in her history of Louisiana, and her archival research was exacting. Even nearly thirty years after its publication, this text is still a reckoning and a required reading. Thanks to *Africans in Colonial Lou-*

*isiana: The Development of Afro-Creole Culture in the Eighteenth Century,* we now have a more muscular body of Louisiana historical literature. Although my work is not exactly colonial, I could not write about my distant ancestors, nor about the ways in which Creole people are connected to our distant history, without Hall's work nor the recent works of Emily Clark, Jessica Marie Johnson, Cecile Vidal, Tessa Murphy, and Sophie White. Their work centers the lives of women of color and casts them as actors and agents. Building a solid counternarrative to the old histories of Louisiana, these historians acknowledge the consistent and important presence of African-descended women in archives. They also make this autoethnographic work possible.

Finally, looking at the stack of thick and thin volumes before me, I write this book with deep gratitude for all of Natasha Trethewey's works. I feel a deep kinship with her writings; part of me feels very strongly that she has rendered in poetry the lives of many of my ancestors. In her poetry collections, *Bellocq's Ophelia* and *Thrall: Poems,* Trethewey works with race, color, sex and sexuality, desire, violence, gender, New Orleans, and the broader Latinate South. She also writes with aching beauty about her parents, a mixed couple who defied the law to get married, and their enduring presence in her embodied life. Trethewey's prose and mixed-genre publications, *Beyond Katrina: A Meditation on the Mississippi Gulf Coast* and *Memorial Drive: A Daughter's Memoir,* consider fractured histories of the Deep South that are so often bracketed by disaster, bookended by catastrophes that leave all of us grasping for what is left, holding onto what remains from the past, what is floating in the literal and the figurative waters around us. Whether it is her brother's life trajectory before and since Hurricane Katrina or the brightness of her mother's memory, Trethewey's willingness to write what is difficult opens a door to me as I write sometimes difficult and personal histories.

I imagine *Sunset Limited* as a living discourse not only between texts that share some skeletal and some more meaty traits but also between generations, between those who remained in our traditional homelands in the lower Mississippi River valley and those who left for California. Of course, my understanding of Creole is shaped by my childhood in the latter place, where ideas about our history and our culture remained frozen in time, gelatinized in the shape of Louisiana at the time of my grandparents' departures. My Louisiana education was given to me by people who missed their home state, who dwelt in nostalgia for the old days back home. But life in Louisiana moved on. The Louisiana that I learned about reflected 1930 and 1945, the years when my maternal and paternal grandparents, respectively, left. My understanding of Creole is also shaped by my return to New Orleans in the year 2000 as a doctoral student at NYU, as a Creole returnee, as a kind of anthropologist, as a kind of artist, as I trace the routes of those whose bodies moved before mine.

How Creoles define ourselves shifts with age, with experience, and with history. What constitutes Creole culture in the post-Katrina world does not look the same as it did prior to that catastrophic storm. When I came to New Orleans as both a student of history and as a descendant of Louisiana Creoles, I engaged primarily with the Jim Crow generation of my grandparents and their peers. I sat with elders who used the term "Colored" without correcting themselves, who defined themselves as proud "stomp-down Creoles," an expression that initially said to me "a passionate and dedicated Creole" and now suggests a weaponized identity. I also spoke with others who scoffed at the term "Creole," who agreed to meet with me to make sure that I knew that we were Black. Of course, I knew: we were Creoles of Color, the "color" attributed to our African ancestry. Yet, many California Creoles didn't experience blackness as a special affinity. It was one element of our multitudinous identity. Our family's status as middle-class suburbanites felt more real to me than any one race.

Still, when I arrived in New Orleans, I felt immeasurably fortunate to be in the city where Creole meant something. I held our history with pride and care, feeling like it represented me. But many people confronted my accent, my vocabulary, the way I carried myself, the way I greeted others, the way I wore my hair, my incorrect pronunciation of local names (including my own surname) and made it clear to me that I was an outsider. They told me, "You are not Creole. You are from California," as if being "from California" cancelled out "Creole." I was also told, "Your family might be Creole, but you're not," communicating to me that, in New Orleans, I would always be someone from somewhere else. I learned from my Vietnamese friends that I was the Creole version of a *Việt Kiều*—an overseas Vietnamese—in my case, a Creole who lives somewhere else, whose existence is shaped by other realities.

I respectfully argued back, "Yes, I am Creole because my family is." It was a clear example of Creole as discourse. My new peers in New Orleans defined Creole as an embodied cultural identity, shaped by daily life in this city; I, a product of a diaspora, defined Creole as an identity that I inherited in the wake of my grandparents' leaving, regardless of outward markers or performances of place. My primary and lengthy definition of Creole was this: a Francophone culture born equally of the African diaspora and the French colonial world; Roman Catholic faith and the syncretic spiritualities that manipulated and reframed it; African and Indigenous American ancestry; a seafood-based diet with traditional, celebratory foodways; French, Spanish, or German settler ancestry; the cultural geography of New Orleans and Louisiana, which is tied to the Caribbean and the circum-Caribbean; and resistance to Anglo-American cultural hegemony.

It is clearly an academic definition: long-winded, layered, locative. But how was all of this *lived?* That is what was missing from my version of Creole.

Still, if all four of my grandparents were all these things, if they were *all* Louisiana Creoles, then what else could I possibly be? They left Louisiana—so what? I was raised in a predominantly middle-class, Jewish suburb of Los Angeles—so what? I felt that I was equally as Creole as those whose families had never left. Like my elders and peers who lived in California, I was both things—Creole and Californian: indeed, I was a California Creole. One truth of diasporic people is that we push definitions of self and identity beyond borders; a diasporic being is a transgressive fusion. Through my fieldwork, through my interactions with extended family, through time spent in lower Louisiana, I came to understand myself as equally Louisianan and Californian.

I am the only member of my family who has returned to Louisiana. My son Aubry was born here, and he has been shaped by his lived experience in New Orleans, by his diasporic mother and his Louisiana-born father. Named for my beloved Uncle Aubry, who left New Orleans to practice barbering on the west side of Los Angeles, my son dreams of life outside Louisiana just as I imagined life in it. This is a text of imagining. When my ancestors and their peers boarded the Sunset Limited train in New Orleans and arrived in Los Angeles, they imagined new lives. They hoped for freedom from a life of segregation. The Sunset Limited has been and still is a symbol of that hopeful migration. When California Creoles remember their family's movement westward, they signify that train. Many of our elder men, including mine, worked as porters—as servants—on those segregated train cars. It is an irony, then, that the iconic train represented both the past and the present, both what was being let go and what was being grasped. A segregated train brought our ancestors out of segregation, carrying them toward the sunset, to the imagined Shangri-la that was California.

As a chronicle of Creoles in Louisiana and in the diaspora, *Sunset Limited* is also a truly and deeply American story. As such, there are facts and there are fables. There are myths taken as truths. There are records with many faces. There are archives collected at kitchen tables. There are many answers to a single question, many renditions of a single event. There are borders that are fluid and expansive. There are many, many unanswered questions. There is the racial binary and there are those who resist it, those who reject it, those who are swallowed by it, and those who fully celebrate it. As an American story, this book incorporates articulations of Creole people before and after the lower Mississippi valley became part of the contiguous United States.

The reader is invited into the cultural fusion of Creole via the syncretism of the text itself; as the text bends around historical narrative, oral history, biomythography, historiography, geography, and poetry, the reader is invited thus to see Creole as multidimensional, prismatic, and dynamic. The reader is asked also to embrace the call to see the imagined and the creative as an essential aspect of Creole. This book includes stories and poems that construct lives out of skeletal census records, inherited objects, and the often-overlapping histories of mixed-race women, enslaved women, Black women, Indigenous women, and working-class women. The reader is asked not to dismiss the poetic, the speculative, and the creative as somehow extraneous appendices to the historical record. Without the maternal source, Creole becomes a list of dates, empires, markets, and men.

Taken together, Creole is imagined, it is lived, it is documented, and it is contested. Thus, this text yearns to reflect the beauty and richness of my people and our history, and it invites the reader to consider this as a multifaceted dialogue with the past. This text is not my autobiography; although it follows the trajectory of my family's history and my return to Louisiana, it is not a chronology of me. I ask the reader to consider this text an unpacking of mixed race and a reframing of race that centers the mixed-race experience. In these pages, I do not center France as the originator of Creole nor whiteness as the basis of Creole. I recognize the powerful ideology of the racial binary, but I do not engage it as a given or a simple truth. This text is not postracial or antiracial; it is not a denial of race as a powerful feature of our society. Nor is it a denial of blackness. It is an invitation to visit the malleability of race and to recognize what many other scholars have written: that race is constructed, and that bodies are racialized in different ways, under different conditions and contexts.

Those of us whose ancestors lived with the difficult realities of colonialism, exploitation, racism, and migration speak new languages, birth new words, and walk in new skins. Through our existence and the articulations of it, we resist the dominant narratives that render us footnotes to history; we too resist calls to silence our history, even if those calls come from our loved ones. Telling this story involved difficult choices. Which stories to include? Which to exclude? Which names to use? Which names to change? Which voices to render nameless? In telling difficult stories, this text confronts what it is to be American in the broadest sense, what it is to be African descended, what it is to be multiracial, what it is to come from the place that we now call Louisiana. And if there is a "New World," I argue, we are it.

May Crowning. New Orleans, 1945.
Photo courtesy of Xavier University of Louisiana.

# 1

# The Marian Apparition

There are books written about my maternal grandmother's face; monologues composed by playwrights and epics penned by poets; monographs written by historians spending hours in windowless archives squinting at birth records, bending over obituaries, and turning the pages of books with illustrations of girls and women with pink cheekbones and dark eyebrows and rosebud mouths. There are books written about my grandmother's face: her skin smooth as mirror glaze, pale and flawless, and her nose French as her mother's family name. There are opuses to her skin and études to her eyes, but I have written none of them.

My maternal grandmother had many names. To the men at Saki's corner store, at the Boys' Market, and at the Louisiana Meat Market, she was Mrs. Burns. To her husband, she was Sug. To her lifelong friends, she was Doll. To her grandchildren, she was Mema. But the name given to her by her mother, the name sung to her by the talkative winds that blew through the sugarcane surrounding her childhood home, was Marietta. Marietta. Sweet Little Marie.

In a childhood memory, Mema spread her hands before me, her white fingers splayed like a kangaroo fern, the blue-green veins erect, the skin loose and tender. I carefully applied the pink polish to her fingernails, beginning with the index finger and ending with the thumb, and she smiled as she watched me, dark haired and brown as a spent leaf. Two heavy braids hung down my back, the ends bound with elastic bands and curled around my mother's fingers, hers, the same color as her mother's. There, in my grandmother's face, were so many stories told about Louisiana. She was Louisiana herself. And of Louisiana was she.

• • • • •

In the Louisiana Room at the main branch of the New Orleans Public Library, I went looking for my maternal great-great-grandmother. And I found her: a nineteen-year-old girl listed on page 602B of the federal census for St. James Parish. Located halfway between New Orleans and Baton Rouge, incised down the middle by the Mississippi River and bloated on both sides with sugarcane, St. James Parish recalls an apostle of Jesus, the first to be martyred. There she is: the second child of six born to Justilien Michel and his wife Justine Numa: he a farm laborer, she keeping house. You can imagine her, with long hair bound in two braids, opening the front door to the census taker, a white man who probably spoke English, a language that the Michels barely understood. Justine, the mother of the house, born free in 1845 not with one name but two, grabbed her teenage daughter away from the door, shielding her from the census taker, her broad body in a protective stance.

My maternal great-great-grandmother, like both of her parents, is listed as *Mu* on the 1880 census, and *B* on the 1900 census. My grandmother called her "a mean old Indian woman."

Her name was Marie Adolestine. Having no photograph of her, we must imagine her into being. Imagine her face, her eyes. and nose; imagine her hair, imagine her limbs, the stance of her shoulders, the width of her hips, imagine her skin. We can take the photograph of her daughter and imagine her features back into the past, even though Adolestine could have looked like her father Justilien. A war baby, she was born in 1865, the same year as the surrender at Appomattox and the same year that the Thirteenth Amendment outlawed slavery throughout the Union—a momentous change that assured the same liberties to formerly enslaved people that Adolestine and her parents enjoyed. Her birth in a three-room shotgun, surrounded by sugarcane, tall and languid in the heat, smooth and sanguine in the light, its winds singing a kind of *shhhhhh* through open windows, telling her *breathe, girl, breathe.*

On June 16, 1881, my maternal great-great-grandmother Adolestine married a Joseph Roussel, a Francophone son of a white farmer and his Mulatto wife. There he is: a nineteen-year-old young man, listed on page 41B of the federal census for St. John the Baptist Parish, Louisiana, a *Mu* occupying the space next to his name too. He who left us no photograph is another whom we must envision: I see his knuckles like large beads of sap, like the marbles his father had given him, which his father's father had also given him. Was his father's father Afro-Creole or French? You can see him with a worker's hands, the nails flat and cracked, and a quiet face—his mouth like his mother's and his eyes large dollops of amber. This imagining is a dangerous act. How do we dream the mixed-race man? Shall we give him the features of the European or the African? Which European? Which African? Which features? How he is empowered, made beautiful, made familiar or dignified or aspirational by the fictional face that we give him, yet how plain he likely was.

Joseph and Adolestine settled nearer her family than his in a village called Vacherie, whose name recalls the French word for cattle: people there built their lives on cane and cows, sugar and milk. Vacherie was not a citified place. Shoeless children cut their feet on dirt roads punctuated with oyster shells. People lived country lives in clapboard houses with unfinished, creaking galleries facing the Mississippi River. The old Big Houses creaked and crumbled too, their charmless pomp undone by the war that Adolestine and Joseph's parents had lived through. Oak Alley and Laura and St. Joseph Plantations still stand today, crepe myrtle purpling the pebbled walkways, sugar kettles decorating the lawns.

Several times every year, I drive out to Vacherie to visit what was my grandmother's birthplace in what is still a mostly rural community; it is a place only somewhat familiar to me. I coast slowly through the little town, imagining my grandmother as a little girl somewhere around here. I gaze at the fields of sugarcane, take some photos with my cellphone; I mark the historic places that she saw. I park my car along the levee and walk up onto it, standing on the ridge that lines both sides of the Mississippi River. Although Vacherie is still a quiet place, it is surrounded by massive industrialization. Activists in St. James Parish struggle against the diligence of racial capitalism, which pollutes the air, the water, and the soil of all the parishes between New Orleans and Baton Rouge, shortening life expectancy for predominantly Black, Creole and Cajun, immigrant, rural, and working-class people. I drive down the road to B&C Seafood where I purchase a few links of boudin, a few redfish fillets, and a couple of pounds of unpeeled and unbeheaded shrimp the size of my palm. On some days, I continue down the River Road to Wallace, where I stop for beignets at Fee-Fo-Lay Café, just up the road from Whitney Plantation. Inside the café, I look at the framed photographs of the owners' extended family. Is that person a Roussel, I wonder to myself. Could that be a distant cousin? Is that what my great-great grandmother Adolestine looked like?

Women like Adolestine married at the age of twenty and gave birth to eleven children, and, of them, buried three. In the segregated cemeteries, where would her children rest? Inside the clean lines of the white cemetery? Within a walled crypt encased with brick and stone or underneath a concrete slab? Were their names recorded? Or would they rest wrapped in cloth, a ritual textile, a cotton gauze? On their own property, at the base of a live oak? Under the ground in a wooden box where African-descended people were buried, overgrown with vines and colonized by fire ants, blessed by the Irish accent of the priest and women's voices reciting the holy rosary? Women like Adolestine prayed to the Blessed Mother; repeating more times than they could count the Marian prayers—the Memorare and the Hail Mary; the Hail Holy Queen, the Magnificat; and the Angelus—they felt her beloved presence all around them. They knew her sacrifice, sending their children to an early grave, their children Jim Crowed into sickness, exclusion, and death. And, yes, women like Adolestine saw a Marian apparition. Was it moss shivering in the wind, or was it a linen gown? A fluid movement, compassion in the silence. Was it her hair they saw draping down her back? Were those tears against her perfect skin, the apparition camouflaged against the woods at night?

But there was no Our Lady of La Vang or Our Lady of Fatima in these plantation lands, no Our Lady of Laus or Our Lady of Zeitoun. Just the women of Vacherie, who looked with their mouths and spoke with their eyes, grey and green and hazel and blue and brown as the Mississippi River, brown as a palmful of almonds, almonds being a prophecy of a Marian apparition. Women like Adolestine were good Roman Catholics, their faith passed down from the fathers of their fathers, who were good Roman Catholics too, except for the ones who kept slaves. On Fridays, they chanted the novenas, and on Saturdays, they hung garlic from the eaves, and they gave their sons the first name Joseph and their daughters the first name Marie.

Adolestine named her two sons Joseph Stephen and Joseph Ansell.

She named five of her six daughters Marie Ella, Marie Nora, Marie Alma, Marie Rosa, and Marie Adorestina.

The second of the six daughters was Ida. Born on the thirtieth day of July 1884, and recorded on page 292B of the federal census for St. James Parish, Louisiana—

Ida of the ash-brown hair
Ida of the copperplate eyes
Ida of the cochon de lait
Ida of the duckfat bath
Ida of the moss mattress
Ida of the fierce tempest—

Ida of the hunter's moon: conceived in October and birthed with the hot July wind singing out to her, *breathe, girl, breathe.*

Ida of the Singular Name: for a reason unknown to me, my maternal great-grandmother Ida was never blessed with Marie.

• • • • •

*"Colored girls must protect their hair. It shouldn't be shown to strange men. Mixblood girls must oil, brush, plait, bind, twist, truss, and wrap their hair. It shouldn't be washed too often. Creole girls mustn't let their hair blow in the wind. It shouldn't be loosed in public. It mustn't be pulled, removed, snatched, stolen, ruined, sold, or cut."*

The words of her grandmothers and their grandmothers before them, told and repeated, told and repeated while scraping the stubble from the hog's skin, dropping fish heads into the pot for stock, flouring the pink legs of field rabbits, pulling the feathers from ducks and saving the fat—all the sticky work of their caste. Ida listened and told and repeated the lessons of her grandmothers chanted like the Marian prayers. Her hair upswept to reveal her neck, rose oil behind her ears. "Unmarried, who might be smelling

Of the Singular Name. Ida Roussel, my maternal great-grandmother. Vacherie, Louisiana, ca. 1905.

behind your ears?" her grandmothers dared to ask her while she was still in their midst. Unafraid of the answer but scandalized nonetheless, her grandmothers passed down from the mothers of their mothers, the old ways and old words, the Louisiana French, the maternalized language of men.

"You made me this," she dared not answer in reply. Ida of the Singular Name, and her grandmothers, of switch and paddle, mean as the land that grew them.

A month before my great-grandmother Ida's twentieth birthday, a young doctor from New Orleans arrived in Vacherie. He had thin hair, a long, narrow nose that hooked at its tip like the beak of a bird, and eyes the color of a grey heron, so light that they could have faded into the surrounding whites. His skin resembled unbaked biscuits and his fingers walking sticks, which Vacherie children fearlessly plucked from the woods out beyond the cane.

My great-great-grandmother, Adolestine, sat herself in a cane-back chair outside his office, her jet-black hair in a dense bun at the base of her head, her hands resting in her plentiful lap, her wide ass seeping over the edges of the seat. Instead of knocking, she waited for the doctor to open the door and see her sitting there. When he did, the wind held its breath, eating its words. Adolestine examined him top to bottom, not interested in silencing the things that her eyes said, not the least bit afraid of him. He wasn't dressed like a doctor but not like a cane man either. He smelled foreign. Like an oil she'd never cooked with.

"I have a girl work good for you," Adolestine told him in what was surely her second language but perhaps was her third—English, feeling in her mouth like salt. Adolestine, the child of free people of color, raised on a farm in rural Louisiana, probably had no schooling at all. "She clean good," she said.

The Grey Heron didn't answer at first because he didn't have to.

"How old is she," he finally exhaled, standing in the sun—sounding like *ha-awld izhi.*

"She clean good," Adolestine answered, sun reddening her brown face, her voice firmed by her mother's heavy hand, her mother insisting that she be unafraid of white men. She may not have understood his question, spoken, as it was, in the skin of another land.

"Bring her here," the Grey Heron said, sounding like "*bringa-heah,*" as he shut the door behind him.

The next morning, he arrived at his office hungry and oil-smelling. A light-colored girl was sitting in the cane-back chair, her hands resting like her mother's, most of her uncut hair bound together in a frayed ribbon. She was the daughter of Adolestine, the granddaughter of Justine and the great-granddaughter of Eugenie: Ida of the Singular Name.

The Grey Heron greeted her in an accent she hadn't yet heard, the grandfather oaks ceasing their tempestuous sway that followed Ida wherever she walked—abruptly pausing, carefully listening, ready at any moment to bend or shake or let go their limbs in her defense.

He inserted the old key into the door, telling her to come in. Her dress clung to her back. Sweat dimpled her upper lip. The wind teased her earlobes, reminding her to listen and to take heed. She followed him into the doctor's office.

By the time she turned twenty, she was pregnant: a little pink fiddler crab in her belly, its arm outstretched to suck its jelly thumb.

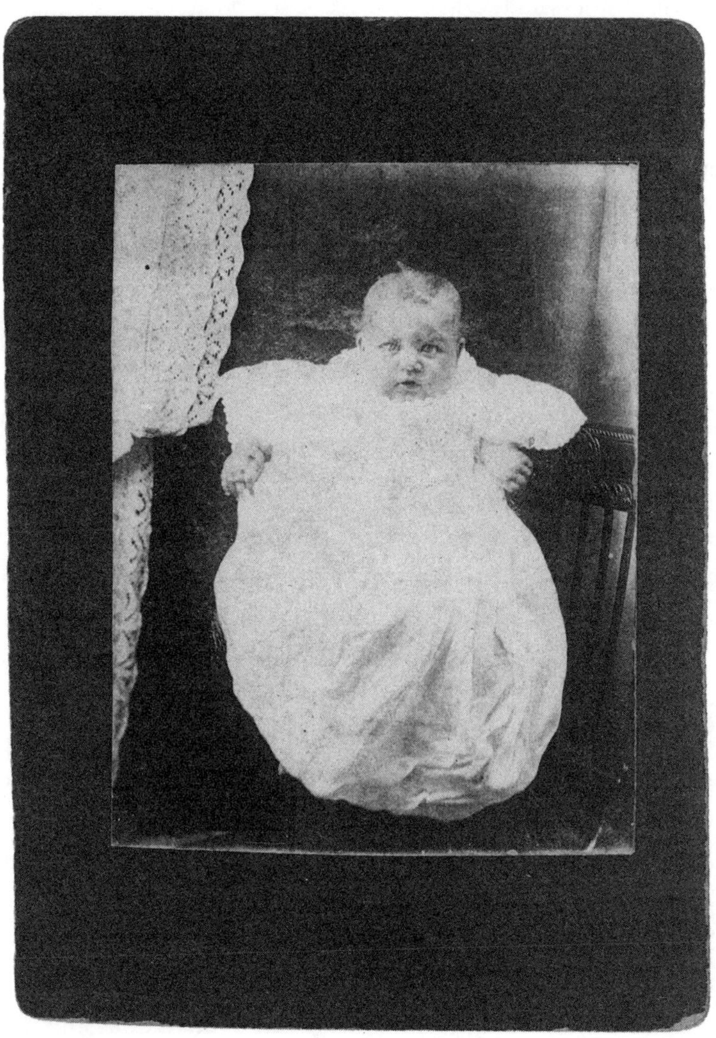

Sweet Little Mary. Marietta Roussel, my maternal grandmother. Vacherie, Louisiana, ca. 1905.

• • • • •

It would be impossible to count the number of Creole girls giving birth on kitchen tables, on woven rugs, on moss mattresses, in clawfoot tubs, on handsewn quilts, with their mothers and aunts and nanáns sitting and standing by, boiling water, wiping their hands, and tugging babies into this world, other babies born to light-colored girls and white men, light-colored girls whose mothers had seen a Marian apparition, hoping that their daughters had seen it too, hoping that their daughters would be like Mary—a light-colored, virginal girl—but knowing that their daughters were not and could not be. It would be impossible to count the number of girls whose mothers and aunts and nanáns knew the dangers their daughters faced—their daughters working for white men, working in their offices, in their homes, in the kitchens of their wives. Their daughters like themselves were born free, but were never free from their perceived sexuality.

Ida of the Singular Name gave birth to a radiant little girl with blue-grey eyes. "That's that Roussel nose," Ida's mother Adolestine said, emphasis on the first syllable, *Rou,* carefully inspecting her brand-new granddaughter, the other women in the room mhming. "But them eyes," she said, "them eyes not we."

Adolestine washed the baby and gave her to Ida of the Singular Name for feeding. Wiping her hands on her apron, she walked outside into the sun, addressing her sons Joseph Stephen and Joseph Ansell, who were standing under the pecan tree, holding their hats in their hands. "Your sister fine," she told them. "*L'enfant blanc.*"

On April 25, 1905, the eight-day-old baby was dressed in a fancy, lacy, layered white gown and taken into Adolestine's arms for the wagon ride to Our Lady of Peace, where the Irish priest poured cold holy water over the baby's head and implored the adults to renounce the devil. (They renounced him.)

The baby was named Marietta. Sweet Little Marie.

On the baptism record, the space for Father's Name _______ was left blank.

After the baptism, my great-great-grandmother Adolestine held my grandmother Marietta against her hard shoulder as she walked through Vacherie, the heat of the months ahead still just an insinuation, the irate wind pushing her tired legs forward, the smells of town sharp. She reached the doctor's office and sat herself in the cane-back chair outside, waiting for the Grey Heron to open the door and see her sitting there. The door opened, and the man was visibly startled.

"See what you done," Adolestine said, her voice flat and centuries old, her eyes biting, meeting his, and then suddenly noticing the fresh gold band around his third finger. She shoved the newborn out from her, as if the baby were an open book or a birthday cake on a platter. "See what you done."

The Grey Heron looked at the radiant child, whose new eyelids were straining against the glare, his expression unchanging. He walked back into his office and shut the door behind him, determined to keep the sun from his face.

• • • • •

Her grandmothers would not abide her. Perhaps they would not abide themselves.

Some daughters left home to be with men of their choosing, some daughters left home to be with men who were not of their choosing, and some daughters were offered to men, given to men in a ritual of heredity. Daughters were given and daughters were sent, daughters were farewell and daughters were lament, but mothers were never supposed to leave their daughters.

By 1910, Ida of the Singular Name appears in the city directories of New Orleans. She exchanged real trees for paved ones: Willow, Plum, Oak, and Fern—

Ida of the ash-brown hair
Ida of the copperplate eyes
Ida of the *Belles Calas*
Ida of the dance corset
Ida of the silk ribbon
Ida of the masked ball
Ida of the Basin Street Blues—

her grandmothers would not abide her.

Ida of the Singular Name couldn't stay out in that country, out in that sugarcane field, that cattle field, out where the trees bend and remember and cry. She couldn't stay out there where every woman who passed her by grunted her breath, sucked her teeth, bent her neck, cut her eyes: every woman out in that red rice field knew that her child's father was a white man. Every woman out in Vacherie knew because they too knew their own stories and the stories of their daughters and the stories of their mothers before them: the fathers and grandfathers were white, and they loved and didn't love them, and they knew and didn't know them, and they met them once in secret and never met them, and they desired them and wanted to be desired by them, and they passed them on the road and never laid eyes on them, and they knew their names but never named them. Because their skin was as white as theirs and they would never be as white as them, Ida of the Singular Name left Marietta behind. Marietta, Sweet Little Marie, she was Louisiana herself.

And of Louisiana was she: born without a man to call daddy.

In New Orleans, Ida climbed the stairs to the little room that she rented. Oil lamps lit her way and gave her cheek a golden glow, or so she was told. She had a bed, a mattress stuffed with cotton, a pillow that was flattened and grey; she had a trunk and a lamp, a Singer, a pitcher and a bowl, and Jesus on the Cross. In the evening, she took down her hair and brushed it one hundred times. The brush, mother-of-pearl; the brush, the bristled tool of her New World beauty. One hundred brushes as a dog barks; one hundred brushes as the rain drops; one hundred brushes as a man knocks; one hundred brushes as the bread bakes; one hundred brushes as the bed breaks; one hundred brushes as a woman sings; one hundred brushes as the church bell rings; one hundred brushes as the dress is torn; one hundred brushes as another child is born.

Her second child was Marguerite. Sweet Marguerite whose eyes were forever crossed; St. Marguerite whose heart was kept as a relic.

Out in Vacherie, little Marietta sat as her grandmothers and great-grandmothers shaved the long necks of sugarcane, as they shucked the oysters and shelled the peas. "*Fallen hair should not be buried in the ground. Fallen hair should not be sewn into clothes. Fallen hair should not be swept from the floor,*" Marietta listened as the old ones told the stories like prayers on rosary beads.

On Mondays, Ida cooked the beans while the clothes boiled: she was a laundress. On Tuesdays, she snatched her arm from a man stepping off the streetcar: she was a quadroon. On Wednesdays, she stitched the socks and repaired the hems: she was a seamstress. On Thursdays, she ignored the "*Hey, gal*" that echoed down an alleyway: she was a mulatresse. On Fridays, she shunned meat: she was what her grandmothers made her. On Saturdays, she ignored the pitiful stares of high-dressed Black women: she was a tragedy. On Sundays, she scrubbed the muck from the floors: she was a maid.

While the floors dried, she took down the books from the shelf like she took down her hair every evening, and she brushed the dust from the foot and the head and the spine of each book. Someone authored books about her: there she was on watermarked pages. The story of her body was bound and printed, displayed on a bookshelf in a house whose kitchen she bleached and swept. She could read enough to recognize herself. She had become a character. A trope. A pathetic, no-nation girl. A hopeless child of strangers. A warning to race-mixers: she was what happened when you crossed the color line. A tragic Mulatto. An object of beauty with a seductive sadness in her eyes.

Who wrote this story that wasn't her life? She was a free woman; she was not a tragedy.

The sun set, and she returned to her room for rent: one hundred brushes with her sore back bent. "*Don't take your hair down for nobody,*" her grandmothers told her. "*Her hair is a woman's glory.*"

But when her daughters and her granddaughters read those books on those shelves that she dusted and scrubbed, when her great-granddaughters write books of their own, they will truly see Ida of the Singular Name, and they will recognize her: a plain Creole girl out there in Vacherie, who saw a different life for herself, a different path, a different road, and regardless of what anyone thought, she took it.

• • • • •

Nearly a decade after she left Vacherie behind, my maternal great-grandmother, Ida of the Singular Name, raised the bottom of her skirt and climbed onto a bus. She opened her wallet and handed the driver the three-cent fare; in return he tipped his hat, punctuating his "thank you" with "ma'am." A moment after the exchange, he'd probably regretted the "ma'am" as he watched the russet woman walk to the back of the segregated vehicle.

"Another one a' them," he must have thought to himself. "Pretty soon, we won't know what from what." The back of the vehicle should have been a contrast to the front, an easy distinction, the bus a "ground of difference." But Ida of the Singular Name and many others like her, proved the task uneasy: multi-hued bodies didn't easily fit into one space or another, in front of the placard or behind it. There was no section of the bus for the nonwhite children of white men; according to the laws of Louisiana and other southern states, they didn't exist.

Stepping down from the bus at the Vacherie stop, she saw her brother, Joseph Stephen, waiting by a wagon and mule. They greeted each other with a country embrace, and he put her bag in the bed of the wagon. They rode along the curved levee, passing crumbling old Big Houses and unpainted three-room shotguns, all-hued children hanging from their galleries, spotted Catahoulas lounging in the heat.

Turning from the Mississippi River and onto a dirt road, Ida of the Singular Name pulled her scarf over her face. Joseph Stephen noticed: "She citified now."

The mule and wagon stopped in front of a house where a pre-pubescent girl stood under a tree, its limbs outstretched like the arms of a father, curling and twisting out: these were limbs that changed their shape with her, lengthening as she lengthened, aging as she aged; limbs that held her hands as she learned to walk; limbs that held her steady as she learned to climb; limbs that pushed out leaves to offer her shade and let go their leaves to soften the ground under her feet. The girl picked up a pecan from the ground. She cracked it, crushed it, removed the shell, and proceeded to eat its meat, blinking in the direction of her mother who had left years before—her mother who went to the city.

When Ida of the Singular Name crossed the road toward her child, the air awoke with memory. A sudden bluster arose from the dust. The trees bent, the air shivered, the house gasped, the magnolias opened, the pecans dropped, the Catahoula howled, and those passing by on the road turned their heads. Ida of the Singular Name stood in the wind that remembered her, the wind that gazed at her, the wind that glazed her, and now she shone like a Marian apparition, light flirting with her dress, sun glinting off her edges: she stood beside the road and glowed.

Ida's hair was arranged in a big chignon, twisted and clipped together with rhinestone barrettes. The child, Marietta, wondered how long it was. She wondered who gave her mother those rhinestone barrettes. She wondered how all that heavy hair sat on her mother's head. On the only photograph that exists of my great-grandmother, someone wrote, "*Touse.*" It might have been a reference to the Creole word, meaning "to cough." It might have been a nervous habit or a childhood sickness, or maybe she was coughed out into this world.

"I came to get my girl," Ida of the Singular Name, the One Who Coughs, called to her mother, my great-great-grandmother Adolestine, who was watching the air change its shape around her estranged daughter who left her own daughter behind.

Before Marietta left the country, her grandmother Adolestine brushed her hair, her hair bent like the Mississippi River is bent, full of trawl and sediment; the river and her grandmother: dark-eyed sisters born from the same sack. She brushed her hair, from scalp to ends, from crown to waist, one hundred brushes, the ritual, while telling her the stories one last time: "*Fallen hair should not be made into thread. Fallen hair should not be eaten by men.*" She watched as her daughter and her granddaughter left for the city; she watched with her mouth, and as her mother and her grandmother had taught her to do, as she had always done, she spoke her goodbye with her eyes.

• • • • •

In the city, Marietta and her mother lived on Burdette Street, but they were surrounded by Spruce, Pine, Hickory, and Birch; by Willow, Plum, Oak, and Fern. And those were blustery days of mother and daughter reunited; the daughter, lighter-skinned than the mother and with blue eyes; the mother, hazel eyed. Marietta dared to ask her mother why she left Vacherie: "Why did you trade real trees for these paved ones? Why didn't you stay with me?"

No one knows what Ida answered.

From the time of her birth, Marietta was called Doll. The great-grandmothers say that when she was born, her skin was delicate as porcelain and beautiful. But beauty means little to a fatherless child.

Beauty means little when mothers leave daughters for the city.

I have a photograph of my grandmother Marietta as an adolescent that I imagine was taken on the one and only day that she saw her father. The story that I have inherited goes like this:

One day, they rode the bus along Jefferson Davis Parkway to Mercy Hospital. They sat in the whites-only waiting room. And they waited.

An older man with thinning hair walked by. He wore the white coat of a physician. Ida of the Singular Name, the One Who Coughs, said to Marietta, "There," pointing with her lips as her grandmothers had done, she told her. "There's your father. Now you've seen him."

And that was it.

In the photograph, my grandmother's hair is brushed back and styled into a hard angle at the base of her head. At twelve years old, she is wearing a homespun country dress. She is half-sitting on a stool, her hands resting in her lap, her lower lip appears swollen, and her mouth is turned down. Her blue-grey eyes are looking into the camera, her eyes telling a story about a Marian apparition, about every woman who came before her whose very existence becomes a matter of belief.

Look with Your Mouth. Marietta Roussel, my maternal grandmother.
New Orleans, 1917.

How long can they look at us and tell us we do not exist?

—SYBIL KEIN

Pale as Wax. Rita Elizabeth Roux, my paternal grandmother.
New Orleans, ca. 1930

# 2

# A Blond Roux Is the Lightest One

My paternal grandmother, Rita Elizabeth Roux, was a master seamstress. She was sewing pins held between thin lips and a pincushion wrapped around her wrist. She was bolts of colorful fabric and Simplicity sewing patterns on onion paper. She was buttons and needles in little boxes, scissors with sharp and jagged edges, colored thread on spools by the window that faced the driveway. She was the mechanical thrum of the Singer, its motor quickening and relaxing with the press and depress of her foot on the pedal, like a foot on the pedal of the standup piano in the living room, its notes sewn together with the foot pressing, and a sudden quietness when the pedal is released. But Rita Elizabeth Roux never played the piano.

The finished pieces were hung around her home on Twelfth Avenue: beautifully tailored suits, wedding dresses, and prom dresses. And the stoles for priests' robes, and tall panels with felt appliques that she sewed for Holy Name of Jesus Catholic Church, where she and my paternal grandfather served for more than forty years. She handled me rather brusquely when taking my measurements—bust, waist, and hips, shoulder width and length, back, arms, and inseam—turning me around to press the tape. But then, very gently, she fitted onto my body the pinned onionskin shells of the pieces that she would sew together in fabric. My Easter suits and Christmas dresses were sewn to perfection, their ribbons always following the straight line that Grandma mastered on the Singer. Because my paternal grandmother had two daughters and one son, six granddaughters and one grandson, she sewed dresses for years. My sisters and I often wore matching dresses sewn by my father's mother.

My paternal grandmother grew up in downtown New Orleans, "downtown" meaning the area of the city downriver from Canal Street or "below Canal Street." Directionality in this city is determined by our primary water deities: the Mississippi River and Lake Pontchartrain. We live on the East Bank and the West Bank of the river; we live on the North Shore and the South Shore of the lake. We live above Canal and below Canal. We live along Bayou St. John, upriver or downriver. Built on the imprint of Bulbancha, the precolonial name for the settlement that would become New Orleans, the city remains a water-bound and a water-defined place, so much of our surrounding land slipping away due to over-industrialization, environmental degradation, and saltwater intrusion.[1]

Funny, then, that my paternal grandmother's family lived in a camelback shotgun—"camelback," a reference to the hump-like shape of the addition built upstairs at the back of the house. A strange desert word in this watery place. And a shotgun is a style of home that is long and narrow, one room built behind the other, with front and back doors parallel, so that if a person shot a bullet from the former, it would pass through the latter. The neighborhood in which she and her four siblings grew up was called the Seventh Ward, and they lived on a street named after a governor of Louisiana when it was a Spanish province; years after my grandmother's family migrated to California, their family home was among hundreds torn down to make way for the contentious building of I-10. Every time I pass by the fire station on the corner of North Miro and Elysian Fields, I know that the Roux house once stood on that very spot.

My paternal grandmother was a Roux, an appropriate name for her. An amalgamation of flour, oil, and heat, a roux is the base of gumbo, a savory soup that is the heart of Creole Louisiana food. Built on a brown roux, gumbo is made with poultry or seafood stock. It could include chicken or sausage, seafood or game, or okra, depending on the region in which the soup is made. Roux is the base of other dishes also common to southern Louisiana, like étouffée, courtbouillon, grillades, and gumbo z'herbes, which is not a soup but rather a hybrid blend of leafy greens and andouille. The roux is the building block—the thickener—of a sauce or a gravy; there are blond rouxs and brown rouxs and rustic rouxs, depending on the cooking time and the method of cooking. When my maternal grandmother Mema died in my seventeenth year, my paternal grandmother became the matriarch of our family, and she was in many ways our base, our foundation. She and my paternal grandfather were also known for their delicious rendition of gumbo, with chicken wings, shrimp, okra, and blue crab legs.

"My father owned a printing press before the Depression," Grandma told me; his name was John Baptiste Roux. He, like so many forefathers in my paternal and maternal family lines, was interchangeably recorded in the U.S. Census as *C* for "Colored," *N* for "Negro," and *Mu* (or *M*) for "Mulatto." Having somehow acquired the printing press from his brother-in-law Albert Bourgeois, my great-grandfather John Baptiste Roux "printed the 'Colored' newspapers, the church bulletins, Mardi Gras ball announcements, all that kind of stuff."[2]

John Baptiste Roux's paternity is heavy with speculation. "Larue," "LaRoux," "LeRoux," "Leroux," and "Roux" appear throughout Louisiana's colonial record, and the hyphenated given name Jean-Baptiste was very common in Catholic communities throughout the colony. For example, historian Jessica Marie Johnson identifies an Etienne Larue, "a [ship] pilot" who arrived in New Orleans in 1747, "most recently from Saint Louis on the coast of Saint-Domingue on the ship *L'Unique*." Described as "a free African man, born in Senegal and likely never enslaved," Etienne Larue was potentially the child of a Senegalese *mulâtresse* Marie Louise Larue and her spouse, "S. Larue, an *ancien captaine*" who worked in shipping and transportation on the Senegalese coast in the eighteenth century. Etienne Larue engaged in a scuffle with three colonial soldiers on the riverfront of the city, during which he fired his pistol in self-defense and was arrested and then jailed.[3] Was this man John Baptiste Roux's great-elder? Was the *La* lost from the name in the generations between Etienne, Jean-Baptiste, and John? We will never know.

Another potential seed of paternity is in one Claude Antoine dit la Fleur Le Roux II, who came from the Châteauneuf-du-Pape region of southern France and immigrated to Louisiana sometime before the birth of his daughter Marie Jacobine in 1735, three decades prior to Louisiana's transfer to Spain and long before the Louisiana Purchase in 1803. Marie Jacobine married the son of Ambroise Heidel, a German immigrant and the founder of what is now the Whitney Plantation.

Heidel, Schexnayder, and Tregre are all German-origin surnames that are linked to the LeRoux family, each of them mentioned when talking with Grandma about her history, although she played down what German ancestry she might have had: "There's some German in our blood too," I recall her saying. But when my father had his genome sequenced in 2018, he was shocked to learn that the results showed an abundance of German ancestral pings, even more than French ones. What might explain that?

These surnames mentioned by Grandma represent families who settled in the German Coast region of southern Louisiana, also called the Côte des Allemands. They practiced the Catholic religion, engaged in plantation agriculture, intermarried with French immigrants of various backgrounds (like LeRoux), and adopted the rural French regional dialect. Some German-descended Louisianans Latinized their names: for example, the elder ancestor arrived as Heidel, and some of his descendants are now Haydel.

Today, the Whitney Plantation is a well-known and lauded institution that aims to educate the public about the history of slavery and to preserve enslaved peoples' histories on that land. Located on the River Road between New Orleans and Baton Rouge, the Whitney neighbors other river-facing plantations that have historically welcomed guests to marvel at the curtains, the four-poster beds, the hand-carved plaster medallions, and other material culture of slaveholders; they paint a benignly hollow image of a place that existed and thrived on the labor of enslaved people. The Whitney, however, "exists as a laboratory for historical ambition," writes poet Clint Smith, "an experiment in rewriting what long ago was written. It is a hammer attempting to unbend four centuries of crooked nails. It is a place asking the question, '*How do you tell a story that has been told the wrong way for so long?*'"[4]

One Jean-Baptiste LeRoux is a third-generation descendant of this slaveholding family and this legacy of labor exploitation and violence at the Whitney. Was he John Baptiste Roux's great-elder? Was the *Le* lost in the naming from one generation to the next? From one racialized ancestor to the next, from Creole to Creole of Color, from white to Black?

Another Jean-Baptiste Roux, born in 1763 in Lyon, was a chasseur in the French military who served as a French combatant in the American Revolution, fighting on the side of the Continental Army. Given the nickname "La Gloir" (The Glory), Roux fought in the decisive Siege of Yorktown under Captain de Sireuil. After the victory at Yorktown, which signaled an end to the Revolutionary War, Roux's regiment, the Gâtinais, was sent to the French Caribbean colony of Saint-Domingue. There, he served until his dismissal in 1783. And then what? Is he the same Jean-Baptiste Roux who owned a coffee plantation on that island? Might he have immigrated to New Orleans after the St. Domingue Revolution, which began just eight years after his discharge?

Was this John Baptiste Roux's great-elder? The record remains unclear. And, with such a ubiquitous name in the history of New Orleans—so many Jean-Baptiste (La)(Le)Rouxes—the possibilities could fill pages. (Is this great-elder the one who was arrested for sleeping on the street? Or whose enslaved laborers were jailed? Or the man who freed one enslaved laborer for "faithful service"?)

Contrary to what historians often find in documented history, John Baptiste Roux's maternity is a clearer story. His mother was named Isidora Philomene Barbarousse. She was the daughter of Joseph Amédée Barbarousse, a free man of color born in 1799 in Port-au-Prince, and his legal wife Marie Helene Perilliat. Thanks to the preservation of historical records, Barbarousse will be remembered for at least one thing: a New Orleans probate record, dated 1833, in which two bricklayers, an M. Fernandez and a Fred Roy, sue him for $380, the cost of building three tombs. Even though Amédée "amicably requested" the tombs, he later "neglect[ed] and refus[ed] to pay the said sum."[5] In the probate, his occupation is given as "dealer," and he requested the three tombs for three free people of color who were buried in them. He was likely a dealer of cemetery tombs.

Although Barbarousse's arrival in New Orleans is not documented, based on the probate record we know that he was in the city and established in his profession prior to 1833. The probate tells us that he resided in a home at the corner of Gallatin and Hospital Streets, which today is the corner of Governor Nicholls and French Market Place, just one block from the Mississippi River wharves and probably very near where Etienne Larue was accosted in 1747. A death record reveals that he and his wife Marie Helene lost their son Joseph in 1838. And Barbarousse's own death was recorded in 1849; like many other Catholic free people of color in New Orleans, he died in the Hospice of the Sisters of the Holy Family, an order of Catholic nuns of color that was founded in 1842.

Without a complete chronological record but with the help of other histories, we can speculate that Barbarousse came to New Orleans as a child or a young person in the years following the St. Domingue Revolution, which was still roiling the island in the year of his birth, 1799. At that time, free Mulatto troops, or *le mulâtre libre,* battled against the majority African-born or African-descended insurgents in the War of the Knives. This may have played a part in the migration of Barbarousse.

The racial and socioeconomic implications of the War of the Knives reflect what historians call colonial St. Domingue's tripartite racial system, a hierarchical social structure. At the top were the landed and landless French settlers, often referred to in historical literature as "*grand blancs*" and "*petit blancs,*" respectively. At the bottom of St. Domingue society were "*des esclaves,*" the enslaved, the vast majority of whom were born on the African continent and transported to the Caribbean through the transatlantic slave trade; without their exploited labor, St. Domingue would not have existed as the leading sugar producer in the eighteenth-century Caribbean. In the middle was the third population in the tripartite structure: the "*affranchis,*" free persons of African descent. Alongside the *affranchis* were the "*femmes du couleur libre*" and the "*hommes du couleur libre,*" the free women of color and the free men of color, also referred to as "*le mulâtre libre,*" the free Mulattoes.

Among the general population of *le mulâtre libre,* we find artisans, entrepreneurs, educators, tradespeople, militiamen, and inheritors named in the wills of *grand blanc* fathers, grandfathers, partners, and husbands. As free people, they could accumulate and flaunt the symbols of the middle class, they could legally marry other free people, they could control the fate of their own children, and they could inherit property. *Le mulâtre libre* were equally shaped by their middle status, their Francophone culture, their African ancestry (as people of color), and their circumscribed and gendered access to freedom and the white world of French men.[6]

Following the St. Domingue Revolution, refugees from each of St. Domingue's three populations migrated to Louisiana and joined the Francophone peoples already there. The arrival of St. Dominguan refugees tripled the population of New Orleans and surrounding lands, making southern Louisiana an even more Caribbeanized space and Louisiana's Frenchness distinctly Haitian. Among them was my great-great-great grandfather, Joseph Amédée Barbarousse. As a free man of color with a profession, an economic record, an address, a probate, and a death certificate, it is very likely that he originated from the *hommes du couleur libre* population in St. Domingue.[7]

His wife Marie Helene Perrillat is somehow connected to an F. Perilliat; they shared a surname that was extremely rare in the nineteenth century. He is listed on the 1850 New Orleans slave schedule as the owner of one thirty-five-year-old woman. Marie's father, Joseph Zamora (another very rare surname), is listed on the 1860 New Orleans slave schedule as an owner of four human beings: three women and a little boy.

Although wrongfully viewed as simply "domestic labor," urban enslavement in the port city of New Orleans was truly expansive. Linking the wharves, the river, the port that carried ships connecting New Orleans to the rest of the American South and to the Caribbean, to the plantations upriver, the markets and public spaces, and the neighborhoods and domestic spaces in the city, urban slavery is a study of the relationship between confinement and mobility. Enslaved people were legally confined and defined by their unfreedom, but they were also mobile persons, laboring within and between all these spaces.[8]

I imagine the enslaved laborers held by my ancestors Zamora and Perrillat engaged in all the tasks of their dwellings and the spaces around them. I see them serving and caring for the master's child(ren) and those of extended and visiting family. I see them conducting business in ways that connected Zamora's and Perrillat's domestic spaces with the rest of the city. I see them engaging in transportation, portage, and communication. I also imagine them caring for Zamora's and Perrillat's bodies and the bodies of their families. Further, there is the bitter labor that is sex, which could also include laboring "as sex workers at their masters' bidding or to earn money for themselves," making masters' homes potential sites "in the geographies of New Orleans prostitution."[9]

My grandmother, Rita Roux, inherited her paternal ancestors' proximity to whiteness as defined not only in the body but also in socioeconomic linkages to slavery. Her family was not by any means wealthy, but her relatively stable childhood, spent in a home inherited from departed elders, cannot be interpreted as solely the result of her father's labors. It cannot be denied that John Baptiste Roux inherited something miserably tangible from his slaveholding predecessors.

"What's so special about having a slaveholder in one's ancestry?" a person at a recent workshop on Black Louisiana history asked. Nothing. "Don't we all?" We probably do. What is so special about having a slaveholder in one's ancestry? What does it mean to me as a historian, granddaughter of Rita Elizabeth Roux, great-great-great-granddaughter of both enslaved people and slaveholders? It means a lot. It demands that I and we reflect on how we talk and write about our family histories, the long-term legacies of that ownership, and how we are shaped by it. How was Grandma shaped by it? How was her father John Baptiste Roux shaped by it? And do we claim the "owners" as "ancestors"? Or do we see them as white men who caged our true ancestors?

When I asked for a photograph of John Baptiste Roux, this great-grandfather of mine, I was told that it was lost, that he was brown-skinned, and that he looked like my Great-Uncle John.

During one of our many conversations about our family history, Grandma gave me the First Communion photograph of her mother, Rosella Susanna Beauvais. The 1896 photo that had been tragically cracked in half was a carte de visite, an inexpensive kind of visiting card that was popular in the nineteenth century. In it, my grandmother's mother is dressed in a decorative white gown, with a veil, gloves, tights, and white lace-up shoes. A rosary is wrapped around the wrist of her right hand, and she holds a white Catholic prayer book and a white candle that is almost as tall as she. Ah, the imagined color of purity, the Catholic endeavor, white on white on white. Her name was shortened to Rosie Beauvais, and later, after she married, to Rosie Roux.

Rosie's father, Victor Beauvais, was born in 1860 to a Louisiana Creole, free family of color. An auspicious year, 1860 marked the presidential election of Abraham Lincoln, a Free Labor Republican from Illinois, whose win triggered the secession of the southern states that then inaugurated the Civil War. In New Orleans—a commercial center that dominated the antebellum

FMC. Victor Beauvais, my great-great-grandfather.
New Orleans, ca. 1890.

domestic slave trade—men assembled to form militias, among them, the Confederate Guards, the Orleans Home Light Guard, the Mounted Guards of Jefferson, and the Confederate Guards.

There is no record of Victor's father Guillaume serving on either side of the war, but his family likely did what they could to avoid the conflict, given that somewhat prosperous free people of color were pulled in opposing directions. As people of wealth and property, some of whom owned slaves, they might have felt pressured to defend Louisiana and to sustain the cruel economy that helped to define their precarious middle status; as people of color, descended in part from enslaved people themselves, they might have felt an urgency to defend the Union, especially later in the war, when ending slavery became an articulated strategy to defeat the Confederacy. As southerners, they certainly wrestled with the realities of slavery around them; as literate people whose travels took them beyond the U.S. South, they must have been exposed to the arguments of abolitionists, who defined slavery as a moral failing. Whether the Beauvais family supported the North or the South or strived to remain neutral, they persevered through those strained years.

A thin mustache above his upper lip, deep-set eyes like Grandma's, fine hair cut short and gently parted to the side, and wearing a suit jacket that doesn't appear to be formal, my great-great-grandfather Victor Beauvais proves his own existence: we don't have to guess at his appearance. Dating to 1890, the photo is the oldest in my family. It is a precious item; it is rare to be a person of color with a portrait of a family member from the nineteenth-century South. Victor's ability to even have a photo (likely an albumen print) taken of him—his financial means plus the time to have the image made, plus access to a photographer—reveals something about his status.

"They say he helped the Negroes back then, after the Civil War," Grandma told me, a reference to the racial justice work that former free men of color engaged in to assist the tens of thousands of people liberated from enslaved labor in and around New Orleans. Her use of the term "Negroes" should have struck me, but it didn't; I'd previously heard her describe an ancestress as a "Negress." Writer Fatima Shaik traces some of these men and their fraternal associations from 1791 to 1919. Through political activism, radical journalism, social organization, and economic solidarity, these literate, skilled, independent, and well-connected Creole men in New Orleans helped advance the liberation of Black people in the years of Reconstruction and beyond.[10] Is this what Grandma was referring to? Maybe Victor Beauvais, described as both a tinsmith and a cigarmaker, belonged to one of these associations, his name scrawled among a list of members that I have not yet found?

In March 1883, Victor Beauvais married Eulalie LaCroix, second daughter of Gideon Charles LaCroix, of New Orleans, and Rosella Fernande, whom my paternal grandmother described as a Cuban. Rosella's surname is sometimes spelled as Fernande and sometimes as Fernandez; like so many aspects of our family's history and my people's history, her name holds two truths in the same hand. *Fernande* could have been an attempt to Frenchify her original Spanish name, *Fernandez; Fernandez* could have been the Spanishification of her original French name *Fernande.*

Rosella Fernande(z) was, in fact, not Cuban. She was born in New Orleans to Rosemond Fernande and to Elisa Rousseau, who was Cuban. Elisa, my great-great-great-great-grandmother, was very likely a person of Haitian origin, who fled that island during or after the revolution and took refuge in Cuba, awaiting her fate—either to return to her original home of Haiti or to migrate to another Francophone place, like New Orleans. However, describing Rosella as Cuban can be seen as an erasure of her Haitianness, either deliberately or by accident. Seeing her as Cuban whitens her, even though she could have been any combination of West African, French, Spanish, or Indigenous descent, and she could have been virtually any color.

What did she look like? Can we see her in her descendants' faces? In mine?

Rosella's husband, Gideon Charles LaCroix (my great-great-great-grandfather), also left few traces, but like Amédée Barbarousse, he left a probate record, dating back to 1898. Born in about 1826 to William Charles LaCroix, Gideon Charles is described as an upholsterer in the New Orleans City Directory of 1875 and as a carpenter in several censuses. In 1875, at the approximate age of fifty, he must have had a thriving business, or he must have been a master furniture maker, upholstery being a highly sought-after skilled craft in the nineteenth century. Gideon Charles may have born enslaved and apprenticed to a furniture maker. Or he may have been born into freedom and inherited the craft from a father or grandfather.

Having lived a relatively long life, on his death in 1895, Gideon Charles LaCroix left behind a piece of property in downtown New Orleans on North Roman Street, where it met Aubry Street and Elysian Fields. Apparently, the property caused conflict within the family. According to the probate record, his three children—Joseph, Eulalie (my great-great-grandmother), and

Eliza—argue that they are their father's only "legitimate heirs," thus the only lawful inheritors of the Seventh Ward property.[11] The probate case appears to be aimed at a fourth sibling, a Charles Jr., who was born in the same year their mother Rosella Fernande(z) died. Charles Jr.'s birth record indicates that he was born in 1858 to "Geobon LaCroix and Rosella Fernande," but only two years later, Gideon Charles names an Elizabeth as his wife in the 1860 census.[12] A rational reading of this story is that Joseph, Eulalie, and Eliza, being confident in the law and their ability to use it, contested Charles Jr. as their true sibling, thus excluding him from his share of the LaCroix inheritance.

Eulalie and her husband Victor Beauvais lived in a double shotgun on North Roman Street at the time of their daughter's birth; that is, Rosella Susanna Beauvais, my grandmother's mother. By the time of my grandmother, Rita's, birth, a camelback had been added to the top, indicating some accumulation of wealth or a necessary expansion to contain a growing, Roman Catholic family. The LaCroix family, the Beauvais family, and the Roux family residing on the original LaCroix land appear throughout the census as *Mu* and *W* (white).

This variety of racial designation in census and other public records is not unique to the LaCroix family or the Roux family that Eulalie's daughter would marry into. Multi-hued families were often recorded differently from one census decade to the next, from one church record or death certificate to the next. Seemingly random assignments of race reveal its instability and its unreliability as a social category. The varied records of Homer Plessy and his family are another example. "What color was Homer Plessy," author Steve Luxenberg asks of the man whose Supreme Court challenge to racial segregation in public transportation would, unfortunately, be lost to segregationists. In 1880, in the New Orleans census record, Plessy was *Mu*. In 1900, Plessy was Black. "He would be '*B*' again in 1910," Luxenberg writes. "Then, in 1920, at the age of fifty-seven, Plessy would be '*W*,' completing his journey across the color spectrum and leaving a paper trail of racial confusion"[13] that other New Orleans Creoles would find in our own family histories.

Why was Charles Jr. rejected by his older siblings? Had he been associated with his birth mother's death and with her subsequent replacement by the mysterious Elizabeth, who doesn't appear with the elder Gideon Charles in any future records? Was Charles a troublesome character? Could he have cast dangerous doubt on his family's race at this venomous time when Jim Crow laws were being laid like railroad tracks, further dividing and codifying populations—sometimes families—into Black and white? Or did it have nothing to do with race? An incomplete historical record leaves us to speculate.

Victor and Eulalie's daughter, my great-grandmother Rosella Susanna Beauvais Roux, was of French and Cuban, Haitian and Spanish, African diasporic and European colonial heritage, of sea and river, of headwater and brine, whose race swivels between *Mu* and *W* throughout her life. She attended the St. Louis Cathedral School, as did her sister Eliza. At the time, it was an institution for white children. I wonder what Victor and Eulalie endured to send their daughters across the color line, to the "white side"? Did they endure anything? Perhaps this wasn't a risky move; perhaps it was simply what they were, what they could be, what they could be perceived as, what they could take advantage of, what they could possess: what historian George Lipsitz called a "possessive investment in whiteness."

And who knows what they called themselves. Did they speak the word "Creole," or did they simply live the only way they knew? Turning skin color into a tool, a hammer to press the nail, a putty knife to scrape the paint, a needle to draw the thread—Rosella did what she could with her skin as an instrument.

Her five children would adopt different racial identities throughout their lives—these children whose skin was described as "ruddy" and "sallow" on official documents, who looked with their mouths and spoke with their eyes, who raised their children under different racial banners, and their children's children, too. Some of them came to Rosella's funeral and sat anonymously in the back of the church.

"My mother was French," my grandmother told me in explanation, leaving out the large proportion of German ancestry in her family line. "So was my father," she added. "French and Negro."

"But not American Negro," Grandma was sure to make clear to me, "not like the *Jac'amelicans.*" When I asked her to explain the distinction, this

Of the Cathedral School. Rosella Susanna Beauvais Roux, my maternal great-grandmother. New Orleans, ca. 1896.

is what she told me: "Well, we were Catholics, and we spoke the Créole French. We didn't learn English until we went to school, and even then, the teachers didn't teach us good English. We didn't dance and tambourine in church on Sundays. We had solemn Latin Mass. We pray to Mary. We didn't eat meat on Fridays. We eat seafood gumbo. We wasn't no better than them; just our culture was different. . . . We weren't American Negroes," she reiterated, the distinction that arises again and again, like the fin of a fish that persistently bobs to the surface of the water, a pointed anomaly along an otherwise calm sea. "We were French. We were Creole."

Sun Fire Leo. Augustus Lawrence Burns, my maternal grandfather.
Venice, California, 1930.

# 3

# Sun Fire Leo

It's true, he was a gambling man. But don't jump to conclusions. Not until you've heard his story.

You can see him, a sharply dressed man in a three-piece suit and a fedora with a ribbon around the brim, his wide kipper necktie distended at the top of the vest. His pants sat high at the waist, belted, seams ironed flat, with wool-blend fabric fluttering out around his long legs and shoes shined to perfection—a daily habit, that shining. He shined his shoes, he shined his car, he shined the stove, he shined doorknobs, he shined drinking glasses, he shined his lucky coins, he shined everything that could be shined or needed shining. You will not see a chain leading to a pocket watch, but you will see his habitual pen peeking out of his pocket. Always at the ready to post his bets, Augustus Lawrence Burns was a dapper one.

My maternal grandfather died seven years before I was born. The only grandparent I never met, he still lives vividly, in my imagination. In New Orleans, I imagine him on the Jim Crow streetcar, restless and impatient behind the insulting sign that separated Creoles of Color from white passengers, his hat pulled to his brow, a vibrant energy and colors swimming all around him, fingertips tapping a complex rhythm on his lap. Planning his next move, anticipating his stop, Jackson Avenue, Louisiana Avenue, Napoleon Avenue, the extravagant houses of the city's Anglo *nouveau riche* occupying double lots facing the avenue, the single shotguns and double shotguns, the cottages and the bungalows of their servants farther up the side streets—Upperline,

Dufossat, Valmont, Lowerline, Cherokee—up to the Riverbend along St. Charles.

I imagine him as I ride my bike in his old neighborhood, uptown, to the three-room shotgun on Burdette Street, now an updated home that recently sold for more than $300,000. Unbelievably, it still boasts the original front porch where my maternal grandfather must have sat, must have stood, must have imagined, must have schemed, must have daydreamed. I ride my bike across Carrollton to St. Joan of Arc Catholic Church, where he and my grandmother Marietta Roussel married in 1922. St. Joan of Arc was once a segregated parish, and today, Black priests and nuns serve mostly Black parishioners. On some days, I park my bike and go inside. The stained-glass windows in the intimate, modest church cast my vision in red and rust; I picture my young grandparents reciting their vows here. Once, a priest came into the church while I was sitting alone in a pew. He greeted me warmly, and I shared with him that my mother's parents married here almost one hundred years earlier.

"That was a long time ago!" he said. I agreed.

And then I told him, "My other grandfather was a deacon in Los Angeles." He asked his name. "Deacon John Gaudin." The priest inhaled deeply, smiling.

"I knew your grandfather! He helped train me at Holy Name of Jesus Church years ago. He loved the Church!"

Of my four beloved grandparents—John Gaudin, the deacon, the carpenter, the venerable worker, the lover of family and Jesus; Rita Roux, the seamstress, the inheritor of beige aristocracy who lost so many relatives to whiteness; Marietta Roussel, the beauty, the abandoned one, her tongue the sharpest knife, my muse; and Augustus Lawrence Burns—Augustus is the one who excites, the one who moves, the one who laughs in my dreams. He is the bird in the sky, free, quick, watching, strategizing, hunting, pivoting, inventing. With feathers slick and glistening, Augustus Lawrence Burns is the one who shines.

As a child, when I spent the night at my maternal grandmother's house, I began the night sleeping in Pop's bed, "Pop" being the name that the children called our grandfather Augustus Lawrence Burns. My grandmother kept the door to his room closed, so the room remained cold and dark; his bed was neatly made, and for as long as I can remember, a copy of *Valley of the Dolls* sat on his bedside table. On his dresser were a Holy Bible and a little golden box that held an image of Christ; beside a jewelry box stood a statue of Jesus with his right hand upheld in a blessing. In his closet hung his unworn clothes; under his bed were unopened gifts, some still colorful in Christmas wrapping paper. Sometime in the night, I left Pop's room and walked quietly into my grandmother's room, where the Virgin Mary and the Immaculate Heart of Jesus hung over her bed, and I climbed in beside her warm body.

In the morning, my grandmother scrambled an egg and toasted some bread for my breakfast. I can see her as an old woman, as I knew her, in her housecoat and fuzzy pink slippers. In the breakfast nook, I sat at the yellow Formica table with the matching yellow chairs, the Formica table on which Augustus Lawrence Burns used to write notes to his wife every afternoon when he left for work on the night shift. Using one of the names he called her, "Dear Sug," he wrote in pencil on the surface of the table, "Electric bill in the mail today, red beans on the stove. Love, Lawrence." Every day, another note, which Mema wiped clean when she came home in the evening. The next day, on the Formica table, "Dear Sug, bet Shoemaker 7–1 today. Love, Lawrence."

Hustler, he: my maternal grandfather learned at an early age that he had to rely on his own wits to make it in the bifurcated world that opened up and welcomed him on August 21, 1900, in uptown New Orleans; that is, above Canal Street, where Bordeaux crosses Chestnut, not far from St. Stephens, the white parish where he was baptized as an infant boy. August Gauff and his sister Matilda, friends of the elder Augustus, served as the infant's godparents. One month before my maternal grandfather's birth, the Robert Charles riot had riven the city, ignited by anti-Black racism enacted by New Orleans police and by anti-Black and anti-working-class policies and practices that targeted the poor, the unemployed, and those in informal economies. The riot terrorized Black citizens of the city, who were attacked by white mobs, volunteer militiamen, and police officers. Historian William Ivy Hair, whose book *Carnival of Fury* is considered the first study of the subject, postulates that even if Charles, a Black migrant to New Orleans from Mississippi, hadn't been the focus of violence during the summer of 1900, a race riot may have erupted in the tense city nonetheless.[1] It was not an easy time to be a man of color in New Orleans.

My grandfather's father—after whom he was named—was a New Orleans Creole of Color who was working as a plasterer at the time of the riot. Presumably of Fon and Yoruba, Irish, French, and Indigenous ancestry, speculations born of histories of the Burns family, Augustus the elder had likely learned the trade from his own father or grandfather, plastering having been a profession frequently passed down through the generations since the antebellum period. Lacking a photograph or any physical description from oral histories, we imagine him as we imagine the visages of other Creole ancestors. Can we see him in his son's face? He, of nut-colored skin and wavy hair, of distinctive nose and broad brow. Would he himself have been targeted by the mobs hunting Robert Charles and those bludgeoning Black people's bodies in the streets? Would his son?

My mother recalls one of her father's nicknames: "*You ol' Irishman,*" his friends called him.

Augustus Lawrence's mother was a laundress named Elizabeth Margin, sometimes called Lizzie. Her maternal line, the Turners, migrated to Louisiana from Virginia right around the time of the Louisiana Purchase—they, of Angolan and Eastern Woodlands Indigenous descent, marked as *Mu* on the census. The Margins, her paternal line, are a mystery. In searching for her father Peter Margin, I found myself at the two ends of a very broad spectrum: I found one Peter Margin, an enslaved man who was forced to labor for the Confederacy; he earned $20 for his unspecified efforts. Another Peter Margin is listed on the New Orleans slave schedule as an owner. Is there some relation between them by kinship or ownership? There is little material evidence and much to speculate on. Augustus Lawrence had several siblings, whom my mother distinctly remembers "didn't look like him," which isn't uncommon in Creole families. There is also this: he is the youngest child and the only sibling with the surname Burns.

My mother describes his siblings from memory, always using the same terminologies around phenotype. She met them when they came to Los Angeles to visit their brother and again when she visited Louisiana as a young child, she and her mother having taken the Sunset Limited to New Orleans in 1944. Aunt Pansy: "olive skin, very Indian looking, with dead straight hair." Aunt Hun: "brown skin, with kinky hair, not Indian looking. She was darker than Aunt Pansy." No one was her father's color. Mom never met her father's brother, Uncle Joe, whose last name was Wilson.

Throughout his first twenty-five years, Augustus Lawrence, a laborer, popped up at several different New Orleans addresses. A restless young man? An unstable family? Poverty? Unemployment? Opportunity? Each one is a possibility, as Augustus Lawrence kept his cards close to his chest, sharing very little about his youth with my mother. As a young man, he learned to play the clarinet, the ukulele, and the spoons. "He once played in a funeral march, in the street, with Kid Ory's band," my mother recalls, a reference to the New Orleans tradition of the second-line parade from the site of the funeral mass to the cemetery. Edward "Kid" Ory, a Creole bandleader born on Woodland Plantation in the 1880s, his father of French descent and his mother of "Afro-Spanish and Native American" ancestry, brought his band to Los Angeles in 1919 when Augustus Lawrence was only nineteen years old.[2] Did he really play with Ory's band, or did he use Ory to signify the music he learned to play as a young man? Was the mention of Ory a tie to his cultural upbringing in New Orleans? Was it an historical invention, a wish for a shinier past?

Out stretches my historical imagination, attempting to fill in the blanks that are left in his history. Who taught him to play the clarinet? The ukulele? The spoons? Was it his father, after whom he was named? Did he have formal musical training? Did he learn on the New Orleans streets or in the servants' car on the Sunset Limited, where he may have also learned to play the horses, the greyhounds, the cards, the dominoes, the dice?

My paternal grandfather didn't follow the usual Creole path: he didn't follow his father into the plastering trade. This is probably because he wasn't reared by his father, who it appears was not part of the household for very long, if at all. Instead, sometime before 1930, Augustus Lawrence, a handsome man of color and intrigue, took a job with the Pullman Company as a porter on the railroad. The Pullman Company, named for the enterprising George Pullman, employed men to be attendants on their luxury sleeping cars, eventually employing the largest number of African Americans of any company in the United States.

Pullman porters occupy not only a romantic but also an important historical position in Black history and in popular media. There is *Pullman Porter Blues,* a play. And *The Sleeping Car Porter,* a novel. One can watch *Rising from the Rails: The Story of the Pullman Porter,* a documentary film. On streaming services, one might find *The Porter,* a Canadian television series. And reaching further back in time, *The Pullman Porter* was a 1910 short slapstick film produced by the Foster Photoplay Company, the first Black film company in U.S. history. The Pullman porter has been analyzed, interviewed, complicated, and made modern; he has even been queered, set within broader histories of transgressive men of color. His voice has been recorded, his memories transcribed. And with good reason.

As a Pullman porter, Augustus Lawrence was a figure of magic; holding two truths in the same hand, he was simultaneously past and future. Just as porters were servants on the U.S. railroads, who "catered to passenger needs and performed the intricate task of transforming a coach car into a rolling dormitory for the night," they represented a long history of servitude among southern men.[3] Servile: the way of the past, the way of the South, the white expectation of Black and otherwise nonwhite men like Augustus Lawrence. Even as the child of free parents and of free grandparents before them, Augustus Lawrence still bore the racial ambiguity, the easily tanned skin, the deeply wavy hair of a person of color. As a Pullman porter, he was clearly in a position of Black subservience—those jobs weren't done by white men. In fact, "conditions on the sleeping car . . . had a lot in common with the plantation," writes journalist Larry Tye.[4] As a sleeping car porter, my paternal grandfather saw to the needs of passengers as they rode across the southern states. He emptied night jars, he carried soiled clothes, he made up beds, he delivered food, he emptied trash.

Sleeping cars weren't desegregated until 1956, more than a decade after he left the railroad, so he surely witnessed the haughtiness and hostility of white passengers of privilege. Certainly, my grandfather experienced what some other porters experienced; for example, continuously being called "George," or "being asked to bark like a dog or let a young boy ride him like a horse."[5] I cannot imagine it. When my mother sees images of Pullman porters on television, she sighs in disbelief. "None of these men look like my father," she says. "They're all Black!"

But Pullman porters like Augustus Lawrence Burns also represented change, modernity, the speculative future, and "the making of the black middle class." Pullman porters, whom Tye describes as "the aristocrats of Negro labor . . . paragons of the community" and "paradigms of sophistication," were professionals who were represented by a union.[6] It originated in porters' informal organizations and attempts to unionize and then was formally organized as the Brotherhood of Sleeping Car Porters in 1925 under the leadership of the brilliant labor organizer A. Philip Randolph. Railroad service came to be seen as an admired and sought-after profession that eventually paid a decent, reliable salary.

Pullman porters diverged from the past because servility on a moving train, like the Southern Pacific, carried them far from their cloistered immediate surroundings. Men who worked on the railroad weren't circumscribed by geography; they weren't the house servants of the nineteenth-century South, the butler, the wagon driver, the manservant. They saw the country. They saw alluring spaces that weren't racially segregated; they must have seemed otherworldly. Traveling from St. Augustine to Santa Monica, from New Orleans to Chicago, they saw Mexican American communities and Native American reservations in the Southwest. They saw tenements and shtetls. They saw the Indigenous lands that became Texas, New Mexico, Arizona, and Nevada and those we call Illinois, Indiana, Ohio, Wisconsin, Michigan, and Minnesota. Natives of flat land, of swamp and bayou, the Deep South, the Black Belt, and the Mississippi River valley, Pullman porters from Louisiana, like my grandfather, saw mountains and forests, cornfields and vast plains, and the former lands of the majestic buffalo; they saw deserts and adobe homes, cliffs and cliff dwellings, cities and ranches and beaches.

And they saw California.

In 1930, a young husband to my grandmother Marietta Roussel and father to two children, a daughter Lawrencia and a son August whom everyone called Sonny, Augustus Lawrence Burns took the gamble and moved his family to California. He had seen it already: he was the first in my family to see the Pacific Ocean. The railroad meant that he worked out of town, frequently leaving a young Marietta to care for their two children with the help of her mother, Ida of the Singular Name, the One Who Coughs. What drew Pop to California, the final stop on the Southern Pacific line, the farthest west that he could go? Was it the sequined waves on the ocean, the icebox

Two Pullman Porters. Right, Lawrence Burns, my maternal grandfather; left, his friend, Theodore Hundley. New Orleans, ca. 1929.

Pacific breeze, so different from the hot, wet winds that blew from the Gulf? Was it the intense sunsets over the ocean? Was it the missing signs on the beach, the absence of "White" and "Colored" spaces that doubled the consciousness of people of color in segregated Louisiana? Was it restlessness? Opportunity? Was it freedom?

Augustus Lawrence Burns, he who is most alive in my imagination, the wishing star in the night sky, he who habitually shined all the surfaces around him—perhaps a habit learned from his time as a porter—moved his family to a place where they had no one. A few friends who became my mother's beloved elders followed Augustus and Marietta later in the 1930s. Nanny Rose, Aunt Vee, Aunt Lil, Daddy Hundley, Uncle Bev, Uncle Marlborough: their names pepper my mother's memories. Among my maternal grandfather's papers is the original *Receipt and Agreement Covering Prepaid Order* for my grandmother's ticket, via Pacific Greyhound Lines, on May 31, 1930, from New Orleans to Los Angeles via El Paso. The ticket costing $50.80 was paid by Augustus Lawrence—the fare lower than what he would have paid to send for his young wife on the Sunset Limited. They moved into a rental at 524 San Juan Avenue in Santa Monica, California. The house still stands; I have photographs of my grandmother, young Marietta, in a bathing suit, standing and sitting outside that bungalow, her hair gathered in a loose bun at the back of her head.

When the Burns family arrived in Los Angeles, Marietta worked in a tearoom on Venice Beach, and Augustus continued working on the Sunset Limited. Among the few kept objects from Pop's life is a postcard. On one side is a full-length photograph; I examine the photo—his face, his posture, his hands, the lightness of his eyes, the depth of his tanned skin. On the other side of the postcard is his handwritten message, one of only two remnants that I have of his handwriting. It reads:

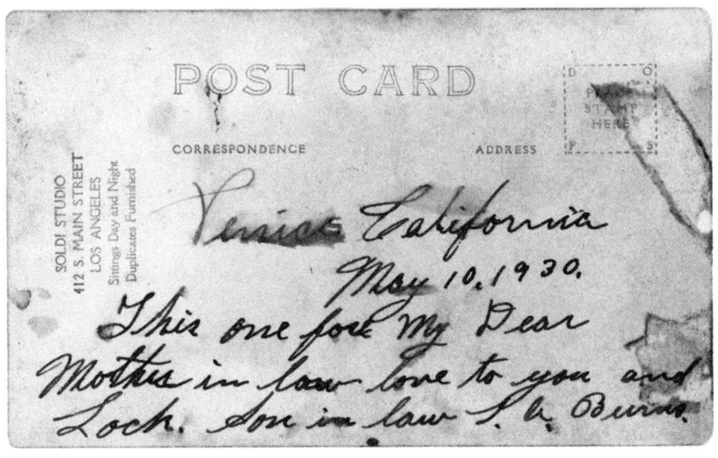


Venice, California. May 10, 1930. "This one for my Dear Mother in law love to you and Lock. Son in law L. A. Burns."

Lock is a reference to his daughter Lawrencia (whose nickname was Lockie because of her long locks of hair), who was left behind in New Orleans to be raised by her grandmother, Ida of the Singular Name, the One Who Coughs. This message is one of many pieces of evidence that my grandfather reversed his names, being known in California as Lawrence August Burns. Why did he switch his names? Did he simply prefer Lawrence to Augustus? Was it a kind of spatial separation: Augustus was the man whose home was New Orleans by birth, and Lawrence was the man whose home became Los Angeles by choice? Did he leave behind gambling debts, a rumor attached to his name, a story he wished to escape? No one will ever know.

After leaving the Pullman Company, he began a series of service jobs in Los Angeles, starting as a chauffeur to patrons of the Santa Monica Beach Club, one of the segregated beach clubs established in the 1920s. Using his Pullman experience, Lawrence August was also a custodian at the Beach Club; in later years, he worked nights as a custodian at Fairfax High School, Los Angeles City College, and Orbach's Department Store. When working nights, he gambled during the day, not only playing the bookies at Hollywood Park Racetrack but also playing dice and cards. My mother remembers the difficult times: "They used to call my father 'Yalla Lawrence,' because of his color. Sometimes they called him 'Gussie,' I guess short for August, and 'Irishman,' too." She continues, "The seventh of the month was payday, and my mother hated that day. He'd come home and leave his pay on the same table he wrote sweet messages on. He'd lay one-dollar bills on the table, a row of one-dollar bills, which was never his full paycheck. So, my mother had to work."

Lawrence August Burns checked the newspapers for the racing results, forever doodling in the margins. He knew that he would hit it big, and once he did. In 1952, he won. "My father won $6,000," my mother shares. My grandmother "took that money and used it for a down payment on the house that they lived in for the rest of their lives, at 3215 West 30th Street. He also bought a 1952 Chevy, two-tone green, with Power glide."

What did gambling offer him? An escape from the contestations of the railroad? A chance that he might win and cast a golden glow on his life? Was it a compulsion? Something he began and couldn't stop? In my mind, my grandfather was a man who took the biggest risks, living his life always on the threshold of a win. Inheriting no wealth from his ancestors and benefiting from little formal education, Lawrence August played the high-stakes game of a working-class man of color. What did he have to lose, except the little money that he had?

I imagine the hardships that my grandmother must have lived with, being married to a man who risked his salary on the luck of the draw, the jockey on the horse's back, and the chances of rolling his lucky numbers.

*He got lucky, didn't he?*
*He blew the dice, his jacket draped over his bent leg,*
*shoes shined, never dusty at the toe,*
*he sprinkled salt over his shoulder*
*or only gambled*
*when the moon was full*
*or new,*
*he played his lucky numbers*
*the 08*
*the 21*
*and he got lucky, didn't he?*

*That's the knife that cuts, the sharp end*
*that she chose when she chose him.*
*Did she choose him?*
*Or did he choose her?*
*Did he see her as a winning hand?*

*His mustache neatly groomed*
*on the seventh of each month*
*he cleans his ears and combs his hair,*
*the waves broad as Greek antiquity,*
*he shines his shoes*
*and she feels that sick feeling—*
*he got lucky—*
*he chose the right jockey and won big*
*once*

*and now, that knife cuts like a new blade,*
*his hazel eyes*
*glinting with the thrill,*
*the willingness to risk it all*
*for the slim chance*
*of winning again.*

*Her mouth a straight line, her blue-grey eyes*
*neutral, finding a distant point of focus*
*in no one's direction, keeping*
*her thoughts masked by the unnecessary powder on her face.*

*He lost again, didn't he?*

*The greyhounds are hungry,*
*slick with sweat in the summer, and thirsty,*
*so desperate to race, paws in panicked unison,*
*and sometimes, he even sweats*
*under his suit,*
*beneath his hat, he lost again,*
*didn't he?*

*A Schlitz and a Camel on a Saturday afternoon, under the trees in the backyard—*
*he worked last night,*
*slept through the morning,*
*hogshead cheese in a glass dish,*
*coffee waiting in the tin.*

*His voice is as silk as his hands.*
*Then, the apology that she's steeled herself against,*
*again,*
*she gazes off into the blurred distance, saying nothing,*
*which actually protects them both.*

*He lost again, didn't he?*
*It isn't violent*
*but it feels like an assault*
*so she sets her mouth into that firm line, lips pressed into a long story—*
*or is it a short one?*
*and she exits to her own bedroom*
*in that house that his winnings won*
*and she shuts the door*
*behind her.*

On the ancestor altar in my home sits my grandfather's fourteen-carat gold Elgin pocket watch. The second hand in the little bubble will move for just a second or two if I shake it, but the unmoving hands of the watch point to 4:43. My mother had no memory of this watch. After her brother, Uncle Sonny, died, she received a phone call from a family member saying that they would send her father's pocket watch to her. "My father never had a pocket watch," my mother said to me and my sisters. She remained in disbelief until it appeared in a little box in the mail; she still would have disbelieved had the watch not had an engraving in the back.

*Sun Fire*
*L.A. Burns*
*Leo*

Did he win it? A lucky day at the races, and it remained a hidden winning for all my mother's life? Was it a gift from a woman? Was she a fire sign too? Was Sun Fire a reference to the thoroughbred racehorse that raced in the 1920s? Did my grandfather bet on the horse and win, and this became his lucky watch? No one will ever know.

For me, my grandfather's affinity for gambling is not only made material in the pocket watch or the two remaining receipts of his playing the Irish sweepstakes but it is also confirmed in my maternal family's migration to California. I know that it was a source of stress and instability for his immediate family, particularly my grandmother, who sewed women's gloves in a sewing factory and cleaned homes to supplement his unreliable income. From a distance, I see his bookmaking through a different lens. He took risks. He trusted in rituals. He looked for clues in the world around him—a full moon, the day of the week, the stars, the weather—to tell him which move to make. He pivoted in some directions that might fail or others that might win. He avoided the things he thought were unlucky; superstitious, he.

Not afraid of losing a simple bet, he died at the relatively young age of sixty-three; he had a heart attack but refused to get medical attention. "He was afraid of hospitals," my mother says, perhaps a carryover from his childhood in Jim Crow New Orleans, where a Black person's trip to the hospital could end in sterilization, in confinement, in experimentation, in death.

Perhaps in his youth he had heard adults talking in the next room, saying, "*Don't trust no doctors, they'll kill you.*" A believer in Christ, a believer in numbers, a believer in lines, a believer in patterns, a believer in signs, Augustus Lawrence Burns was willing to gamble; he made a decision that changed his life, my grandmother's life, and the lives of their descendants. A guiding light in the sky, the Western Star, he arrived in California fifteen years before my father's father. If it weren't for my maternal grandfather, Pop, earning a living on a segregated railroad, reading the stars, and making a dicey move, my mother would not have been born nine years later, in the city of Los Angeles. And I would not have this life that I have today.

*Thank you, my Sun Fire Leo.*

What are we if not what the light says we are?

—OCEAN VUONG

A Man. John Norah Gaudin, my paternal grandfather.
New Orleans, ca. 1940.

# 4

# Holy Name

On a recent Saturday morning, as the sun was rising, I departed New Orleans and drove upriver toward my paternal grandfather's birthplace. The scenic route that I often choose when driving out to the River Parishes takes me through Bridge City and Boutte to Des Allemands; along the outskirts of Hahnville and Edgard to the Mississippi River bridge that carried me to Gramercy; through Lutcher, Union, Convent, and finally, to the tiny community where my paternal grandfather spent his memorable childhood: Darrow, Louisiana.

I would say that the place is wide open and spacious; that the sky is large and generous, offering me blues of every shade and clouds of every shape; that this place is the green of healthy stalks of sugarcane and corn, and okra, its butter-colored hibiscus bleeding red at its center. But that's just a dream. Or maybe it's the distant postindustrial future, or perhaps it is the memory that my paternal grandfather had of this place: "Farms and crops as far as the eye could see, so beautiful," as he once told me. On that day, Darrow, Louisiana, had me squinting in the unforgiving sun. While my lungs filled with air, my nose realized something was very wrong here. Acid. Sulfurous rot. My throat tried to keep it out. Breathing in short cuts, I inhaled nicks of pollution. On that day, all that Darrow was offering me was stench.

Grandpa would weep today if he were to walk the roads of Darrow. He would weep from the desecration of Mother Mississippi, whom his mother's people may have called *Misha Sipokni,* from the Choctaw, meaning "beyond age." He would not abide the many transportation and logistics industries built on the river: Darrow is located, like New Orleans, within a sharp double bend, a risky two turns for deep-bellied river vessels. He would point a bent finger at Buzzi Unicem, a cement manufacturer located just up the road from Houmas House, an old plantation that my grandfather often saw as a child—the environmental pollution of the present snug alongside the moral pollution of the past. He would revile Impala Terminal, a coal exporter, and Veolia, a chemical plant, just downriver in Burnside. He would despise C. F. Industries, a nitrogen fertilizer plant just across the river in Donaldsonville. He would be appalled by the environmental degradation in this place, which is part of the region now sadly dubbed "Cancer Alley," due to the astronomical, disproportionate rates of cancer found among residents here. Chemical plants are built directly on top of what once were river-facing plantations, which were built directly on top of what once was Indian land. He would retch from the heady smell. One can hardly breathe in this place. It reeks not only from pollution but also from the pure and simple disregard for land and life.

Grandpa would weep.

• • • • •

I knew, even from a young age, that Grandpa was someone special and that it was my great luck to have him as a grandfather. He never shouted, argued, or bullied; he was tender, soft-spoken, thoughtful. He spoke with a strong Louisiana accent and sang in a tenor voice, the nostrils of his narrow nose flared, which made my young cousins and me giggle. Perhaps, in part because he lived his life surrounded by talkative women, he was contemplative and careful. Grandpa chose his words wisely, he said what he meant, and then left it alone. He sucked his teeth loudly after he ate, and he loved seafood gumbo and monkey bread. When his allergies flared or when he caught a cold, the tip of his nose turned the color of a blood-red beet. When his knees finally went bad, he had knee-replacement surgery and walked with a kind of double limp, no one leg being favored over the other. I remember his smooth-handled mahogany cane, which he kept dangling on the edge of the bar countertop.

Grandpa recited the Holy Name Novena before going to bed every night. He repeated the Hail Mary along the trails of a rosary that he may have acquired in Rome or in Quebec. He kept holy water in bottles shaped like Our Lady, Star of the Sea. I felt a little guilty as a young girl, preferring sleep to prayer. I remember his distinctive voice reciting the prayers at the long kitchen table, where Grandma laid out her sewing patterns during the daytime.

Grandpa was mostly bald throughout my childhood, his fine hair forming a faint ring around the outer orbit of his head. He often shielded his freckled, smooth scalp with his beloved Basque beret, which he had purchased on a trip to Seville. It sits in a little enclosed box in my office, along with my son Aubry's first pair of Stride Rites: things that don't go together but somehow do. Grandpa died when I was seven months pregnant with Aubry. I was heartbroken that he would never meet the person he called his "last great-grandchild," but he was very pleased that the child would be born in Louisiana and that I chose a family name for my son.

• • • • •

I'd heard from my paternal grandfather, John Norah Gaudin, that his father lived for more than one hundred years and that he died admiring the fruit in the orchard on his little piece of land that faced the Mississippi River, out in Ascension Parish. I'd heard that the Cajuns nearby walked across his farm, uninvited, to test the land for oil. "Eh, Nonc," they called him, their work boots trampling the grass. "Nonc," the Cajun word for uncle, carried with it the onus of racism: it was unfathomable to call a man of his color, a brown-skinned Afro-Creole man, "Mr. Gaudin." The second time they came, my grandfather's father met them with a shotgun and some blunt words in their own language, and they never called him "Nonc" again.

My grandfather said this about his father: "He was nice and calm, he was a man, you know what I mean. But don't walk over him. The minute you thought you was going to step on him, you were stepping on a rattlesnake. And he would let you know it in a minute."[1]

I'd heard from my paternal grandfather, John Norah Gaudin, that he grew up knowing that some of those Cajun men in Bayou Manchac and Crowley Ditch and Welsh Gully were kin to him and his father's people, but he also knew to keep that information to himself. The Cajun men had no "visible admixture," no obvious trace of African ancestry, only the occasional rumor, although they were outlandish; they were thick tongued and sunburned, they of squirrel tail and nutria pelt, of racoon musk and oyster breath. There was little advantage to being ethnically Cajun in those days when they were sometimes called "rednecks." Yes, they spoke a variety of Louisiana French and a variety of Louisiana English too. They practiced Roman Catholicism; they lived mostly rural lives of hunting, fishing, shucking, and skinning, their skin, sometimes a darker brown than that of Afro-Creoles, their culture practically identical to the one that defined the Gaudins' lives. But the Cajuns were hybrid whites; they were ethnic whites; benefiting from their marginal whiteness, they were the defenders of whiteness still.

They called his father "Nonc."

Grandpa's father, Joseph Norah Gaudin, was born in 1870. The Gaudins lived in rural Ascension Parish for many generations, their spoken French far outliving that of Grandma's family: New Orleans Creoles were much more likely to drop the language of the old people for the language of the new. For some, replacing French with English gave them opportunities that they might not have had if they'd clung to their ancestral tongue; for others, speaking French was accompanied by humiliation, punishment, or ostracism. Interdisciplinary artist Monique Verdin (Houma Nation) writes that a similar fate befell Houma French: parents did not teach their children to speak it to protect them from punishment in Anglophone public schools.[2] In the Ascension Parish of my paternal grandfather's youth, however, Créole and Cajun French—the creolized languages produced by colonization and diaspora—were still commonly spoken.

"My granddaddy was a Union soldier," Grandpa once told me, pride in his voice, a serious sharpness in his grey eyes. Sometimes, my grandfather became animated when he spoke, his tenor turned baritone at an elevated volume, whispers of that rattlesnake he inherited from his father Joseph Norah. "My granddaddy hated that segregation, and I hated it too." One of the themes that often arose in our conversations, especially after I began majoring in history in undergraduate school, was racial segregation in the Catholic Church. Grandpa detested it; an infrequently angry man, it angered him. He thought it was a betrayal, a cruel hypocrisy. How could a religious institution uphold an evil, unbiblical law? Decades after desegregation, the subject still turned Grandpa's face red. A repeated refrain: "I never could understand that, and I never will. The House of God, and Black people had to sit in the back. It wasn't right."

A lifelong devout Catholic and a man completely committed to his wife and children, Grandpa served the Catholic Church in all the ways that he could. In 1979, when I was nine years old, he retired from his work as a carpenter, entered the seminary, and came out a deacon, the closest he could get to the priesthood. To his ordination, my cousins and I wore our best Grandma-sewn dresses; my cousin Edris, the only boy, wore a suit that Grandma made. We grandchildren even sang with the church choir. After Mass, my paternal grandfather came down from the altar in his clerical robe, his joy saved for later, his face serene.

Grandpa's granddaddy was named Celestin Gaudin, an alliterative name in its nasal French endings, tongue flattened in the mouth, the *n* silent; the Anglo-American census takers sometimes spelled his given name "Celestan." He married a woman my grandfather described as "a Choctaw Indian"; Grandpa said her name was Clementine Joseph, but it actually was Clementine Peters. It seems her father was a man by the name of Joseph Peters. I think my grandfather remembered Joseph and forgot Peters. Clementine's mother is lost to history.

In Grandpa's family narrative, Clementine is a Native woman, a descendant of the great mound builders of the Mississippi River valley. Our Indigenous foremothers and forefathers remain in the narratives of our elders, while those very people often disappear from official records, which invisibilizes Indigenous people to one end: to justify the unabridged confiscation of their land. Racial designation laws that were written in the post–Civil War period undeniably defined blackness as a negative mark, as a stain that erases any legitimate claim to any other identity. Categorizing mixed-heritage people as Black, reinforcing anti-Black racism throughout all levels of public life, and then limiting the rights of Black people, succeeded in disempowering a much larger population; likewise, categorizing mixed-heritage Native people as Black—not Native—shrank their population, making them seemingly "invisible" and thus terminating their historic land rights.

Verdin's very personal record of the Louisiana Houma sheds light on the complications here. She writes, "Some lines of our genealogy can be traced back to France. In other colonial documents, our relatives have been listed as 'griffe.' During the Spanish era, this designation was for mixed people of African and Indian ancestry." She goes on to note, "As Louisiana changed from a territory to a state, Indian identities were erased in census records by American obsessions with race. With Indian people classified first as 'people of color' and later as 'black,' tribal identities were not acknowledged." The "mixed status" of the Houma people, among many others, is one of the reasons why the tribe has struggled against bloodline definitions of Indianness used by the Bureau of Indian Affairs.[3]

There are so many histories. There are histories of Native peoples who adopted and incorporated Black people into their nations. There are histories of Native peoples enslaving Black people; after emancipation, those freed people incorporated Native identity into their African American one, both identities becoming equally meaningful. There are histories of Native and Black fusion, histories of solidarity that caused generations of European settlers and white Americans to pause and consider this a dangerous alliance. Black and Native people have both experienced racialization in different ways but to somewhat similar ends: as alienated people, an ocean of force between the African motherland and U.S. soil, the racialization of Black people has defined them as undeserving of full citizenship and fundamentally unequal. Deliberately dispossessed people of their own land, Native people are racialized in ways that define them similarly as undeserving of full citizenship, including access to their land and all its resources, and fundamentally unequal.

Claiming, and reclaiming, our Indian ancestresses, then, has meaning for historically disempowered people. Clementine (Joseph) Peters existed in flesh and blood, not only in memory. We have no photograph of her, but we do have one of her daughter Aliska. Did the daughter favor the mother? Can we read something real, something tangible, in her photo? Its sepia tone, the blurred background, the stoic faces? Reclaiming Clementine is an act of resistance against her erasure. Importantly, it is also a declaration that people can be more than one thing at once; contrary to the "one-drop" myth of race, a person can be proudly Native and Black (and white). The racial concept of hypodescent argues that racial identity can be both essentialist—defined by one thing that is seen as its "essence"—and reductivist: reduced to one thing, usually something viewed as negative. Hypodescent declares that "one-drop" of "Black blood" defines a mixed-race person as Black, but "one drop" of white blood does not define a mixed-race person as white.

Historian Frank Deloria (Dakota Nation) points out, "Indians have reason to exclude Americans—both white and Black—who amplify a drop of 'Indian blood' to claim Indigenous authenticity and perhaps tribal benefits." He adds, "But then there's the troubling 'one drop of Black blood' logic of the Dawes Rolls, which defined both Black freedpeople and mixed-blood Black Creeks as unequivocally Black, but allowed mixed Creeks who had white ancestry to remain among the 'full-bloods.'"[4] In what is a transparent deceit, a pure invention, whiteness is treated as compatible with indigeneity, but blackness changes the whole calculus. Hence, the "essence" of Creek people, in this example, is not erased by "one drop" of white blood.

For many of blended ancestry, hypodescent is a painful erasure. Mel Michelle Lewis, a Black and Poarch Creek writer and artist from Bayou La Batre, Alabama, writes about such contradictions. Their long-form poem, "Erosion," considers the function that tribal membership rolls play in Indigenous identity. Reflecting my own thoughts on the subject, Lewis writes:

> In some cases
> Census says
> The same person
> Is Indian
> I
> Is White
> W
> Is Black
> B
> Is Mulatto
> M
> Depending
> How the taker
> Took them.

Another powerful stanza reads, "Mother, we are Sehoy's Wind Clan children / Although / We do not appear / On the roll."[5]

Grandpa remembered his grandmother this way: Clementine (Joseph) Peters was a "Choctaw Indian from Mississippi," with "light brown skin and thick black hair," who spoke only "broken English." She was as "stern" as Grandpa's mother, her daughter Aliska. I have not found her, my Native foremother, listed on the Dawes Rolls, the first federal government census of enrolled members of Cherokee, Choctaw, Creek, Chickasaw, and Seminole peoples, but her mother and her grandmothers might be there. Alas, she is as Grandpa remembered her; so it is.

On October 10, 1918, Clementine (Joseph) Peters Gaudin, my great-great-grandmother, filed a "Widow's Application for Pension" in Ascension Parish, Louisiana; she was eighty-five years old. Her husband Celestin, had died on the ninth of October, one day earlier, leaving her "depending on my sons," one of whom was Joseph Norah, my grandfather's father, the rattlesnake. At ninety-eight, Celestin had died of "old age." Clementine declared Louisiana as her home "all her life," which contradicts Grandpa's memory but affirms a persistent pattern of migration, sometimes forced, in Native histories; perhaps her mother's people had been from Mississippi, and they migrated to Louisiana before she was born. At the time of the pension application, Clementine had property valued at $1,000, which had been "mortgaged for $200 to Mrs. Van Hop of Donaldsonville," a town across the Mississippi River from Darrow. The censuses of 1900 and 1910 confirm this, listing Celestin as the owner of property that was mortgaged.[6]

In the years 1896, 1900, and 1919, Clementine's in-law, Cyril Arnaud Gaudin, saw her through what had to have been the tremendously difficult dissolution of the Gaudin family land. In each of those years, Clementine and Cyril sold off one tract at a time. Just as the LaCroix–Roux home was demolished to make room for I-10 in the city of New Orleans, the Gaudin land was sold as part of Ascension Parish's descent into industrial madness.

Celestin and Clementine's economic status in the first decades of the twentieth century reflects the state of poverty that was endemic in rural Louisiana. Family farms were lost to bankruptcy even before the Great Depression, and plantations became largely impoverished places with the collapse of racial slavery and its replacement with sharecropping and tenancy. The industrialization, mechanization, and modernity that represented the postbellum New South reached Ascension Parish plantations like Rebecca,

Ben Hur, Point Houmas, and Cofield, which were available for tenants and for sale in the 1910s and the 1920s. Clementine and Celestin were not planters, but they were also not alone in their indigence.

It is no wonder, then, that on the day after great-great-grandfather Celestin died, great-great-grandmother Clementine applied for her husband's pension to continue; she needed the money. Her application reads as follows:

> Mrs. Celestin Gaudin . . . a resident of Darrow . . . declares that she is the widow of Celestin Gaudin who entered the service of the Confederate States during the civil war under the name Celestin Gaudin at Pelican Battery from the state of LA that he honorably served until End of war at [left blank] on the [left blank] Applicant's husband was a pensioner on the Rolls of State of LA that she was married to the said soldier under the name Clementine Peter . . . on the 6 day of July 1852.[7]

Having found this application, I paused, my hand came to my mouth, and I read it again. Heart pounding. Out loud. *Celestin Gaudin. Confederate States. Pelican Battery. Darrow.*

I took a moment to look up Pelican Battery. Without any Civil War histories in my immediate grasp, I began with the simplest and quickest inquiry, Wikipedia. "The 5th Louisiana Field Battery was an artillery unit recruited from volunteers in Louisiana that fought in the Confederate States Army," I read. "The Pelican Artillery . . . recruit[ed] men mostly from St. James Parish, Louisiana." St. James Parish borders Ascension Parish, and in the distant past, they were one unit. Writing in my research notes, "Look @ Civil War history, LA, Black troops fighting for the South, sources." I continued reading the short Wikipedia article. The battery "saw action on Bayou Teche . . . at Gaudet's plantation . . . at Kock's plantation . . . and served during the Red River campaign." Surrendering in Tyler, Texas, in 1865, "2 were killed in action, 5 died from disease, and 1 drowned."[8] I added to my research notes: "Confirm Pelican Battery / Artillery."

Pause. Reopen Clementine's application; read it again.

"*My Granddaddy was a Union soldier.*" I can hear Grandpa's voice, his accent, the tone. Read it again.

I began reviewing U.S Census records for Celestin Gaudin, the only man with that name in Ascension Parish, who was always listed with Clementine below him. I had read these census records dozens of times throughout my research. Celestin is consistently categorized as Black, and his wife and children are repeatedly marked as Mulatto. As the census decades pass, I see familiar family names. There's Alice, who wrote letters to my grandfather after he moved to Los Angeles. There's Percival, whom Grandpa lovingly called Percy. There's Earl, who graduated from Xavier University of Louisiana, the first known college graduate in my family. I opened another census record and zoomed in close, my glasses on my forehead as I peered closely at the words on the screen. And then I saw it, in the column on the far right of the screen, what I had never noticed before.

> 1910 Census, Ascension Parish, sheet 2B. Gaudin, Celestan. Race: B. Age: 84. Column 30, "*Whether a survivor of the Union or Confederate Army or Navy.*"

Below him in the record is Clementine, his wife. And there it is written, clearly, with a check mark beside it: "*CA.*" Confederate Army.

Call Dad.

"Dad, do you recall Grandpa saying that his grandfather had been a Union soldier?"

Dad: "No."

"What did he say about his grandfather Celestin? Do you remember anything?"

Dad: "No."

"Well, apparently, he fought for the Confederacy."

Dad responded, "Oh. Well, it's a historical fact, so that's the way it is." Dad, a retired biology professor and current beekeeper, isn't really interested in history, including our family history. Fighting for the Union or the Confederacy holds no ethical meaning for him, he who loathes racial politics. He who supported me in choosing history as a major in undergraduate school, but then scoffed when I told him I'd be studying race. I wondered whether he simply did not care.

Dad never met his great-grandparents, and he saw no photographs of them, if they'd ever had photographs taken. As a child, Dad did meet his grandfather Joseph Norah when he visited the family in New Orleans. Here is Dad's description of him: "He was light-skinned, my color, and he had wavy hair, not close-cut; it was kind of long, like he hadn't had a haircut in a while. He had a mustache, and he wore a suit. He sat in a chair and leaned it back against the wall. He smoked, and he was very pleasant, smiling." My father's first childhood memory is of his trip to Darrow to attend the funeral of his grandmother Aliska. Dad remembers, "There were pecan trees planted in a row on the path to the house. One of my uncles picked up the pecans two at a time, he crushed them, and gave me the pecan meat."

I struggled to wrap my mind around all this information; I wasn't sure how to hold it all. I'd studied southern U.S. history, so I knew a bit about the Civil War, although I had no expertise in that truly enormous field. I knew that most African American Union troops were men from the North. Some Union regiments of southern men existed, so I always assumed Grandpa was referring to one of them. There was the 1st Louisiana Native Guard, or the Corps d'Afrique, one of the first Afro-Creole regiments in the Union Army, made up mostly of free men of color from New Orleans; there was the 1st New Orleans Infantry Regiment and the 2nd Louisiana Mounted Infantry and others. These men are remembered for their radical act of military service, an act of resistance to racist ideas that portrayed them as weak men who couldn't be relied on to soldier in a war. They killed, risked their lives, experienced injury and capture, and sometimes died for what they knew was a most important cause.

And here is Celestin. On every record, Celestin is Black. The 1910 census definition of Black reads, "All persons who are evidently fullblooded negroes," and that of Mulatto reads, "All other persons having some proportion of perceptible trace of negro blood."[9] Full-blooded? Perceptible trace? There was no doubt in the mind of Joseph A. Reddix, the census enumerator who showed up on the Gaudin farm on the sixteenth day of April 1910.

What did Celestin Gaudin look like? Was he tall and slim like his son Joseph Norah, whom the Cajuns dared call "*Nonc*"? (Did they dare call Celestin the same?) How is he visible in my face or in my father's?

More digging found Celestin Gaudin's original application for a veteran's pension in 1911. "Soldier's Application for Pension" reads as follows:

Born: December 1825
Where were you born: St. James, Ascension Parish
When did you enlist in the Confederate service: in 1[8]62 in the Summer
Where did you enlist: near Ayraud's plantation in Ascension where the co[mpany] was
In what command: Pelican Battery
Give the Branch of service . . . : Artillery
Give the names of the regimental and company officers . . . : (he gave them)
Were you wounded: No.
Reason for discharge: end of war.

When the war ended, Celestin Gaudin was "paroled in Texas, Henderson County, then came home to St. James." Asked if he ever "took an oath to the United States Government at any time during the war," he answered, "*Never.*"[10]

"*My Granddaddy was a Union soldier.*"

Another pivot: maybe Celestin had been enslaved and was conscripted into the military in a servile capacity, an experience that was common throughout Louisiana and the rest of the former Confederacy. But his pension application says nothing of servitude; it makes no reference to his previous condition nor to his race (that scrawled *Col* or *B* so common throughout family records). I didn't find him in the records of enslaved men who worked for the Confederacy and were paid a small sum of money for their labor. If he'd been an enslaved servant or a porter, he probably would not have been paroled in Texas at the end of the war; he very likely would have absconded with the passage of the Emancipation Proclamation in 1862, the same year that he said he enlisted. Furthermore, formerly enslaved persons who served the Confederate militaries were not entitled to pensions.

How did the clerk of court look at him when he walked into that office to file that pension application? This Afro-Creole man, regardless of his skin color. And how about his two character witnesses, a Herman B. Landry and a J. B. Boudreaux? Is it only strange to us, today, that a Creole of Color would enlist in the Confederate Army, but it wasn't strange at all at that time and place? So not strange that two white men backed his story? Was he seen as a "good Negro," a true ally to the southern cause? I clench my jaws at the thought. My grandfather always painted his elders as proud men, unafraid to confront white men in dangerous times. This didn't add up.

Although Celestin Gaudin was not a free man of color living in New Orleans, and although his life would have been significantly different from theirs, I still wondered about his enlisting and the discordance with his racial affiliation. Of the free men of color who defended the Confederacy, writer Fatima Shaik considers, "Were they men who feared being enslaved themselves" (was he?) or "slave owners whose economic interests or skin tones gave them more affinity with the planter class" (was that it?). There is no record of a Celestin Gaudin owning enslaved people in St. James or Ascension Parishes. Or "men who sought the respect of New Orleans whites"—did he similarly seek the respect of whites in his midst? "Or Blacks simply loyal to the Confederacy?"[11] Does that explain it?

Speculations abound. Did Celestin Gaudin serve as a white man or as a racially ambiguous person, despite his census record consistently listing him as Black? Was he a white man who demanded that census takers record his race as Black? There is evidence of white men who did this as a strategy to marry women outside their race. But this seems unlikely.

We will never know why Celestin Gaudin fought on the side of the Confederacy. My conclusion is this: if my great-great grandfather did indeed fight for the Confederacy, which the historical record appears to prove, he may have been coerced by other landholders in the vicinity. He may have also joined because he felt it was his duty. On his pension application, he says that he joined in the summer of 1862; at that time, Union forces shelled and set fire to plantations around Donaldsonville. He likely joined the regiment in response. Celestin was a simple farmer. Perhaps he felt the need to protect his farm, to defend his land. And he gained nothing from his service: his family ended up selling off their property and succumbing to a life of sharecropping.

I grapple here with what was lost—the Gaudin family land—and what was gained: this story about my grandfather's grandfather who fought as a Union soldier. How did my grandfather make this acquisition? Was there a deliberate act to obfuscate, to change the story, to change the actions of

Celestin Gaudin? Were his actions shameful to his son Joseph Norah, my grandfather's father? Or did Grandpa know the truth and instead choose to tell me a more pleasant version of his and my ancestor? What a proud statement that any African American might make, that they are the descendant of someone who fought to overthrow the slaveholding oligarchy of the South, to liberate fellow Black Americans! What is the statement that I will make? Will I venerate Celestin the same? Will I apologize for him?

The poet Caroline Randall Williams offers one Black perspective on the Confederacy in the essay, "You Want a Confederate Monument? My Body Is a Confederate Monument." It begins with a sharp image: "I have rape-colored skin. My light-brown-blackness is a living testament to the rules, the practices, and the causes of the Old South." In response to recent conflicts over Confederate monuments and pressures to choose sides—take down the monument as a relic of racism and segregation or leave it up as "history"—Williams offers some of her thoughts. "My blackness does not put me on the other side of anything. It puts me squarely at the heart of the debate. I don't just come from the South. I come from Confederates. I've got rebel-gray blue blood coursing my veins."[12] Reading Williams's essay, I wonder, might she have any Black Confederates among her ancestors? And if so, would her interpretation be any different?

Is Celestin Gaudin represented by Confederate monuments in the South? Certainly not. He was buried in a Catholic cemetery in Donaldsonville, just across the river from Darrow. Did he seek to be buried in a Confederate cemetery? Did his color make him ineligible?

One final pivot, an addendum that will put Celestin to rest. Attached to his application for a veteran's pension is this note, from the Adjutant General's Office of the War Department in Washington, dated December 8, 1911: "There are no rolls on file in this office of the 5th Louisiana Field Artillery, Confederate States Army, and no record has been found of the capture or parole of a man named Celestin Gaudin as of that organization."[13] Reading this, I felt some hope for the complicated memory of Celestin. Did he make up the whole story of serving in the Pelican Battery? Was he impersonating a veteran to get a pension? This is hard to imagine, but it's possible. I also remembered that the federal government did not issue pensions nor keep records of pensioners in the former Confederacy—that was a responsibility held by the southern states—so it makes sense that they would have no account of him.

Still, somehow, on December 15, 1911, his pension application was approved. And on his death, his widow Clementine received a continuation of his pension of $23.98.[14]

My grandfather's father, Joseph Norah Gaudin—son of Celestin Gaudin, Confederate soldier in record, Union soldier in memory, a man of unclear motives who left no explanations, no justifications for his actions—was a quiet man himself. He married a woman named Aliska, whom some called "Mai-eh, Mixblood," but they probably only said it once. Aliska kept the family in line with her stern voice and a firm switch, and she healed her eight children with medicine that grew on their piece of land. Grandpa says she barely spoke any English—one of the many ancestors who are described this way: What was it that she spoke then? Maybe his mother spoke a kind of French with German notes, or maybe she spoke Choctaw French, or maybe a combination of both. Grandpa says it was Créole, a language he himself carried in his mouth to Los Angeles.

Joseph Norah Gaudin and Aliska Webre, of woolen suit and ribbon skirt, of cypress pirogue and burnished plow. When my grandfather referred to his beloved mother, he spoke her name as if it were holy. It sounded like *Vay-ber.*

• • • • •

I'd heard from Grandpa that there was no school for children of color where his family's farm once stood, no school for the racially ambiguous children who were so plentiful in the plantation lands of Ascension Parish. And so, each weekday morning, a flatboat carried my grandfather and his siblings across the river to St. Augustine's School in the town of Donaldsonville. Founded in 1886 by the Sisters of the Holy Family, St. Augustine's gave my grandfather his formal education in English, as Créole increasingly became the at-home tongue.

When my grandfather attended St. Augustine's School, he was told that his relative, Mother Juliette Gaudin, had been one of the founders of the Catholic religious order, Sisters of the Holy Family, in New Orleans, in 1842. Juliette, a free woman of color, is often referred to as Cuban because she was born in Cuba to parents who had been born in Haiti. (Did she share a similar history with Grandma's great-grandmother, Rosella Fernande(z)?) Juliette's parents, Pierre and Marie-Thérèze LaCardonnie Gaudin, were said to have come from the Rivière Gaudin region in Haiti's Plain-du-Nord, where plantation agriculture was at its most concentrated, and so was enslaved labor. This is where, in 1791, the early skirmishes of the St. Domingue Revolution took place. Were the Gaudins planters there, in Plain-du-Nord? Were they slaveholders? The historical record is incomplete, but their ability to flee to Cuba, to live there for some time before emigrating to New Orleans, tells us something about their status.

So does the evidence of their experience as new arrivals in New Orleans. According to Sister Mary Bernard Deggs, who wrote an early history of the Holy Family Sisters, Mother Juliette Gaudin was from a "well known and prosperous famil[y] tied to influential members of the white community," a status that made her and the other sisters "acceptable to the increasingly racist white population [that] would threaten the existence" of the nonwhite order. The Holy Family Sisters "educated girls from free and elite families" in New Orleans. "Keeping with the traditions of the [Catholic] Church which reflected the legal system of Louisiana," the early order "restricted their work among slave girls to instruction in religion." Furthermore, the editors of Deggs's chronicle suggest that Mother Juliette may have rejected a potential nun's entrance into the Holy Family congregation "because she was recently freed and had dark skin."[15] Another layer of complexity confronts me in reading about Mother Juliette. Could this be my paternal inheritance? How does this history reflect on me? On the Gaudin family? What are its implications? I settle in and contemplate, making the decision to include the speculative here.

What is the connection between Juliette Gaudin and Celestin Gaudin? Was there any connection beyond the surname? Beyond belonging to the population of free people of color in Louisiana at the same time? Mother Juliette died in 1888. Celestin Gaudin died in 1918. Was he a nephew? A younger cousin? Did Pierre Gaudin have a son or a nephew who moved upriver, who then had sons, among whom was Celestin? Is it coincidence? Without irrefutable proof, I sit in the imagining, in the space of not knowing. Gaudin, an uncommon French name in Louisiana, a small family group. The many layers of possibility, the difficult morality of my paternal heritage.

Grandpa graduated from St. Augustine's in 1926. Since there were no public schools for children of color in Darrow and Donaldsonville, it follows that there was no high school for them either. So, John Norah Gaudin left home to finish his education. He moved to New Orleans, where his older brother Earl was already living. He graduated from John McDonogh Colored High School in 1930 and then returned home to Darrow and began learning the carpentry trade.

College of Pharmacy Graduates, Xavier University of Louisiana. My great-uncle, Earl Gaudin, center, 1938. Photo courtesy of Xavier University of Louisiana.

In 1932, while visiting New Orleans, he attended a Carnival ball. On that night, my grandfather met the woman who would become my paternal grandmother, Rita Elizabeth Roux. The ball was held at the Autocrat Club, which was aptly named. The members were known to have been autocratic about who was allowed in: only those with a fine grade of hair, the correct tone of skin, or a referral by another member. My grandmother arrived chaperoned and proper, in a gown and feathered mask. They met; they danced. When Lent began, my grandfather returned to his father's farm in Ascension Parish; he wrote her letters, including a photograph in one. He is brown and striking, his Amhara ancestry clear in the sharp line of his nose and in the set of his mouth. A foot resting on a bent knee, he is relaxed, sitting reclined, against a backdrop of his father's corn and cotton fields. Someone wrote his name, "John Gaudin," on the photo. He isn't what my grandmother's family wanted for her—a man from the city—but he is the one my grandmother wanted for herself.

I'd heard from my grandfather about one of their dates on a night in 1934, at a segregated theater in Donaldsonville. As they were leaving the theater in my grandfather's brother's car, some white men began honking at them, flashing their lights and attempting to run them off the road. My grandfather drove into a field, he told me decades later, "cut the engine, turned out the lights, and hid until they was long gone."

"They thought I was driving in a car next to a white woman," he said. A fatal flaw, a deadly crime for a man my grandfather's color.

The incident was one of many that drew my grandfather's attention away from Louisiana and toward a place where his—and our—brown skin would not be treated and seen as a curse.

You will always be someone from somewhere else.

—DAO STROM

California Creoles. Rosella Gaudin Aubry (my father's sister), Eleanor Burns Gaudin (my mother), and John Norah Gaudin (my paternal grandfather). Twelfth Avenue, Los Angeles, 1957.

# 5

# Sunset Limited

In 1941, he finally felt like a man. Like *a man.*

He was twenty-nine years old.

The expression—feeling "like a man"—didn't mean a lot to me when I interviewed Grandpa. Yet, as I write about it now, more than twenty years later, I summon James Baldwin, I am reminded of Richard Wright, I bow to Frantz Fanon, I thank Ralph Ellison. The feeling "like a man," robbed from Black men in the South by segregated spaces that kept them in the back, in the balcony, in the margins, behind the sign, on the outside; by laws that prohibited interracial marriage; by taxes and clauses that curbed their full citizenship rights; by individuals who humiliated them with what we now call micro-aggressions and with outright aggressions too; who tripped them when they walked down a narrow sidewalk; who fired them from a demeaning job for which they were underpaid; who slapped them for forgetting the "sir"; who left them their shitted drawers to wash, their filthy socks, their fatty fork and sticky spoon, their stained sheets; indiscreet, who called them by their first names when they asked to be called "Mr.," who called them "Nonc," and worse. I think of the poet John Warner Smith, who wrote about being spat on, in the back of the neck, by a child of nine, a white child who was taught his superior place—an action duplicated throughout time and space of committing uncountable harms against the Black body.[1]

The conversation with my grandfather is unforgettable: we were sitting in the room that was my father's childhood bedroom and then became my grandmother's sewing room, and then a binary room of sewing and rest.

Grandpa died in this room. Peacefully, sitting in his favorite recliner, while his wife of more than sixty years, Grandma, was at her water aerobics class. That was in 2013.

In 1941, John Norah Gaudin was one of thousands of southern craftsmen who were recruited to build an enormous bomb shelter in Pasco, Washington State. The bomb shelters built there were part of that state's massive transformation in support of the war effort, which, horrifically, included the incarceration of Japanese Americans residing there. (Did Grandpa's labor contribute to the building of the camp in Pullayup? I cringe at the thought; I banish the idea from my mind.) The bunker at Camp Hayden represented one of many throughout the state that were designed to survive a devastating attack from the enemies of the time: the Axis powers, Italy, Germany, and especially, Japan.[2] The website *Atlas Obscura* features an article on Camp Hayden, describing it as "an abandoned World War II bunker that was part of a chain that runs throughout Washington." It featured "a fire control radar and harbor entrance radar, as well as 45-foot guns that covered the Strait of Juan de Fuca."[3]

The wartime opportunity to make a decent wage at sites such as these, and to see a different part of the country, led John Norah Gaudin to leave his wife and young children back in Louisiana, and he traveled for the first time to the West Coast. There, he said, he finally felt like a man. And while working on the bomb shelter, my paternal grandfather saw something he'd never in his life seen before nor ever expected to.

According to Grandpa's recollection, early every morning, the workers rose from their barracks, ate a basic meal, and rode to the job site, all of them, white men and Black men and Creole men from Louisiana, men of drawl and twang, sitting scattershot on the bus. "All these poor white men from the South, throwing around the word 'n——,'" his voice in a soft rasp as my grandfather tenderly said the word to me.

My grandfather continued: "When that bus was full, they knew how many seats they needed, and they counted the guys as they came on. And a white guy, must've been from Oklahoma . . . he said, 'I got a seat for one more n——.' The colored guy that was sitting [on the bus] got up and, before he knew it, that white guy was flat on the floor of the truck. He hit him upside his jaw here with his fist," Grandpa showed me, "and blood was coming out his mouth. *Pow!* I couldn't believe what I was seeing." The Black man on the bus commenced to beat the white man's ass, right there on the bus, with all the many-hued southern working men watching in silent awe. When the fight was over, everyone remained sitting on their benches and rode to the job site. "Nobody did nothin' about it. And the guy that hit him didn't lose his job," my grandfather said, still astonished after all those years. I remember his face as he told the story, his eyes wide, his mustache characteristically twisted, curled, and waxed at the ends. "If that happened down South, that Black man would've been lynched."[4]

At that moment, my grandfather says, he decided to move his family out West.

In World War II–era Louisiana, John Norah Gaudin had belonged to the Colored Carpenter's Union. Regardless of my paternal grandfather's West African, Afro-Caribbean, French, German, and Mississippi Choctaw heritage, he proudly joined that union of skilled men. Grandpa shared with me that carpenters of color in rural and small-town Louisiana were given the worst jobs among those in the building trades. In New Orleans, however, things were better than they were in Grandpa's native Ascension Parish. Creole craftsmen in the city, especially those originating in the city's Seventh Ward, were so specialized and had such talent that they were known and admired far and wide. "Anywhere you went, if you was from New Orleans, they were known for their articular craftsmanship," recalls master plasterer Earl Barthé. "When you said you was from New Orleans, you had a job. You had nothing to worry about."[5] New Orleans Creole craftsmen were sons and grandsons of woodworkers, plasterers, lathers, bricklayers, masons, blacksmiths, and tinsmiths, proud of their work, proud of their heritage. Yet, despite being "imbued with the mission of perfection," master craftsmen who were men of color still had to contend with the humiliations and violence of segregation.

Many couldn't tolerate it; instead, they chose to leave: In my paternal grandfather's words: "I realized: no, this is not the place for me. I said, I got to find a better place to live for my children. Said, they can't grow up here. Said, they can't grow up under the conditions I grew up under. I had to tolerate that because that was the way of life down here. I said, let me get out from here. Find a place where my children can be somebody."[6]

Instead of Washington State, John Norah Gaudin chose California, where there was already a Louisiana Creole population and where a wartime building boom drew skilled craftsmen to Los Angeles via the Sunset Limited line of the Southern Pacific Railroad. Boasting a "Ladies Lounge" with a bath and a maid, a "Commodious Observation Platform," "steel sleeping cars," and a porter (like my maternal grandfather Augustus Lawrence), the Sunset Limited carried thousands of Louisiana Creole families to the West Coast. The train has since achieved somewhat mythic status. Mark Broyard, performer and coauthor of the play *Inside the Creole Mafia,* remembered his family's migration to California in 1961, almost twenty years after the Gaudins settled there. "Six months after my father and uncle drove to Los Angeles in a rental truck full of furniture and appliances," Broyard recounted, "my mom packed up the three kids, and we boarded the Sunset Limited through Louisiana, Texas, New Mexico and Arizona, and got off at Union Station in Los Angeles."[7]

For many Louisiana Creoles, going to California was like "migrating to the colonies," albeit on a modern sleeper train rather than a stinking and fetid ship. Risking everything, they left everything behind: parents and siblings, extended family and neighbors, employers and schools, intergenerational customs, Catholic parishes and fraternal organizations, lifelong friends, betrotheds, and businesses. Mark Broyard shared, "My father closed up Broyard Construction, sold his trucks and cement mixers, scaffolding and tools, and left behind the family business." Broyard's mother too "closed up the beautiful yellow brick house that my father built for us on Eads Street, where we lived around the corner from her mother, down the street from my dad's parents, and down the block from my dad's grandmother and aunt. We said goodbye to them all."[8]

The migrants left behind the places where their names were recognized and where their idioms made sense. They left behind the cemeteries where their ancestors were buried, the above-ground crypts in the old wards, crumbling brick homes sheltering the dead. Reflecting on this westward migration, I consider that which carried Ruth Behar's family from Cuba and Dao Strom's family from Vietnam, their narratives foundational to this one. The catastrophe of civil war and invasion and communist revolution—the dramatic stories of loss, leaving with a box of photographs or gold sewn into the hems of clothes—might not match the Creole migration of the mid-twentieth century, but the wider story of diaspora certainly does.

One Creole migrant to California, Bernard Brulé, called himself a "sort of a pioneer," having arrived in Los Angeles in 1929, one year prior to my maternal grandparents' arrival. "Pioneer" carries a heavy load today and understandably so; gone are the narratives of a toughened, romanticized, white family under covered wagon, fearful of "Indians" and driven by manifest destiny. History tells us other stories. Here, Brulé's story implies choice, a nostalgia of westward movement, a train gliding into the horizon; the trauma of segregation, a door permanently closed behind them. "I didn't know anyone out here . . . but I never thought about going home, no." Brulé added, "You could just see the opportunities."[9] In the absence of formalized Jim Crow, California and the West Coast represented a fresh beginning, a new life. In recorded conversations and interviews with my elders, California was described as "the land of milk and honey," a place imagined as "so wonderful, you could go and pick up gold in the streets." Another newcomer, Leonard Tureaud, reflecting on the migration to California used a stark description for what the West offered Creoles of Color from the South: "In Los Angeles, I can't walk down the street and say my grandfather built that staircase, no. But I can point over there and say, 'Look, I built that hospital.'"[10]

The image of the Sunset Limited is glazed with romanticism, but California was no Xanadu. Its streets were not paved in gold, and Creoles did not arrive in a place free of race, racism, or hardship. They arrived in a place with its own trauma, its own history of Catholic missions, of racial repression, of Indigenous people's removal, of forced labor. Creoles who migrated to California encountered job discrimination, racial and color prejudice, and neighborhood covenants that attempted to keep marginalized populations out of desirable areas. Some, like my paternal grandparents, used other means at their disposal to navigate Los Angeles–style racism. As my grandmother shared with me in a recorded interview in 1999, "I thought that, in California, we wouldn't have to worry about all that color stuff. But some things were the same out here. Daddy couldn't sign the papers for this land: he wasn't light like me. So, I had to do it. I guess you can call it passing, I don't know. I just went in to sign the papers, and that's how we got the land that we're still living on. They thought I was white and that, plus the money, was enough."[11] With the mortgage signed, Grandpa and his brothers-in-law commenced to build the house, their varying shades of brown skin shining in the sun.

Given the extent of Creole patterns of settlement in the Jefferson Park / Crenshaw area of West Los Angeles, many families can tell similar stories of the lightest-skinned members of the family negotiating business with white Los Angelenos. It must have helped them as newcomers in the West. Back in New Orleans, a person's race could be revealed in their other-colored sibling, in the parish or elementary school that they attended, in the clubs they frequented or the beaches they frolicked on or in the labor union they belonged to. It could also be exposed in the varied and sometimes racialized spelling of their French, German, and Spanish surnames, although race and surname were not exactly aligned. In New Orleans, my grandfather's surname, Burns, told the listener that he is from uptown and a questionable Creole, uptown being associated with Anglo-Americans; my grandmother's surname Roux indicated she was from downtown, a true Creole, from the old people, the French. The diasporic writer S. Sukardi reminds us that names contain generations of meaning. In Chinese naming traditions, "all the members of a family's generation would share the same first syllable of their given name." Sukardi adds, "With little ease and patience, you could approximate a person's age, reconstruct what village and province they belonged to. More than being the contents of an archive, the name was a small, complete archive unto itself."[12]

In California, however, migrants' unfamiliar surnames and lack of local history sparked no flame of suspicion. Being taken as white may have helped them purchase land wherever they wanted, and circumventing a racist law by performing whiteness may have represented a kind of resistance—but this action did not help dismantle racist neighborhood covenants, which kept out those with Spanish surnames, those who were marked as Japanese, or those without the socioeconomic benefit of lightness of skin.

California-style racism that targeted Mexican Americans may have also negatively affected racially ambiguous Creoles; racism that targeted African Americans certainly did.[13] Some Creoles used their skin color as a tool to quietly negotiate familiar realities in a new place. "When we came out here [to Los Angeles], people couldn't tell if we were white or black," one Creole migrant to California remembered. "I was looking for a job and I passed a restaurant with a 'help wanted' sign in the window. The sign said, 'Whites Only Need Apply,' but I walked right in anyway and got the job."[14]

"Whites Only Need Apply" may not necessarily make a person think immediately of California, but systemic prejudices against racialized populations certainly abounded on the West Coast. After all, racism is an American problem, not just a southern one. So, Louisiana Creoles adapted. They assimilated into their new surroundings, they transplanted as much of their original culture as they could, they colonized whichever Roman Catholic parish was near their home, and they sent for family members to join them. Families back in Louisiana pooled money to send a father, a brother, or an uncle to California, where he joined others in community, bought an empty lot, and built a house. Then others arrived, staying in that original house while the skilled craftsmen in the family built another house, and the practice continued until a whole family had settled in the same area.

My family was no different: with his own hands and with the help of his wife's brothers, Grandpa built a camelback shotgun. The house was long and narrow, each room followed by another room behind it, from front to back, with the bedrooms and bathrooms along the sides of the house, and the middle opening up for the spaces where we gathered as a family. In the living room, or the front room, my grandparents hung portraits of their grandchildren, and we all sang holiday songs while my Aunt Sandy played the piano. In the dining room and the kitchen, we ate seafood gumbo with white rice and stuffed mirliton on Sundays. In the sewing room, my paternal grandmother's Singer hummed and buzzed. It was not a traditional shotgun with the front door and the back door in parallel formation, which a breeze could blow straight through, but this was not Louisiana. Grandma and Grandpa's house on Twelfth Avenue was an adapted architectural form.

The camelback apartment upstairs was for my grandmother's sister, Aunt Lalie (short for Eulalie), whose hair was dyed red and stayed red until shortly before her death. My grandmother's other sister, Aunt Yvonne, lived four doors down. Aunt Lalie married a Despues, and Aunt Yvonne married an Allain, both fine-dressing, sweet-smelling, nut-colored men from New Orleans and both Creole men skilled in the building trades. Within a two-block radius was Uncle John's house, Uncle Albert's house, and Uncle Aubry's house.

My father, the only son of a skilled craftsman and a master seamstress, grew up surrounded by the families of young boys like him: French-named families who had left New Orleans behind and built brand-new houses with their own hands and who attended Mass on Sundays at St. John the Evangelist, St. Bernadette, Transfiguration, and Holy Name of Jesus. My father grew up with other Creole boys whose mothers wore Yardley complexion powder and carried parasols in the sun and whose homes were adorned with holy water bottles, rosaries, and portraits of the Sacred Heart of Jesus. They represented a broad spectrum of families from downtown New Orleans, of multi-hued fathers who dressed neat as a pin and of multi-hued mothers who could sew a gown for a Carnival queen. Most were middle-class Creoles of Color, the population that had just enough money to move their families across the country.

The pattern of the Los Angeles Creole diaspora was like that of other diasporas: when one family arrived, others arrived, settling on the same street, and then an avenue over, and soon the pattern sounded like the recitation of a prayer. "There were the Broyards, the Dupres, the Tureauds, the Delereys, the Theards, the Gagniers, the Rousseves, the Olivers, the Fontenots, the Antoines, the Anthonys, the Conants, the Aubrys, the Metoyers, the Loquets, the Roques, the Guenveurs, the Bacquets, the Desvignes, the Domaines, and the Gueringers. There was the Bordenave family and the Hardins, the Honores, the Vavasseurs, the Pajauds, the Prudhommes, the Monteguts, the Saulneys, the Lacroix family, the St. Cyrs and the St. Juliens, the Pichons, the Dumas, the Chevaliers, the Feltons."[15] And there were the Burnses. And the Gaudins.

My grandparents attended the Catholic church closest to their new home, Holy Name of Jesus Catholic Church, which originally served a predominantly white parish in the Jefferson Park area of Los Angeles. It came to be called "Corpus Christi West" or "Little Corpus Christi" because so many of its parishioners, by the early 1950s, were Creoles from New Orleans's Seventh Ward where Corpus Christi was the principal community church. Catholic Creoles founded and dominated the Knights of Peter Claver, a

Pioneers. Marietta Roussel and Augustus Lawrence Burns, my maternal grandparents, living well in Los Angeles, 1963.

Catholic fraternity and good works association popular in New Orleans. In church halls, they hosted community suppers replete with Louisiana music and food. They carried with them the tradition of socializing and sharing gossip following the recitation of novenas. And, of course, they were the sharpest dressers.

In Los Angeles, up sprang Creole clubs like the Pelican Club, Autocrat West, Le Club Sans Nom, the Versatilians, the Socialites, the Crescent City Lodge, the Jolly-Jokers, the Bon Ton Social Club, and my father's club, the Cajons: these gave Creoles ample opportunities to gather outside Catholic services and holiday celebrations. The writers of the *Bayou Talk* newspaper, a “Cajun Creole communication vehicle” to assist Louisianans in communicating with relatives “back home” and finding relatives in California, reported on these culturally significant clubs.[16] Autocrat West was organized by “a small group of [originally Seventh Ward] men with common interest and the desire to associate socially.”[17] Some clubs reflected more than others the Creole tendency to insular clannishness. For example, the Jolly-Jokers, “organized in 1965 by eleven Louisiana ladies,” began as a Christmas savings group but came to focus on the preservation of “Louisiana culture and philosophy for their families.” Its bylaws “restricted the number of members to the original number of eleven.”[18]

By limiting the size of a club, its members also justified the exclusion of any persons who may not have met certain criteria; for example, having a French surname, practicing Roman Catholicism, intending to arrange the marriages of their children, sharing the phenotype of the rest of the members. They also assured themselves a comfortable and stable social network and provided an acceptable example of proper association for the next generation. Another Creole club, the Bon Ton, required that new members “must be a Louisiana native . . . be nominated by a member of the club, and pass a review by the membership committee.”[19]

In Los Angeles, Creole migrants persisted in their Deep South practices of keeping to themselves in tight-knit Catholic communities and socializing only with those whom they defined as “their own people.” Admittedly, “their own people” was sometimes interpreted as someone of their own color, an indication of Creoles’ practice of colorism; that is, the preference for those of lighter skin or those who are read as racially ambiguous. Some California Creoles carried with them an inherited prejudice, one with origins in colonialism, in slavery, and in segregation and characterized by an obsession with skin color. This fixation was not absent from my own family group; I can recall many lengthy conversations about skin color and hair texture.

But this should not be overstated. For every example of a family that preferred a certain shade of skin or grade of hair, there is another example of a family that did not. Creole families are multi-hued families: it is very common for varied phenotypes to appear among siblings. The image of the “light-skinned Creole” is a stereotype; it is contextual, deeply local, and not representative of the group. Creoles in downtown New Orleans married into other downtown families, choosing their partners from within the community, hence reproducing similar traits; Creoles in uptown New Orleans did the same. If we reach beyond New Orleans and consider lower Louisiana—communities closer to the Gulf in Terrebonne, Lafourche, and Plaquemines Parishes or the parishes along the Mississippi River, where my maternal grandmother and my paternal grandfather were from—or Acadiana, the communities around Lafayette like Frilot Cove, Ville Platte, Opelousas, Mamou, and Plaisance; or the Cane River communities in northern Louisiana; and if we reach beyond Louisiana into the Gulf Coast regions of Mississippi and Alabama, we will see Creoles of every beautiful shade of skin. We will see people whose progeny shared the features of those around them, because most people in small communities made their families from within the population. "Their own people" referred to many things.

Historian Tyina Steptoe explored this subject with another migrant population, Creoles of Color who settled in Houston in the decades following World War I. Steptoe writes, "They spoke French, practiced Catholicism, and established musical traditions like the accordion-based 'la-la,'" which is linked to the Zydeco musical form that originated in southwest Louisiana. Steptoe continues, "Foods like boudin, gumbo, and étouffée became staples of Creole cuisine. When they evoked a Creole identity, then, they did not just refer to their European and African roots; they also referred to the linguistic, religious, culinary, and musical traditions that helped them express who they are as a people."[20]

It was similar in Los Angeles, where there was the strong emphasis on Catholicism. Their nephews, like my cousin Father Julien were parish priests, and their nieces, like my cousin Sister Marie Gabrielle, were nuns. They celebrated the Feast of St. Joseph, a tradition initiated by New Orleans Italians and practiced by Creoles of Color, and they marked the feast days of other Catholic saints. They gathered at the same parishes, initiated Catholic fraternal societies, and made these churches their social universe.

The California migrants ate gumbo, caouane (turtle soup), rabbit sauce piquant, hog's head cheese, andouille, crawfish, boudin, cracklin', and French bread. They shopped at the Louisiana Meat Market, the Louisiana Fish Market, the Big Loaf Bakery, and the St. Bernard Market: these establishments didn't exist when my maternal grandparents arrived in 1930 but were later opened to cater to a growing population with particular tastes and the ability to pay for imported goods. They gathered at Harold and Belle's, the New Orleans Grotto, and Merlin Saulny's restaurants. They patronized Desvigne's, Duplantier's, and Aubry's barber shops. California Creoles also held Mardi Gras balls that, some say, rivaled those in New Orleans.

As members of this community, all four of my grandparents—Marietta Roussel, Rita Elizabeth Roux, Augustus Lawrence Burns, and John Norah Gaudin—sought out "*their own people*"; that is, people who understood their Louisiana origins, people who spoke their language, people who experienced the same dislocation, the same movement westward. All four of my grandparents continued to do whatever they could both to continue their lives as Louisianans and to benefit from all the freedoms that California had to offer. "Like going to the beach whenever they wanted to instead of only on specific days and between certain hours," writes California Creole Mark Broyard. "Stepping through the front door of a restaurant and being welcomed. Enjoying the national parks, the museums and the theaters, and feeling safe as they traveled, stopping in whatever motel or hotel suited their fancy and their wallet." California made possible Creoles' "newfound sense of . . . long-hoped-for liberation."[21]

Creoles in California were people with a history that was centuries old, but they were also new people in a new land. In California, they could be African American. They could be multiracial. They could be Latin American. They could be Mediterranean. They could be Creole. They could be racially nondistinct. As my mother has said, "I can be anything. I am whatever people see me as." This characterization is not only a reflection of California as a place where the migrants' phenotypes did not immediately racialize them; it is also a leftover of the Louisiana from which they came. Historian Kim Lacy Rogers describes it as "a mixture of blacks, white Creoles, people of Irish, German, and Italian descent, people from numerous parts of Latin America, and the descendants of Louisiana's 'gens de couleur.'" Furthermore, in southern Louisiana, "black and white Creoles claim[ed] to possess Mediterranean looks," including "dark hair and eyes, fair or olive complexions, Anglo or Spanish features"—resulting in a humanscape whose "sheer variety of skin color" often made it impossible to "tell the race of an ostensibly black or white community leader."[22] The anonymity, then, that California offered to Louisiana migrants may have reflected the ambiguity of the lands that they'd left behind. California represented a doorway to "a better life," however that might be defined, and many Creoles walked through it.

• • • • •

When I asked my father to define himself, he said, "I'm Dr. Anthony Gaudin. That's it."

Ah, California and the freedoms that my family exercised.

For the racially ambiguous among us, California seemingly offered an escape from the punishments and limitations codified in anti-Black racist laws. Being read as a racial unknown or as white offered tangible, measurable benefits: the "wages of whiteness" that historians and intellectuals such as W. E. B. Du Bois, C. Vann Woodward, Robin D. G. Kelley, Matthew Frye Jacobson, George Lipsitz, and David Roediger have written about. Higher wages and access to jobs only available to those who weren't a member of a despised group; opportunities for promotions, bank loans, and financial incentives of all kinds; invitations to network; benefits associated with nepotism, the "wages of whiteness" locked out populations of color from advancements of all kinds.

For those of any phenotype who migrated to California with resources and skills, opening and owning one's own business were ways that Black people and people of color provided for themselves: they established their own lending institutions, they cared for their own sick, they built their own construction companies, they buried their own dead, they relied on their own industry. Entrepreneurship has a long history among historically excluded populations—if you get the worst cuts of meat at the butcher, open your own butcher shop; if a beauty parlor won't treat your grade of hair, open your own salon.

For those who were not immediately perceived as Black and thus not subject to the worst of racist prohibitions, the "wages of *beigeness*" might have been possible. Even those who could not "pass as white" could avoid the worst expressions of racism by being viewed as an "ethnic other." The comic strip illustrator George Herriman is one example. Migrating to California with his family in 1890 at the age of ten, Herriman is often seen as a Creole of Color, of downtown New Orleans heritage, who passed as white in his adult life. But Herriman was perceived as and called "Greek," an ethnic nomenclature that does not necessarily equate to "white" in the early twentieth century. He persevered throughout his life under that not-Black, ethnic-other classification.[23] In the memories and the narratives of those who watched their family members board the Sunset Limited, the West was imagined as a place where one could get ahead by shedding one self and donning another.

"They went out there to be white," one oral history informant told me very plainly about some members of her family. "That's all they ever wanted to be, so they left here."

Listening to this, I furrowed my brow. Grandpa, I thought to myself, wanted to be white? Why? How? He was brown skinned! Surely the idea of people becoming white in the West was hyperbole, an exaggerated mythology associated with the California migrants. I wondered if it stood out so much in the diasporic narrative because people at home in New Orleans were doing the same, practicing serial passing? A plethora of examples of people "allowing themselves to be taken as white" colored my oral history interviews with those who never migrated to California. There is the example of the woman who "worked as white" at Haspel's sewing factory because she earned more money that way; instead of doing the basic sewing work done by employees of color, she stitched the fine details of men's suits. There is the example of the man who took his two children to the library on whites-only days because he overheard someone on the streetcar saying that different books were available then. There is the example of the man who rode in front of the "White passengers" screen on the streetcar to get to work every day but who attended Corpus Christi Catholic Church on Sundays, where his browner-skinned coworkers shook his hand and kept his secret. Another example: during the Great Depression, a woman's red-haired father stood in the white line for food distribution at City Hall, while her brown-skinned mother stood in the Colored line; they shared the extra perishable food with neighbors and stored the shelf items for leaner days. And another: a woman worked as an artillery technician during World War II, earning three times the salary of her husband, who cleaned the facility;

when they left for work in the morning, they walked separately to the bus stop, they sat in different sections of the bus, and at work they acted as if they were strangers.

The stories call to mind lines from a poem by Natasha Trethewey. A woman who has migrated to the city for work is writing a "Letter Home" to her family. In it, she confesses, "I walk these streets / a white woman, or so I think, until I catch the eyes / of some stranger upon me, and I must lower mine, / a *negress* again."[24]

But, in many interviews, *passa blancs,* the Créole term for those who could pass as white, were consistently imagined as those who left for California. The overwhelming message that I received was this: in the city of New Orleans, there was a degree of anonymity that allowed people to perform whiteness for specific purposes, in truncated form, as an act of resistance against segregation. In contrast, California, and other imagined geographies, offered space for those who wanted to cross over, to *become white,* which suggests that the performance was permanent. One woman whom I interviewed in Plaquemines Parish, whose home was uncomfortably close to a chemical plant, told me of her two sisters who married white men and moved to Maine. The other, sometimes imagined and sometimes experienced place is a blank slate in many of the narratives of diaspora. It is a place without constriction, which is racialized as white. The sentiment resonated in the words of my paternal grandmother's lifelong friend, the late Audrey Garnier Baquet. In a recorded interview, we shared this exchange:

> *Me:* Do you think some people went to California to pass [as white]?
>
> *Miss Audrey:* Oh, that was one of the main reasons . . .
>
> *Me:* Do you think so?
>
> *Miss Audrey:* Oh, yeah, all the ones I know went to California to pass.[25]

She wondered about the relationship of color to identity, however, adding, "To me, if they looked so much like white, why did they have to 'pass?' Why couldn't they just be white if they looked white?"[26]

In a conversation with an extended family member on the Gaudin side, I learned the same:

*Me:* Can you tell me of some instances of people passing?

*Family member:* Well, most of them went to Los Angeles.

The synonymity of California Creoles as *passa blancs* does not reflect the reality of the multi-hued Creoles who migrated. It does, however, suggest a larger understanding of the migrants having markedly easier lives than those they'd left behind in Louisiana. It makes sense: "White is the color of freedom," as articulated so starkly by historian Allyson Hobbs.[27] This conflation of whiteness, migration, and upward mobility certainly stems from familiar roots. Some of those who remained in Louisiana measured their own lives as fraught with toil, both psychological and physical, stemming from the carceral policies and practices of the white South. And the many who measured their lives against that fraught narrative recognized the deliberately disempowered position in which peoples of color dwelt.

Creoles who remained in Louisiana interpreted information given to them through letters, postcards, telephone calls, and visits from those who'd left. My paternal grandparents' visits to New Orleans were a kind of guidepost to California: their ability to take time off from work and spend money on travel, conversations about their children attending universities in Los Angeles, gifts they gave to relatives, photos shared from their other travels throughout Europe, Asia, the Middle East, and the Caribbean. Their vocabularies changed and their geographic references changed. California Creoles spoke "better English," many folks told me, and we spoke without a Louisiana accent. We were perceived as having a better understanding of the white world too and being less hampered by ideas and hang-ups about race. In Louisiana narratives of the diaspora, we in California were better educated and better paid. "Ya'll had it easy," one elder cousin said to me frankly. "No offense intended."

"Those who left escaped the fight," the late Ferdinand Delery Jr. shared with me as we sat talking at his dining room table in his New Orleans home in 1999. A friend of the family, a retired master plasterer who also worked in the field of aerospace, Mr. Delery warmly welcomed me into his home and shared with me some of his family history. Regarding the California migrants, he told me, "They didn't have to deal with the ugliness and the racism and all that." Mr. Delery's children helped desegregate New Orleans Catholic schools, and despite the centuries of interracial mixing and the layers of racial ambiguity in the city, those times were not pretty.[28] Civil rights activism in New Orleans, Baton Rouge, and elsewhere in Louisiana slapped many Creoles of Color in the face: any notion of Creole privilege, the idea that we were measurably different from other African-descended people, came crashing down as white parents fought to keep Creole children from attending whites-only schools. Mr. Delery shared frankly that the California migrants "escaped and left us to fight it out."[29]

Harold Baquet, a prominent New Orleans photographer and spirited human being who lost his fight against colon cancer in 2019, drove me around the city several times, sharing bits and pieces of New Orleans history and introducing me to friends and family whom I would later interview for this book. He also publicly shared his thoughts regarding Creoles who migrated to California: "Some people think you copped out," adding, "we can't blame ya'll."[30]

Having abandoned the South for the West Coast, my family clearly avoided the struggles of the civil rights movement. Migrating during the early twentieth century, they could not have known what was coming in the 1960s. But it cannot be denied that my elders' language around identity, their lives spent in a somewhat insulated diasporic community, and the educational and economic options available to them were all shaped by their sheltered California reality. While their extended family and friends left behind in Louisiana were putting their lives on the line not only to desegregate public spaces and to exercise their right to vote but also to insist on the full humanity of Black people, my family was exercising freedom, calling themselves whatever they wanted.

And it is true: in California, my paternal grandfather's only son wouldn't be subject to the limitations of a segregated and deeply unequal society. He would not feel the need to lower the volume of his voice, to shrink back into the corners of life, to strategize a way to survive, to hunker down and hustle. In California, far from the cotton crops and the pecan trees around his father's home in Darrow, Louisiana, my father could fly as far as the winds would carry him.

Professor. Anthony Joseph Gaudin, my father.
Los Angeles, 1958.

# 6

# Taxonomy

*Hurricane, typhoon, tsunami*
*Drizzle, sun shower, cloudburst*
*Thunderhead, rain shadow, downpour*
*Cyclone, hail, waterspout*

Every July, I wished for rain. I dreamed of rain; I conjured rain. The kind of rain that sounds like wind and winks in the night. I wished for curtains of rain to come in waves, to heavily slap the second-story roof of my childhood home and then to quietly tap on it with fingerling drops—only the rain itself knowing what mood it would take, when it would stop. Every July, I waited for rain from the upstairs front-corner bedroom, the bedroom with purple walls and a purple ceiling, with lilac window blinds and puffy stickers on the door, a bedroom of my own in our golden home, with my rectangular view of the world and my rectangular wish for rain, daytime or nighttime rain that slid down the pine needles outside my rectangular bedroom window and the roof of the single-story home next door: made of wooden shingles, kindling, waiting to be lit up.

Every July, the green turned to brush in that artificial landscape, that dry little village at the base of the Santa Susana Mountains, in a San Fernando Valley suburb outside Los Angeles where I spent my childhood.[1] The streets in our little cocoon of cul-de-sacs were named after cities in other places.

Baton Rouge. Los Alimos. Key West. Des Moines. Tulsa. Nashville. Olympia. Cheyenne. Tampa. There was Chatsworth Street of New Jersey, but in our mouths, it prickled of England; and our street Bismarck Avenue, of South Dakota, but when we said it, it bittered of Germany. My father, like his father before him, followed employment and the hopes of a better life when he moved our family from the city of Los Angeles to the San Fernando Valley, an area that had once been part of Alta California, Mexico, that had once been orange groves and ranches of cattle and sheep, that had once been the autonomous lands of the variegated Tongva people. At the time of my family's move, in August 1970 when I was six weeks old, Northridge was beyond the end of the I-405 freeway; it was not quite a white-flight community—we had sidewalks and no residential covenants—but there were very few families of color among us.

Surrounded by dry, rolling hills, summertime reminded us that we actually lived in a space of convergence: the place between the deserts of the Southwest and the fertile lowlands of Central California. Every July, pine dried into brown. Sweet peas smoked into ash. Ivy bristled into crisp. Juniper and dichondra, olive tree and bottle brush. Sparse orange groves blistered in the heat, as brown as the horses on shrinking ranches that kicked up dust into their globular eyes. The thirsty suburb of Northridge swallowed up open land, replacing it with water-hungry dichondra lawns and two-story, four-bedroom tract houses.

July was the longing for rain. The kind of rain that my great-grandfathers prayed would stop—these grandfathers' great-grandfathers who were born before hurricanes were named after women and so close to Louisiana's waters that they saw the homes of their neighbors wash away down the river; they saw the bones of their own grandfathers floating in an ordinary flood. July in Northridge, California, was the pleading for rain to come, a departure from that ancestral voice, my heritage, the voice of my grandfathers' great-grandfathers, who begged the skies and the intercessors for pause. "Saint Medard, protect us."

Oya, blow what harms us away.

Every July, my father joined the other fathers in a summer ritual—our suburban tribe, the tribe of the middle class, of migrants who left cities behind for the sidewalked pristine. In my memory, we gathered outside and watched as an ominous orange glow appeared in the mountains above our homes, as if the sun had squatted just up there where we could see it.

Wildfire.

A throbbing sizzle of heat and ashes falling on the windshields of our Volvos and Volkswagens. Flames in the hills twirling like sequined dervishes. And all of us gathered outside, all of us children with stay-at-home moms and dads who cut the grass, Joni Mitchell's *The Hissing of Summer Lawns* our sunken living rooms' soundtrack. All of us with matching dressers and desks and twin beds with headboards, all of us with wallpaper in the kitchen and laundry rooms off the den, all of us angling our gazes to the glowing summer hillsides, with our mothers under blankets mapping the smoke. And our fathers turned the summer hoses to full blast, aiming the arc of salvation toward the wooden shingles, badly mimicking the rain we all hoped would come.

"St. Florian, protect us."

I wonder whether my memory of fire in the San Fernando Valley is like Grandpa's memory of his Grandaddy, the "Union soldier." Did he hear his Granddaddy talking about the war just once, and then it became a defining story in his memory? Has the memory of one summer fire become a terrible symbol of July? My perception of fire in the Valley is made more real by recent fires that have burned unfathomable expanses of land in California, those fires mongering fear on the TV news that my mother watches throughout the day, and blanketing, as they say, the desert skies. On a recent visit to California, I drove along the I-14 and the I-5 freeways to visit my sister Leslie, who lives a mile from our Bismarck Avenue childhood home. The scorched remains of trees and brush clung to the hillsides, their bodies burned, the ground around them blackened.

All summer long, my best friend Cindy and I rode our bikes around our cul-de-sac, Cindy in braces and blonde, electric hair, her thick bangs bulging out like a wave on the ocean—and my hair not yet cut, growing down and out for twelve years, hanging down my back in a dense braid. Our bodies were still mostly straight lines, not yet having grown into our mothers' bodies. Cindy was most definitely her mother's daughter, the maternal in her pale, freckled skin, but I was regularly thought to be adopted: my mother's skin was much lighter than mine and her hair, much straighter than mine.

We spent entire summer afternoons in the swimming pool in my backyard, my sanctuary, which held our little vegetable garden and our dog and our ducks and our rabbit. There, Cindy and I could still be little girls.

A summer baby, a Sun Fire Leo, I had just turned twelve. Cindy had been twelve for nine months, so she was nine months older and nine months taller; she was nine months slicker, my mother said, nine months sassier than me. She had lived nine months longer in her house on Bismarck Avenue, two doors down from mine, her house closer to the hillside that perpetually burns in my memory and my house wrapped around the corner that faced our small elementary school. Since Cindy was nine months older than me, she was always one year ahead of me in school, and when busing sent suburban children to urban schools, where most of the students were Black or Spanish-speaking immigrants, her parents enrolled her at Pinecrest Prep. My best friend Cindy, nine months whiter than me.

My twelfth summer seemed extra hot, the sky somehow smokier than in the past. I roller-skated out to the birch tree in front of Cindy's house where we played as very young children: Cindy's hair shining golden in the sun, and I, in my grape-colored Vans, a singular braid pressed long against my spine, a long rope of hair that tied me to my grandmothers and their grandmothers before them—hair, the dream of sails on our sea of heredity.

Cindy was waiting for me there under the birch tree.

"My dad is moving out."

Cindy looked hurt by the news, because she spent as much time at our house as her parents let her. Cindy came to our house for chocolate and tenderness. She came for the swimming pool in the backyard. She came to our house to laugh without lowering the volume of her voice. At her house, we giggled quietly in the kitchen and whispered in the TV room, which was right next to her father's radio room, where he spoke to crackling voices over the CB wires while her mother walked throughout her house without making a sound.

"I'm sorry, Wen," Cindy said. Having met when we were in diapers, we'd been friends all our lives.

And then Cindy said, "Isn't that what they say, though, that mixed couples don't last?"

Every July, I yearned for rain. I yearned for it to come dropping from the sky, to put out the fires that started as little buds, little glowing crumbs of catastrophe, before they spread wildly through the dry, windy, Southern California air, before they became too large for our fathers' summer hoses and burned our golden homes to the ground.

• • • • •

*Mr. Grofski, Mr. Horlick*
*Mr. Schafer, Mr. Klein*
*Mr. Malamud, Mr. Haas*
*Mr. Baxter, Mr. Stein*

"Hi Daddy!" In my memory, I call from the fence around the yard of my preschool, my hair in a high ponytail, my lace-up red tennis shoes dusty from the yard.

I turn to my friends: "There's my daddy working in the Plot!" My belly is a thermos holding the warm soup of my affection for him.

During my preschool years and some years following, my father helped cultivate a community garden at California State University Northridge, where he taught in the Biology Department. We called it the "Plot." He planted mirliton, tomatoes, cucumbers, broccoli, cabbage, turnips, collard and mustard greens, okra, squash, string beans, beets, lettuces, and cantaloupe in the rows allotted to him; my family watered, weeded, and harvested the vegetables on the weekends, the stiff arms of gardening tools protruding from the hand-cranked windows of my dad's cherry-colored VW Bug. My mother's side of the family sometimes worked in the Plot too, wearing wide-brimmed hats that protected their pale skin. I didn't like digging weeds from the dirt, but I loved running along the ditches that separated one sprouted row from another.

In this early memory, he waves to me from the rows of vegetables he so lovingly tends, and he walks over to the fence. "Hello, sweetheart!" I remember him sweetly saying to me in his seemingly accentless voice—his tenor voice like his father's tenor voice only without the strong tones of Louisiana—wearing his white undershirt and his straw hat, and his lips so thin they seemed to disappear when he smiled.

There's my father in another memory. He is in our backyard just a few miles from the university, in his usual white V-neck undershirt and a pair of belted slacks, pushing a bare-bladed, motorless lawnmower or sweeping the patio with a long-handled broom. There he is, brushing out the sticky insides of our aluminum smoker, where he smoked the fish that he caught in Lake Castaic and transformed into Daddy-made fish cakes, one of my favorite things to eat. There he is, brushing the floor and the sides of our blue-tiled swimming pool, because my sisters and I loved to swim, but we didn't love cleaning the pool. And there he is, brushing the thick, black hair of our dog, the Spanish-named Chico, whose favorite place to loiter was at my father's feet. "Move!" he would shout at the dog, more annoyed than angry, making my sisters and me laugh. There's my father, setting up the ironing board in the den, its legs issuing a familiar staccato as it rises to the height of his waist. Can you see him? With golf on the television, or baseball, he gathers his short-sleeved, collared shirts, the ones with the little penguin at the heart, and he irons his clothes for the week; the dog runs in and out, his pink tongue spotted with black.

There's my father in my memory, saying, "Good morning!" to the neighbor men, whose wives stayed at home, filling their lives with *Life* magazine and sewing machines and soap operas on the TV, whose driveways also inclined toward three-car garages that were two-thirds filled. The neighbor men, whose wives peered at my mother, wondering if she was Jewish, like them, and whose sons gazed at my older sisters, beautiful in their beige shades of brown. The neighbor men, whose fathers were another kind of refugee—not of the Jim Crow South but of World War II Europe—the neighbor men, of ghetto and shtetl, their wives with scarves on their heads. They all wondered where my father came from: he, Dr. Gaudin, French named with wide sideburns, with brown skin, his enunciation impeccable, any trace of Louisiana gone from his speaking voice.

There, in my memory, is Mr. Schafer, sitting on a beach chair at the top of his driveway, his blond hair aging into white, his trash cans clattering with empty beer cans. There is Mr. Baxter, who carried glass bottles of seltzer water into the kitchen, whose daughter, my friend Kelly, danced tap and ballet. And there is Mr. Haas, whose daughter Faith was rejected by so many children, but whom I adored until we parted ways after college; Mrs. Haas cooked us kosher hotdogs after school, slathered with mayonnaise.

And there is Dr. Goldenberg, my kind pediatrician, and there is Dr. Shippow, my sixth-grade social studies teacher who traveled the world during his summer vacations and shared his slide photographs with the class. In my memory, both men look remarkably alike—somewhat tall with rounded bellies, wearing glasses with dark squared frames, and longish hair combed over balding heads. They were older than the neighbor men, but both were ethnically Jewish like so many of the men of my childhood: Creole me, raised in a community of Ashkenazi Jewry. The San Fernando Valley was part of the larger history of white flight from Los Angeles, but it was also part of a Jewish migration: as people sometimes racialized as white, Jews who settled in the Valley activated their racial privilege in leaving L.A. proper, and as middle-class people, they bought newer homes distant from the historically settled Jewish enclaves of Southern California.[2] My father was among the Jewish neighbor men, with them but not of them, not unlike them but not like them either.

And there's my father, that one time on the TV, my sisters and me lined up on the sofa watching. The game show was called *Tic Tac Dough.* A smile. A laugh. A joke. "Professor," the game show host says in my memory, "we've got a smart one here!" My stomach fills with warmth—he is my winner of a thousand races! He is my man on the moon! His last daughter, his companion: I know that I love him the most. He answers the questions swiftly, lightly, effortlessly, with his singular dimple, his warm smile in his brown face.

We all knew he would win because he's our father, and we three girls had everything we wanted: a summer house on Oxnard beach, bicycles on cul-de-sacs, and upstairs bedrooms of our own. We three daughters had our own daydream of Daddy: in mine, he breezed down a windy street with love dust and nighthawks, the sweet earth flying behind him. But he choked on a biology question. I saw it in his body when the host let him down easy ("Oooh no, that is not correct"). He looked down, embarrassed, asking himself, "How could I get that wrong?" And I cried on the sofa with my sisters beside me, for the first time feeling sorry for my daddy.

From the passenger seat of my father's VW Bug, my beloved *Frog and Toad* books sitting in my lap, I watched him shift gears as we climbed and descended the freeways that took us into the city. I did not like going to Los

Fine, Nut-Colored Men. Anthony Gaudin (my father), August Burns (Uncle Sonny, my mother's brother), and Leon Aubry (Uncle Aubry, my sister's godfather). Los Angeles, 1978.

Angeles; the freeways frightened me. "Do you know where you're going?" I asked him over and over again: "Do we have enough gas?" I checked to make sure the doors were locked, fearful that someone would open the door and snatch my body into the wake. "Are we going to get lost?"

Arriving on Jefferson Boulevard, my father and I walked hand in hand into Aubry's Barber Shop. Uncle Aubry was in his white barber's jacket, his salt-and-pepper hair wavy and soft, his mustache trimmed and neat, his cashew-colored face graced with a warm smile. Kissing me on the cheek, sweet-smelling and jovial Uncle Aubry was one of my favorites among all the tender men in my childhood. He easily lifted me up and sat me in a barber's chair—I felt like such a big girl—while my father got his curly hair cut. Uncle Aubry's brother, Thomas, whom I did not call Uncle Thomas, sat in a waiting chair against the wall. Swollen belly, white hair—in my mind, he is perpetually smiling but I cannot hear his speaking voice.

Other nut-colored, sweet-smelling, sharp-dressed men walked into Aubry's Barber Shop, musical accents swimming from their mouths. There was familiarity in their loud laughter, in the lightness of their exchange, and I was usually the only little girl in the space of old-school, transplanted southern gentlemen of color. They loosely shook hands, they embraced, they teased, they talked at the same time. Emotive speech: eyes widened, thigh slapped, sentences unfinished, agreement presumed: "Mhm!" "Oh no!" "Mai-eh!" I heard one of those nut-colored men at Aubry's signify "St. Bernard Avenue." And another "Corpus Christi." And another "the Autocrat." Another man walked into the back of the barber shop to fix himself a bowl of gumbo—yes, Uncle Aubry had an infamous little kitchen in the back of the shop, the smells there an odd mixture of seafood and aftershave. A Playboy calendar hung scandalously from the wall; I peeked at it from the corner of my eye.

I remember once, not long before he died, Uncle Aubry said to a teenage me, "You know, you can call me Uncle Leon. Leon is my name." But that seemed a strange request. He was always Aubry—his surname—to me.

Somehow, I knew that my daddy was different from these men. He looked like them, and he laughed like them: un-self-conconsious, mouth open and toothful. He knew them, and they knew him. But he didn't join the orchestral conversation; the references to New Orleans were absent from his mouth. His speech was organized in a different way; in this place, he sounded like someone from somewhere else. Reflecting on his relationship to the Vietnamese language, Viet Thanh Nguyen writes, "Through Vietnamese [your parents] teach you tradition, discipline, etiquette, religion. . . . Also love." He adds, "But you do not know that and feel that until after you leave home, when hearing Vietnamese being spoken, even by strangers, will evoke for you the sound of love."[3] While my father's parents and peers, the Louisiana-born generation, brought English with them to Southern California, their speech patterns, their accents, their place names, the colloquialisms, the names of the people left behind became foreign, became another language, to my father. It came to symbolize the past, the South, a place he left when he was eight years old, a place he barely remembered. That Louisiana language of memory became, to Dr. Gaudin, a regressive language, the accent he scorned. Why didn't he ever develop a nostalgia, a yearning for this Louisiana language? Did his parents' language ever signify love?

Back at home in Northridge, my father sat at our circular kitchen table and set up his electronic IBM typewriter. Neatly stacking his mimeographed notes, their chemical smell broadcast throughout the downstairs, opening his dog-eared science journals, my father turned the platen knob clockwise to feed the white paper into the machine. The strikers obeyed his poised fingers as he jabbed the proper keys from memory. I loved the echoing sound that my father's typing made.

For my eighth birthday, I was given a stuffed Kermit the Frog and a baby-blue Sears Holiday typewriter. Kermit, my childhood sweetheart! Kermit, the tender, the innocent one, unafraid of interspecies love and eternally pining for a diva-esque pig. Kermit, the articulate tree frog, a magical being: not only could he strum a banjo and ride a bicycle but he could also survive in both aquatic and terrestrial environments—he could breathe air and water. Liminal, he! I placed Kermit puffy stickers on my bedroom door. I carried a yellow Kermit lunchbox to school, with its matching Kermit thermos. When I took a home economics class in elementary school, my sewing project was a pillow with a giant image of Kermit's face on the front. *The Muppet Show* compelled my undivided attention when it came on TV, and the soundtrack to *The Muppet Movie,* released in theaters when I was nine, often played on the record player in my bedroom. "Bein' Green" and "Rainbow Connection" still bring tears to my eyes, the lyrics stamped into my memory. (No, Kermie, it's not that easy being green.)

The baby-blue Sears Holiday typewriter was not as dignified as my father's, and it didn't plug into the wall, but it was my very own. In my memory, I am sitting next to my father at the kitchen table, my fingers pressing the keys of my typewriter, mimicking his movements. But instead of articles and lectures notes, I am typing letters to my freckled friends and one-page stories about my sweet, protected life in my golden home in the San Fernando Valley, one-page stories that I adorned with crayoned drawings of myself with yellow hair and cornflower blue eyes, looking distinctly like my best friend Cindy—drawings of myself that looked nothing like my grandfather, my father, or me.

• • • • •

*Rocky Mountain Tree frog, Red-spotted Toad*
*Western spadefoot, Horned Toad*
*Hyla Regilla, Pseudacris Sierra*
*Rana Aurora, Rana Pretiosa*

In the Santa Susana Mountains, in the wild place behind our house, above the cluster of cul-de-sacs where we carelessly tossed a football in the street and played hide-and-seek, up there at what was once the end of Tampa Avenue, now Limekiln Canyon Trail, there was a sliver of a canyon that we called the "Creek." On spring and summertime afternoons, my family went for walks and short hikes along established trails, and sometimes we brought our lunch for a picnic. But we were thoroughly suburban: our hikes never went too far, never strayed off the path, and we children never left our parents' sight.

My father, who had no brothers and no sons, mastered his VW Bug up the steep hill, its gears hiccupping from first into second, as my friends, Cindy or Faith or Leah, Allyson or Kelly or Esther, and I giggled in the tiny backseat. Walking along a dirt path lined with parched pines, thirsty shrubs, and dry branches scorched from the last burn, we girls followed my dad into the mountains. Horses' hooves stamped into the earth, and the roofs of our houses huddled down below. In his fatherly voice that was also his professorial voice, both voices melding into one, he warned us, "Watch out for snakes!"

Into the cold rush, we put our little fingers. The shallow waterway that gave this place its name tickled and splashed. The Creek was clean and cool. We stood at its dusty edge, and then we hopped over to the other side, my dad reaching out his hands to us, making sure that we crossed it safely.

Among the branches, the shrubs, and the brush, we found them. Amphibians. California tree frog, Yosemite toad, my father easily named them. Sometimes, he captured them and brought them home, setting them free in our backyard, where I played with them on the green lawn, unafraid of them, eager for them to hop and to croak from their pink, inflated vocal sacs.

My father studied frogs. Herpetologist, he.

*Rough skin, smooth skin*
*Horizontal pupils, vertical pupils*
*Enlarged toe tips, straight toe tips*
*Dorsal stripes, dorsolateral folds*

In my father's herpetology lab, I climbed up on a tall metal stool and examined the shelves lining the walls. Glass jars held little creatures floating in colored liquids. There were fetal beings and reptilian beings, long scaly beings and little foreign beings, night-colored beings and translucent beings, their interior organs visible through their skin. There were discolored frogs in mid-leap, suspended in mysterious, tainted water. There were index cards with notes, the classifications of living beings; there were microscopes and long pointy tools, cold instruments, and notepads, a white lab coat on a hanger, an iguana and a head of lettuce in a big cage, and containers with scientific labels that I didn't understand.[4]

In a closet or a secret room, maybe a big refrigerator or a giant box, there were humans too. When my father taught the human anatomy lab, he called them "cadavers." But I was never big enough to see them.

This was the 1970s, and I was the youngest child. Born shortly after he finished his PhD, I likely spent more time with my dad than many of my friends did with theirs, and even more likely than would the child of a STEM professor today, what with the expectations of publication, research, grant writing, mentorship, and leadership. On a professor's salary, with a spouse at home to care for his three daughters, my father could guiltlessly teach, write, and run the herpetology lab. Some of my clearest and most cherished childhood memories are associated with laboratories and classrooms. Dad's office was a safe and sacred place to me, a place where he could be an educator, he could be a scientist, he could be an adviser, and he could be a parent. Dad imbued me with a deep respect for learning. Having felt so completely at home on a university campus, attending preschool and summer school, and afterschool tutoring there, it is no wonder I became a professor myself.

Almost every time Dad brought me to school with him, Dr. Oppenheimer popped in to say hello. A short man with a New York accent, dark, curly hair, and a mustache, he waved at me, smiling. Every time I saw him, he made me laugh, his corny scientist jokes signifying the community that he and my father belonged to. When he inquired how I was doing, he always indicated interest in the answer. Maybe his daughters too sat at the front of his classroom while he lectured about his research, about embryonic development and cancer, about the cellular basis of cancer metastasis. They too must have looked up at their daddy, standing at the lectern, smiling the big smiles of secure little girls.

Dad's students drew out the "Aww!" when he told them, "We have a special guest today: my daughter is here, sitting in the front row." I turned to look at the rows of students in my father's classroom, all of them learning from him.

And down the hall from Dad's lab were those of Dr. Sheeler, Dr. Cohen, and Dr. Bianchi, for whom the campus planetarium is now named, all of them my father's colleagues, who sometimes came to our house for dinner. They looked nothing like Dad, but his voice sounded more like theirs than those of the men at Aubry's Barber Shop. Were these professor men my father's people? As scientists and university educators, they spoke the same language, they shared the same values and the same academic ambitions, they lived very similar lives in the suburbs. Had they also left religion behind, as my father had? Did these men come from a long line of academics, a long line of intellectually driven, college-educated men? My father, being the descendant of master craftsmen, of farmers, of tinsmiths and printers, did not follow in those footsteps, but he did inherit their work ethic, their dignity, their close attention to method and outcome, and their pride in their profession.

In my mind, my father, like other Creole men of color, is also an heir to formally educated Francophone Creole men of color who shaped New Orleans and Louisiana in profound ways, in both the antebellum and postbellum periods. Dad is the beneficiary of inventor and chemical engineer, Norbert Rillieux, who revolutionized the processing of raw sugar cane. He is the beneficiary of architect and engineer, Barthélémy Lafon, who published New Orleans's first almanac and designed the city of Donaldsonville, where Dad's father attended school as a child. Of the master fencer and mathematician, Basile Crockere. Of the attorney, Louis A. Martinet, who founded *The Crusader*, a New Orleans newspaper. Of the Creole composers, Edmond Dédé, Samuel Snaër, Basile Barés, and Lucien Lambert, some of whom were born into slavery, and others, born free. Without the Creole authors Rodolphe Lucien Desdunes, Camille Thierry, Armand Lanusse, Victor Séjour, and Alexandre Dumas, Dad would not have accomplished the things that he did. Without the efforts of Saint-Dominguan merchant Vincent Ogé and his comrade, the political essayist Julien Raymond, both of whom argued for full human rights and equality for free men of color in that colony; and without the work of physician and journalist Louis Charles Roudanez, who founded the French-language *L'Union*, the U.S. South's first Black newspaper, and his brother, Jean Baptiste Roudanez, an engineer and mechanic who appealed to President Abraham Lincoln for voting rights for free men of color, Dad would not have had the opportunity to become Dr. Anthony Joseph Gaudin.[5]

Aren't we all beneficiaries of our ancestors' struggles and successes, of the efforts and strivings of previous generations? Isn't my father a leaf on a branch of the family tree of Creole men of color? In my mind, he is.

Of course, my dad did not write scientific papers that won international awards, and he is not a famous scientist doing groundbreaking research, but he was a celebrity among the show-and-tell crowd at Beckford Avenue Elementary School. While my teachers stood at the back of the classroom, his caged amphibians sent all of us children squealing and screaming. I held the frogs and toads in my hands like they were my pets, running my fingers along their bumpy backs, comforted by the coldness of their feet.

Sometimes, my father arrived for show-and-tell with human bones.

*Fibula, tibia, femur*
*Humerus, radius, ulna*
*Hammer, anvil, stirrup*
*Scaphoid, capitate, hamate*

In big plastic bags were the butterfly pelvic bones and the string bean ribs, the elephant ear scapulae and the mushroom cap patellas. In little boxes, the bones of the hand and the foot and the inner ear rolled around like marbles.

In his fatherly professorial voice, Dad asked, "Can you guess which bone this is?" In the flattened palm of his hand, he held a calcaneus. "It's your heel bone!" he gave away, animated, emphasizing the long *e* in heel, and all us dramatically looked down at our feet, imagining the ginger-root bone inside our shoes.

The biggest prize was the skull. My father carefully pulled it from a bag like it was a basketball, his thumb inside its base and his fingers spanning the occipital bone; my father, the biologist who made his father weep, rejecting the church in favor of science. None of us children could believe that under our skin was this unbending thing. "Here is the jaw," he told everyone. "And here is the nose. Here are the eye sockets, and here are the strong, healthy teeth." The skull smiled perpetually as it was passed from one set of child-hands to another, everyone oohing and aahing. The image is fixed in my mind: me, standing next to my daddy; him: a Bic pen upright in his chest pocket, his wavy black hair in a sharp widow's peak, wearing eyeglasses and a mustache. Was he that different from the neighbor men? From Mr. Klein or Mr. Stein? Like the men at Aubry's Barber Shop, Dad was like them but different.

In my mind, my father knew everything. A scientist through and through, he easily classified the world around me. What kind of rain was that falling? What kind of clouds were those in the sky? What kind of tree was that in the yard? What kind of bird woke me with its song? What kind of insect pierced my foot when I stepped on it? What kind of fish dangled from the line? What kind of egg was that which had fallen from its nest? Why were my eyes mixed green with brown? Why didn't I look like my mother?

"Children enter the sensemaking world through language," writes poet Natasha Trethewey, "by naming things."[6]

My birth certificate reads:

*Father's race: Negro / white*
*Mother's race: Negro / white*

My parents were not a mixed couple after all, as Cindy had falsely assumed. My father explained that to me too: we belonged to what biologists call a *population.* Someone invented the word *miscegenation.* Historians referred to us as *Mulattoes.* Novelists chose words like *quadroon* and *octoroon.* Anthropologists called us *triracial isolates.* We called ourselves *Creoles.*

All of it, a taxonomy of us.

In the Santa Susana Mountains, there was a wild place that we called "the Creek." Before my father left home, he led us up the path, through brush and blackberry bushes, through desert flowers and conical anthills, naming every living being along the way, so far away from the Louisiana that birthed him, so far away from that watery place where all his ancestors were buried. "Watch where you walk," my father said, my hero in Wallabees, my luminary with a lab full of bullfrogs. And I felt so lucky to be me, like an oak toad he held gently in his hands, placed softly and safely in the grass.

. . . South, when you were young, no one asked.
Women said, *I bet I know who your mother is.*
You weren't surprised that they were right every time . . .

—ARDEN ELI HILL

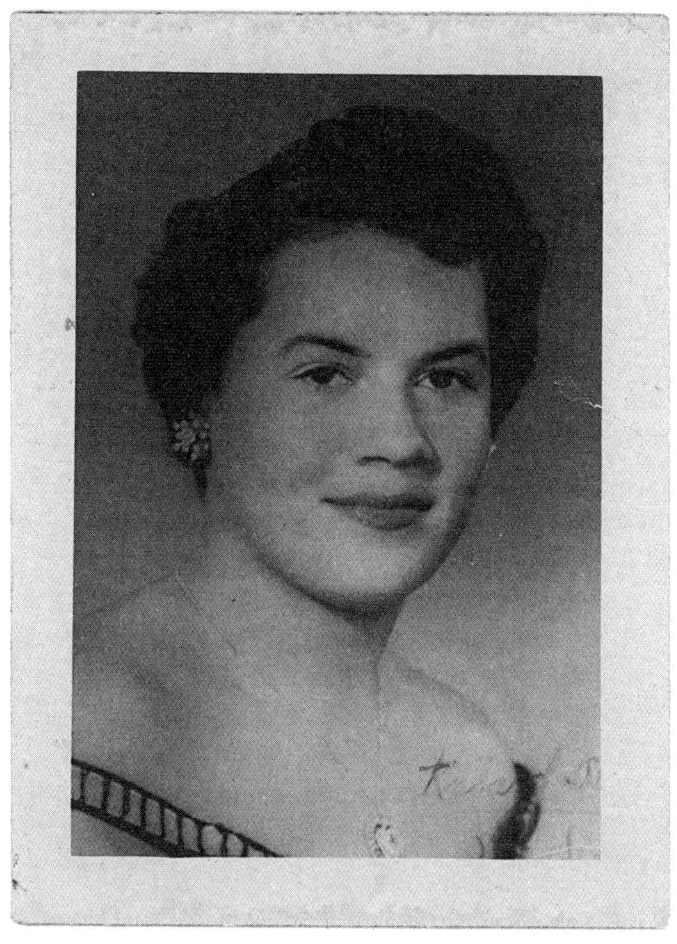

Speak with Your Eyes. Eleanor Marietta Burns, my mother. Los Angeles, 1958.

# 7

# The Habit and the Ghost Shirt

My mother wanted to be a cupcake nun.

There was something sweet about it.

They called them the cupcake nuns because of the look of their habits. A circular, crenulated cloth stood straight up around their heads. Cupcake nuns topped with a pure-white halo, marking them as Sisters of the Holy Cross, trussing them to the nuns with the winged habits and the coned habits, to the Oblate Sisters of Providence and the Little Sisters of the Poor and the rest. To the little girls at St. Agnes Elementary School, the crenulated cloth was the paper lining of a cupcake.

The habits were not sweet, nor were many of the sisters who wore them.

Once, when they were children, playing kickball out on the yard, a gust of wind arrived like an unexpected gift to the little girls: it blew Sister Marilla's cupcake habit entirely off her head, stiff as it was, starched and unforgiving; then Sister Marilla ran into the convent because her head had been exposed. She hardly had any hair. And the children laughed and laughed until the nuns told them to stop. Of course, they immediately obeyed.

Those were the days prior to the liberalization of the nun's habit. Prior to Catholic nuns wearing the clothing of laywomen, even skirts that showed their ankles, prior to the nuns showing a bit of their hairline, and later all their hair—scandalous as it was and still is to my mother, even though she long ago left the Catholic Church.

My mother wanted to wear the cupcake habit. She loved and revered the nuns, even though they often broke her heart.

And she will never forget what they did to St. Agnes.

Piece by piece, they took St. Agnes apart, in a reversal of its construction in 1907. The narthex, the flying buttresses, the nave, the confessionals, the pews—the parts of the church having been shipped all the way from Italy in giant crates made of wooden slats, the ceramic faces of the saints peering through the spaces between, the monstrance hidden beneath layers of paper and cloth wrapping, the chalice hidden deeper still. The mystery of the transfiguration, right there on Vermont Avenue. And decades later, piece by piece, like appendages of a saintly body, they took it apart, and my mother never forgave them for it.[1]

Blessed Agnes, patron saint of the chaste. Of the untouched.

My mother secretly imagined that the church organ was hers. After all, prior to the church's consecration, she played for masses and holy celebrations and choir practices. She spent hours of her time after school in the little cove off to the side of the chancel, hands on the keys, adjusting the organ's thumb pistons and swell pedals, learning the chords, perfecting her playing for St. Agnes. But then Sister Principal told her the church organ was, in fact, not hers and that she had been replaced with another organist for St. Agnes's consecration. But what about me? my mother yearned to inquire but dared not speak the words—never mind her heart that sobbed for the music, never mind the appetite of her heart, the shell mouth of my mother's wide-open heart, her thorn-skinned heart for St. Agnes.

The land and the church were consecrated, blessed by the Archdiocese of Los Angeles and by all the angels and saints; its twin spires seemed to her, then, the tallest things she'd ever seen. They were glorious, the sharpness of them like the nuns' spiked tongues, piercing the sky. A consecrated church was never supposed to be taken apart, and yet it was: St. Agnes was dismembered, desanctified, and my mother never forgave them for it.

Blessed Agnes, patron saint of virgins, of the young and the virtuous. Holy Agnes, cradle of the lamb, birthed and died for my mother: young Eleanor, sitting atop a stool in her mother's powder room, a hairbrush in her mother's hand, her hair dark brown and heavy as a smooth waist-length coat, heavy as the veil the cupcake nuns wore. Her mother Marietta brushing from root to tip, brushing from head to waist, one hundred brushes for her daughter, her little girl with a lavender sadness in her eyes. The powder room, the refuge of mother and daughter.

But then her mother revealed, "I struggled so hard laboring you," a story that my mother has carried her whole life. "You nearly broke my back."

Young Eleanor imagined that her long, heavy hair was her veil. It trailed behind her like the great train of a wedding gown, its filigreed edges taking the patterns of St. Agnes's floor, a fancy Italian tile that my mother thought she'd never forget, until I asked her to describe it and she couldn't. Her mother Marietta bound her hair together in two long braids, two long braids that bound my mother to the women who came before her—to her grandmothers and their grandmothers before them—two long braids that I also wore as a child, binding me to my foremothers.

Braids. Eleanor Marietta Burns, my mother (*right*) with her childhood friend, Carol McCalla. Los Angeles, 1950.

In the powder room, Eleanor looked into her mother's blue-grey eyes, her eyes more a reflection of the Pacific Ocean than the muddy brown Louisiana waters that she came from. "I never questioned why my mother's eyes were blue," my mother told me. "In those days, you didn't ask."[2]

My mother was born in California. Her siblings—her sister Lawrencia and her brother August, both conspicuously named after their father—were born in New Orleans. Augustus Lawrence and Marietta carried three-year-old August with them when they first arrived in California in 1930; they left eight-year-old Lawrencia behind. My mother, whose lifelong nickname is Duckie, was born nearly a decade later, in 1939, when her older siblings were seventeen and twelve years old. "Well, isn't that just ducky?" Aunt Lil said when she heard that her friend Marietta was pregnant once again, and at the age of thirty-four. The name stuck. But its negative connotation—a misfortune—did not; along with frogs and toads, we decorated our childhood home with sweet and wholesome little ducks, glass ducks and crystal ducks, rubber duckies in the tub, and duck magnets on the fridge.

My mother, like her mother before her and her grandmothers before her, was born at home; she, on the kitchen table on East 45th Street. My grandmother's friends were there at that auspicious moment. There was Odalie, the one they called Sis. There was Viola, the one they called Aunt Vee. There was Nanny Rose and Aunt Lil. These were all the women who helped raise my mother, all the women who left Louisiana for California, all the women who should have protected my mother, whom the neighbor men on East 45th Street called "*Lil Peck,*" short for the racial slur "peckerwood," meaning "white."

My mother is not white, but I am her darker-skinned child, the one whom strangers presumed was adopted. And, likewise, its opposite: my son Aubry is my fair child, and our contrast has caused others to ask me, "Are you his babysitter?" Why does it continue to be unimaginable that a mother and child who are not the same color can be born of the same people, the same population? Why do we continue to be a spectacle? As a child, I knew my mother was my unbendable and unbent protector, my parent who rarely took her eyes away from me, but I felt a different connection to my father and to his father, to the men who gave me my color.

My sisters and I had the same set of parents, but we had three different colors of skin. My eldest sister Leslie was slightly lighter than our father; my middle sister Roslyn was my mother's very fair color; and I was the darkest of all of us. When the Los Angeles Unified School District began categorizing students in its classrooms in preparation for desegregation in the 1970s, my mother received three different classifications for her daughters. The school district classified Leslie as a "Hawai'ian / Pacific Islander," Roslyn as "Caucasian," and me as "Native American." The school district went as far as to request my tribal enrollment number, which of course, I did not have.[3]

"Ridiculous!" the adjective my mother attaches to the memory now. At the time, she bravely appeared in the district offices, demanding a change. "How dare you?" she asked them, a rhetorical question. Had my distant ancestors also pushed back against state agents who tagged them with racial labels that did not fit them? Had they issued a similar complaint?

My mother spent hours washing and oiling and combing and brushing and parting and rolling and braiding the long hair of three daughters with three different sorts of curls. Tight waves and exultant frizz and thick spirals covered our heads, and my straight-haired mother mastered it all because she knew that we were not the same as the neighbor girls, our childhood friends. We were not Steins or Buchwalds or Kaufmans. We were French-named Creole girls whose well-kept hair kept us safe, kept us beautiful, might've even kept us safe from racism. (It didn't.) We never left the house with our hair out of place. Nothing wild or untame sprang from our scalps. Our brushed and braided hair, our straightened and blow-dried hair, our hair in pink curlers for the night—our hair was our shelter, our ancestral tie to Louisiana and to the women who came before us. Our hair was a monument to our middle status: it was a geography of our ancestry, a habit that she hoped would shield us from the worst experiences of race.

We were our mother's everything. We were our mother's profession. Protecting her three daughters was our mother's mission in life. A stay-at-home parent, she paid sharp and intense attention to each of us. All our movements, all our habits, all our desires, all our friendships were governed by the magnificent gallery of her tones of voice and her facial expressions. My mother missed nothing, consuming her daughters' lives and remarking with glances, stares, squints, scrutiny, a twitch, a raised eyebrow, a tightened lip, a cutting look. She kept my sisters and me close to home, saying no to summer camps, no to sleepovers, no to day trips with friends, no especially to the fathers and brothers of our friends unless mothers and sisters were also present. Trusting almost no one with her daughters, she watched us from the sliding glass door while we swam in the pool; she watched us from the front picture window as we played on the brick patio; she watched us from the driveway as we rode our bikes up and down Bismarck Avenue. When I grew up enough to walk home alone from Beckford Avenue Elementary School, I could see her standing on the corner in front of our house, watching me as I traversed the three blocks home.

Mom chose the safest man she could imagine to be our father. Like hers, he never shouted, he never grabbed, he never spanked, he never snatched, he never bullied, he never forced, he never slapped, he never pushed, he never cursed.

My mother embroidered shawls of protection around us and dared anyone to snatch them from our shoulders. A fierce seamstress of armor, Mom sewed reinforcements into our clothes, challenging any man to harm our cossetted bodies. It would not happen. Our swimsuits appeared ordinary to the untrained eye; what seemed like flimsy bikinis were fortified by our mother's piercing scrutiny. Our dresses contained unbreakable bone breastplates that shielded our tender hearts. Our matching pantsuits: tough as hide on the outside, so that if we were pushed, our skin wouldn't bruise. Our sweaters: ruffled with cactus, lest the wrong man rub up against us. Our summer dresses: ghost shirts for Creole girls, which bullets could not pierce.

Young Eleanor, where was your ghost shirt? Where was your protective habit whose wool layers hid stretches of scythes?

Maybe she knew what St. Agnes went through. They say that Agnes wanted more than anything to save herself for Jesus, but a man wanted to have her; so he tore her clothes from her body and dragged her through the streets, intending to break her in a brothel. Agnes did not protest, but she prayed. And as she prayed, hair sprung from all over her body, hair long enough to cover it, long enough to protect it—a long shield of hair like the robe of a nun, and the men who came to her were instantly struck blind. She was only thirteen.

Superwoman and Child. My mother and me.
Big Bear, California, ca. 1974.

My mother remembers girls throwing lit matches at her hair, and she remembers St. Agnes's prayer.

St. Agnes, watch over the defenseless children of the world.

My mother remembers meeting her grandmother, Ida of the Singular Name, the One Who Coughs, only once. She had come from New Orleans to California, but her destination was Chicago, where my grandmother's half-sister Marguerite lived.

Ida of the Singular Name was as stern as the nuns. She was the color of wheat and the feel of it too: prickly to the touch, her hair gathered in a tight bun at the back of her head.

My mother wanted to be a cupcake nun, her hair hidden under the heavy habit, her body shielded behind the walls of a robe. She wanted the crenulated halo around her head, sweet as vanilla pudding or buttercream—the sweet little girl that my mother always was, but of course, those were just the daydreams of a child.

• • • • •

Magic.

That's how my mother describes the railroad: "There's something magic about riding a train."

Once, my mother and her mother rode the Sunset Limited from California to Louisiana, an ironic compass taking them toward the sunrise, eastward to the dark place, the Deep South. When I ask my mother to share her memories of the train, a list spills from her mind. The whistle. The dining car. China cups and saucers stamped "Pullman." Linen on the tables. A fresh flower. Porters with towels resting on their arms, their smiling faces serving breakfast: coffee, eggs, and toasted bread. The Pullman sleeping car. Beds turned down. Clean white sheets and a textured blanket embroidered "Pullman." The door sliding open and closed. Privacy. Privilege.

And safety. Surrounded by Pullman porters, men in the same profession as her father, my mother felt protected. Perhaps when they were off duty, they were playing the numbers, throwing the dice. Gambling on a better life, the dull patina of servitude wearing off. Perhaps they were betting on the horses, the greyhounds, the spores of anticipation tingling on their fingertips. No matter: the porters were "friendly men," my mother says. Maybe they knew her father Augustus Lawrence, who had also worked on the legendary Sunset Limited; maybe that information turned a switch in their minds: this woman and her child aren't white.

Pullman men, surround this little girl and her mother.

Saint Christopher, protect the travelers. Watch over them as they cross into Texas.

Once, my mother traveled to Louisiana in the back seat of her father's 1952, two-tone green Chevy Powerglide. It was a hot summer; with no air conditioning, she, her father, and her mother drove from the west side of Los Angeles all the way to New Orleans with the windows down, bugs flying in my mother's thirteen-year-old face. Her braids were so long she could sit on them. My mother remembers her father occasionally dozing off at the wheel and stopping on the side of the road to catch a nap.

Driving through Texas, seeking a hotel for the night, my grandmother, whose eye color signaled an immutable whiteness, entered the motel office with my mother in tow. My grandmother paid for the room while my grandfather waited in the car; later, he secreted himself into the motel room of his wife and child. The next day, they quietly and quickly exited, careful to escape the view of anyone who might hold the dangerous thought that my grandfather was a "Colored" man cohabitating with a white woman.

Continuing east toward Louisiana, they stopped at a roadside restaurant to eat a meal. My mother recalls, "People looked at us really funny, and men outside the restaurant began milling around my father's car." Having not been waited on or eaten anything, sensing that the patrons of the restaurant were wondering what that brown-skinned man was doing with that white woman and child, my mother and her parents quickly left the restaurant. "It was like that," my mother says, casually. Like my parents, they might have been read as a "mixed couple," a dangerous speculation in the South, especially with the inclusion of a white woman.

But Marietta was not a white woman.

Arriving in New Orleans, they found Great-Aunt Ella sitting on the front porch of her shotgun house, waiting for them, praying for their safe arrival. My mother remembers the privy in her aunt's deep backyard and the slop jars under each bed; there was no running water in the house. She remembers her aunt's "pure white, perfectly straight hair, in a big bun"; her skin "coffee with lots of cream in it"; and a large goiter on her neck. While my maternal grandparents enjoyed themselves in the city they'd left twenty-two years earlier, my mother spent time with Great-Aunt Ella and her paternal aunt, Pansy, these women representing the two halves of her bloodline and racialized in two very different ways. My mother noticed the wide range of phenotypes in her extended family—mothers and daughters and sisters and wives who had very different physical features. Her own father, she recalls, looked nothing like his sisters.

Consider this time in New Orleans, this return to the place where my mother's parents said they'd never live again. Nguyen might call them "cosmonauts," refugees who "permanently escape the gravity of home."[4] Did they casually drive by their old three-room shotgun on Panola Street? Did they stroll on the Mississippi River levee, just blocks from St. Joan of Arc, where they were married? Did they share their new California lives with old friends? Did old friends notice their new California skin? New speech: Did they remove the locative references in their language? New movements: Did they float, weightless, against the gravity of segregation, their bodies governed by a new atmosphere, that of the West Coast? Or did they revert to how they once had lived, with feet heavy on the ground?

On one Sunday in the city, my mother and her mother attended Mass. Afterward, they rode the streetcar back to Great-Aunt Ella's house. When they two walked onto the streetcar and sat in the back, the streetcar driver stood from his seat and approached them.

"Ma'am," he said to Marietta, "you're sitting in the wrong seat."

My grandmother answered him, "No, we're sitting in the right seat," and she refused to move. The driver then removed the sign that read "Colored Passengers" and placed it on the seat behind them, effectively stretching the White section to include them.

The memory is not an exceptional one, although it stands out among my mother's memories of the segregated South. Public transportation has long been recognized as a space not only of resistance to segregation laws but also of dissonance between racial laws and human bodies. In 1891, the state of Louisiana passed the Separate Car Act, which required "White" and "Colored" passengers to sit separately. In response, New Orleans Creole journalist Rodolphe Lucien Desdunes wrote that such an "audacious and insulting" law was "a slap in the face of every member of the black race, whether he has the full measure or only one-eighth of that blood."[5] In addition to the outright racism of the Separate Car Act, there is also the ludicrousness of splitting any public space in New Orleans into two parts. Many Creoles tell stories like my mother's: their racially ambiguous presence in a starkly segregated space caused a glitch in what was supposed to be a clearly and obviously demarcated space. The laws of race, which designated all those of mixed heritage, all those with any "visible admixture of blood" to be Black, ran counter to the kaleidoscope of human phenotype and self-definition in the southern city of New Orleans. When my grandmother and my mother sat in the "Colored" section of the streetcar, they exposed the fallacy of spatial segregation. Visually, they did not belong there; thus, the driver moved the sign, so that they would technically be in the White section. But my grandmother and my mother, being of mixed race, sat where the law said they belonged. Jim Crow segregation made no space for the middle: the racial binary was the rule of law, regardless of whether it made sense.

Luckily, my mother and her parents, along with other nonwhite people, were able to sometimes avoid both the color line and confrontations with segregated public transportation by using their own automobiles. I am reminded of a story that one informant shared with me: to avoid racial segregation on public transportation, he bought a motorbike and rode it to work at Maison Blanche, a massive department store on Canal Street, where he was a (white) baker in its industrial kitchen. Otherwise, where would he sit? If he sat in the front, his Black coworkers might see him sitting there; if he sat in the back, his white bosses would know that he wasn't white.

In my grandfather's Chevy, my mother and her parents safely followed the long and winding road from New Orleans up to Vacherie, the country town where my maternal grandmother was born. My mother remembers the Huey P. Long Bridge, a cow in a yard, a field of sugarcane, mosquito netting over the bed, and a metal roof. In Vacherie, she met extended family on her mother's side; she remembers Uncle Peas, and Uncle Ansell, and cousin Honorine, who lived in a modern house across the Mississippi River. Honorine also lived her life as a white woman. She often sent letters to my grandmother in Los Angeles, containing photos of her blue-eyed children. The photos rest in plastic casings, among all my other family photos. What were their names? Did they carry the Roussel family name? Would I know their descendants if I saw them on the road to Vacherie? Might I see my grandmother's face in theirs? And are they still our people?

On their return to New Orleans, Mom's Aunt Pansy took her downtown. My mother followed her aunt to the back of the streetcar, thinking nothing of it, because this is where her mother had sat just days before. The people sitting among Aunt Pansy and my mother, behind the movable "Colored Passengers" sign, were Afro-Creole and African American; they were Cuban, Honduran, Canarian; they were African-descended people from a variety of cultural backgrounds, displaying the wide-ranging palette of skin that defines the New Orleans human landscape. Sitting next to Aunt Pansy, my mother felt protected.

When they reached the Maison Blanche, Aunt Pansy directed my mother's steps, mindful of the actions and behaviors associated with caste: angles, reaches, steps, glances, and expected salutations of which my mother knew nothing. In the 1950s, Afro-Creole and other presumably nonwhite shoppers at the Maison Blanche couldn't try on hats and clothes; they had to take a measured guess, hoping the items fit, knowing that a skilled seamstress or tailor in the family would have to make the necessary alterations. Afro-Creole and other shoppers of color could not sit and eat at the lunch counter, nor could they use the restroom.

My mother remembers coming upon a water fountain. My mother went to drink and then noticed the sign. "White patrons only." She turned to Aunt Pansy, who matter-of-factly told her, "You can go over there, but I can't."

"Being in New Orleans was my first experience with segregation, the first time I really saw race," my mother tells me, as Los Angeles had given her and her family the space for ambiguity, the space to breathe before the moment of racialization. Somehow, being called "Lil Peck" and "stringy-haired little patty" by her African American neighbors in Los Angeles didn't have the same blunt impact as these experiences of Jim Crow. Being in New Orleans may have been my mother's first experience of being Black.

That trip in 1952 was my grandmother's second and final known attempt to see her father. My mother tells the story: "We went to Mercy Hospital, where he was working. My mother told the nurse, 'I want to see [the Grey Heron]. The nurse said, 'Who is calling?' My mother said, 'Marietta Burns.' The nurse came back out and told them, 'He's busy right now.' But I saw his back. He looked like an old man. He walked right out the side door. But I was just a little girl. I didn't really understand, and of course, I didn't ask."

Fifteen years after that futile encounter, her mother Marietta sat on a stool while Mom dyed her hair in the powder room of her own house. By then, both my mother and my grandmother wore their hair short. While my mother applied the dye, my grandmother told her, "I never had a father."

Mom answered, "Yes you did," her response, an attempt at compassion, a reaction to the sadness in her mother's voice. She had forgotten all about the incident at Mercy Hospital in 1952.

My grandmother continued, "No, I didn't. I could never have his name, I couldn't even go near him, and he didn't want anything to do with me."

My mother remained quiet as her mother held her sadness in her mouth. The powder room, the act of caring for hair, from mother to daughter and from daughter to mother, signified a safe place. In this space, they could shed layers of protection that each had worn out in the world. They could let go the thorned vest, the habit, and the ghost shirt that vulnerable girls and women had to wear among unrestrained men.

After a pause, she told my mother his name. She spelled it out. Then she painfully said his name again, this time beginning with "Dr."

# 8

# A Work of Fiction

He could be played by Michael Caine. Or Peter O'Toole. Or Anthony Hopkins. He is an older man in my mind, with grey hair and grey eyes. He is tall, his arms are long, and his shoulders and back are curved forward from years of bending over the surgical table and relaxing into his long, privileged life as a southern white man. Although these actors are not Louisianan, they could easily adopt an authentic New Orleans accent; it is a performance, after all. They could sit with ease on a covered porch, sport a seersucker suit, drive an aquamarine '52 Buick, saunter into Antoine's Restaurant on Rue St. Louis in the French Quarter, and sip a Sazerac or a French Gimlet. They could play the Grey Heron as a more mature man, whose absconding backside my mother saw as a child. If he were a character on a screen, in a Hollywood treatment, or in a classic New Orleans novel, he would not just be a wealthy white man. He would be *a Creole.*

And my grandmother, his daughter, who would play her part? That is a trickier proposal. If she were a character on a screen in a Hollywood treatment, or in a classic New Orleans novel, who would best replicate her face? Her European nose (as it has been described), her grey-blue eyes and pale skin (her father's), her wavy brown hair and turned-down mouth (her mother's)? Would a casting agent choose a white woman? A biracial woman? A Black woman? How about an ethnic European? A French actress? Or a woman from the Deep South or, deeper still, the Caribbean? The trick is in the imagination. Is she imagined as Black, despite her white father? Or white, despite her mixed-race mother? In my mother's mind and in mine, my grandmother Marietta Roussel was indisputably Creole: Francophone, Catholic, bred on the diet of the lower Mississippi River valley, seafood and okra gumbo, dirty rice and hog's head cheese and *maque choux,* immersed in southern Louisiana taxonomies and colloquialisms, a child of those who had lived in Louisiana for many generations. But in the fictional portrayals of her, she would not be Creole. That was a designation historically reserved for Francophone white people. Instead, she would be *an octoroon.*

In works of fiction—especially in works of fiction set in Louisiana—my grandparents and great-grandparents, my ancestors and ancestresses of mixed ancestry, of Indigenous southern and West African and Caribbean and Latinate European origination, were portrayed not as Creoles but as *octoroons, quadroons,* and *Mulattoes.*[1] This linguistic distinction was rooted in the objectification, the exoticization, the monetization, and the sexualization of mixed-race, African-descended people—especially women—in the histories and literatures of Louisiana and the Deep South.[2] A seductive representation, it pulled me into its wake. As a younger person without a racial affinity, without an employable language to describe myself, without any Creole friends, without a parental education about race and identity, without an immersive understanding of Creole, I became convinced that the plentiful fictional characterizations of *octoroons, quadroons,* and *Mulattoes* were representations of my people. Only with time, with research, and with the permission of my elders, did I grasp that we were not simply summaries of our imagined blood mathematics. We too were Creole. And we too had a right to call ourselves by that name.

But ask some of the authors who crafted the fictional Louisiana Creole character, and they will answer in the negative. A true Creole, in their minds, was a person of pure European ancestry. Writer Lafcadio Hearn, for example, author of the 1877 letter "Los Criollos," begins, "The common error of interpreting the word 'Creole,' as signifying a Mulatto, or quadroon or octoroon of Louisiana, and particularly of New Orleans, is far from being a local one, and dates back through centuries." This error, says Hearn, "actually lives in New Orleans, where the word Creole is a term of proud honor among the aristocrats of the South." However, "when one considers that the light-tinted, French-speaking colored element of New Orleans—the relatives and the children of true Creoles—call themselves Creoles, and desire to be so called, the existence of the fallacy does not appear so extraordinary after all." A "true Creole," according to Hearn, is one who can "trace his ancestry back to the nobility of France, or to the grandees of Spain in the days of the conquistadors."[3] Hearn's argument raises the question: Why couldn't the "relatives and the children" of "true Creoles" also call themselves Creole? If they are blood relations, aren't they the same thing?

Journalist and poet Alice Dunbar-Nelson, author of the 1916 essay, "People of Color in Louisiana," explains this argument further: "The native white Louisianan will tell you that a Creole is a white man, whose ancestors contain some French or Spanish blood in their veins. . . . The Caucasian will shudder with horror at the idea of including a person of color in the definition, and the person of color will retort with his definition that a Creole is a native of Louisiana, in whose blood runs mixed strains of everything un-American, with the African strain slightly apparent."[4] Why shudder with horror? Because, especially during segregation, an ostensibly white person and a person of color using the same language to describe themselves would also suggest sameness—and equality—between the two, and that was unimaginable to those who sought to maintain a vested hierarchy based on racial difference. People of color insisting on calling themselves Creole, then, was an act of resistance against white Louisianans who tried to dictate what other people could and could not name themselves.

Through this dated lens, the Grey Heron would be considered a true Creole, and Marietta would be considered his octoroon daughter.

Twelve years after Dunbar-Nelson's original essay was published in the *Journal of Negro History,* novelist Edward Larocque Tinker added this forward to his 1928 novel, *Toucoutou,* which was set in New Orleans: "It would never have occurred to me to define the word Creole," Tinker admits, had he not "come across it in *Modern English Usage*" and found it equated with the word "Mulatto." He continues, "The mistake current among certain misinformed people that Creole denotes a person of mixed white and negro blood is due possibly to the fact that they confused the noun Creole with the adjective creole. . . . When the noun Creole is used, it can mean only one thing and that is a pure white person born of European parents in Spanish or French colonies."[5]

Sociologists added their voices to the debate about who constitutes Creole and whether people of color could be included under the moniker. In 1940, Allison Davis and John Dollard added a lexicological footnote to their study of African-descended youth in New Orleans: "The word 'Creole' has found wide usage to indicate a group of white people in New Orleans who are of French, or mixed French and Spanish, descent. It is denied that they have Negro blood in any case." Adding an important exception, they wrote, "It is affirmed as a matter of social fact, however, that in Negro society there is also a group of persons who have a history of French language and custom in their families; these persons also refer to themselves and are referred to by others as Creoles; to be perfectly clear, we shall refer to the latter group as *colored* Creoles. Whenever the word is used here it means the latter group and not the white group."[6]

Despite this acknowledgment from social scientists—that Creole is a cultural designation shared by people who occupied different racial categories—the image of the Creole as a white person persisted. Folklorist and novelist Lyle Saxon, author of the 1945 collection of Louisiana folklore, *Gumbo Ya-Ya,* wrote, "No true Creole ever had colored blood. This erroneous belief, still common among Americans in other sections of the country, is probably due to the Creoles' own habit of calling their slaves 'Creole slaves' and often simply 'Creoles.'" He continues, "Too, there are proud light-colored families in New Orleans today who are known as 'Creoles' among themselves. But Creoles were always pure white. Any trace of the *café au lait* in a family was reason for complete ostracism."[7] This point is especially baffling to me, given the widespread practices of interracial sex and interracial intimacies in New Orleans; it was not a secret that interracial sex was common at the time of Saxon's writing. The *café au lait* member of the family was probably found among every set of cousins.

In the same collection of Louisiana folklore, Saxon describes the *café au lait,* spotted in the French Market of the city of New Orleans, who is distinctly *not* Creole: "There would probably be one of the city's lovely quadroons in sight, trailed by a single servant. She would walk like a queen, her chin high, her jet brows disdainful, her handsome silk gown lifted just the proper inch or two from the cobblestones. She would be as proud as any Creole lady in the city. And why not? Her father might be one of its most famous residents. Her lover, to whom she is absolutely true, another."[8] This portrayal of the quadroon character, who is "as proud as any Creole lady" but is not herself Creole, includes some notable features: she is lovely, and as indicated by her servant, her silk, and her father, she has status. She is also sexually alluring, suggested by "her lover." Although there is no mention of her color, both men in the description are presumably white, which positions her, and quadroons generally, as white adjacent, as somewhat or almost white, but still women of color.

The quadroon characters that were truly foundational to my early historical curiosity were more recent than these. In 1994, I discovered Anne Rice's 1979 novel, *The Feast of All Saints.* I remember the year distinctly. That was the year of the Northridge earthquake, 6.7 magnitude on the Richter scale, which jolted all of us out of sleep at 4:30 a.m. on a January morning, at the very start of the spring semester of my junior year in undergraduate school. The quake killed more than fifty people. It collapsed part of the I-5 freeway, it pancaked some of the apartment complexes near California State University Northridge, and it cracked the foundation of my mother's Reseda Boulevard townhouse. Because many of the buildings were unsafe or unstable after the quake, the university erected tents and trailers all over campus, where we attended classes and professors relocated their offices. Since then, Cal State Northridge has expanded, with restored and added buildings and facilities. My father's office and lab in Eucalyptus Hall are still there, but, since he retired, they have been occupied by younger generations of biologists.

The year 1994 is also memorable because that was when the film *Interview with the Vampire* was released. It is based on the first book of Anne Rice's thirteen-volume *Vampire Chronicles.* In the film, a young Tom Cruise and a younger Brad Pitt terrorize each other and suck each other's blood and the blood of other humans, stray cats, rats, and children. They mope and brood; they murder; they cry tears of blood; they fly, levitate, and move at the speed of light; they rage; they dance frantically—inebriated, their faces moody and pancaked, their mouths bloody, their incisors sharp. And they speak with inexcusable New Orleans accents. Today, *Interview with the Vampire* is also the basis for a new drama series on the streaming service AMC+. The queer subtext of Rice's novel has become evident, and the main character—the subject of the "interview," a tortured vampire named Louis de Pointe du Lac—is whom sociologists Davis and Dollard would have described as a "*colored* Creole." The original film grossed me out, to use an expression in my native tongue (Valley Girl English), but it introduced me to Anne Rice.

*The Feast of All Saints* is a reference to All Saints' Day, a feast day in Roman Catholicism, traditionally celebrated in New Orleans by cleaning and adorning the above-ground cemetery tombs of one's ancestors. The back cover of *Interview with the Vampire* read, "In the days before the Civil War, there lived a Louisiana people unique in Southern history. For though they were descended from African slaves, they were also descended from the French and Spanish who had enslaved them. They were the *gens de couleur libre*—Free People of Color—and in this dazzling historical novel, Anne Rice chronicles the lives of four of their number, men and women caught perilously between the worlds of master and slave, privilege and oppression, passion and pain."[9] The words "unique," "caught perilously," "master and slave," as well as the French-language terminology, *gens de couleur libre,* all reinforced the image of New Orleans and its people as exotic and enticing.

As an undergraduate student initially majoring in creative writing but later switching to history, I purchased the book and quickly read it, despite its 571-page length. Rice, a master at descriptive prose, built characters inspired by literary tropes in earlier works of New Orleans fiction. The book begins with the main character, the adolescent Marcel, who is described as "part African, a *quadroon* most likely," a "striking figure":

> The white and the black blood in him had combined in an unusual way that was extremely handsome and clearly undesirable. For though his skin was lighter than honey, indeed lighter than that of many white people who were forever studying him, he had large, vivid blue eyes which made it dusky. And his blonde hair, tightly kinked and hugging his round head like a cap, was distinctly African. He had ridgeless eyebrows which were high and gave his expression an appealing openness, a delicate nose, with small, flared nostrils, and a full mouth.[10]

Marcel's Mulatto mother Cecile, "a stunning lady," has "a French face, petite, sharper feature, with no trace of the African, except, of course, for her beautifully textured and very dark skin."[11] A psychologically tormented woman who rarely leaves the confines of her house, Cecile had come to New Orleans as a child refugee from the St. Domingue Revolution. Her Aunts Tante Josette, Tante Colette, and Tante Louisa were wealthy free Mulattoes, descended from St. Domingue's mixed-race slaveholding population.

After migrating to New Orleans, Cecile becomes the concubine of Philippe Ferronaire, described as a "Creole [white] gentleman to his fingertips, and in debt on the next crop to the hilt, his white children crowding the family box at the opera every season."[12] The relationship between Cecile and Ferronaire is obviously influenced by the historical practice of *plaçage,* in which free women of color engaged in semi-formalized relationships with older, established white men, who provided the women a home and a measure of financial security. These relationships were often associated with dances called quadroon balls, which is where the *plaçage* relationships may have begun. There is much historical debate about *plaçage* and quadroon balls: the point of contention is the *interpretation* of actual balls held in New Orleans and of actual relationships between free women of color and European men. Because European men attended balls along with free women of color, who were often chaperoned by their mothers or elder aunts, it seems a fair assumption that the balls were sites of negotiation and betrothal. And because there is archival evidence of European men sharing a domicile with free women of color, and fiscally providing for her and their children after his death, it seems a fair assumption too that the semi-formalized arrangement existed throughout New Orleans. Interpretations of these balls and relationships—which may or may not have been loving ones—give them a romantic air. Whether we call them balls and relationships, or *quadroon balls* and *plaçage,* depends on our interpretation of them; it also shapes how they are seen and understood. Finally, the language used to describe these balls and relationships contributes to the exoticism of New Orleans and the people therein.[13]

In Rice's novel, Cecile's son Marcel and her daughter Marie, the children of the patriarch Ferronaire, are at the cusp of young adulthood. Marcel wishes to study literature in Paris, and his father has promised to support his travels there. Marie, who is described as so light-skinned that she can pass as white, hopes to escape what fate has in store for her: to follow in her mother's footsteps as the concubine of a Creole man. Part of the novel's plot centers Marcel and Marie's conflicted position as simultaneously privileged (they are the free-born children of a white man) and constrained (they are the nonwhite children of an unrestrained, rich white man).

*The Feast of All Saints* is a stew of New Orleans history and literary mythology. It features Voodooiennes and scary Voodoo rituals, drunken and violent French-speaking men, masked balls, a challenge to a duel, slaves on auction blocks and resentful slaves who keep family secrets, a gang rape of a light-skinned girl, afflicted gay men and rumors of them, shadowy bayous, Catholic priests, the romantic background of the French Quarter and the not-romantic plantations upriver, madams and brothels, and *quadroons.* Lots of *quadroons*—most of them romantically and beautifully sad, exotic in the constellations of their physical features, desired by both Black and white men but attainable only by the latter.

As a young reader with no Creole friends who had not yet read any Louisiana history, and who was mostly uninformed about my family history, my mind was blown by Anne Rice's *The Feast of All Saints.* Its depictions of Creoles and mixed-race New Orleanians drew me in. Its storylines widened my eyes. I was, as the book jacket promised, dazzled. I closed the book on my lap and penned poems. I daydreamed about New Orleans, its above-ground cemeteries, its curl around the Mississippi River. I imagined the Place d'Armes, the St. Louis Cathedral, the cottages and shotgun houses, and the French Market; I pictured people like me, moving elegantly through these spaces, at home in their bodies and communities. Because Rice didn't refer to the nonwhite characters in *The Feast of All Saints* as "Creoles"—this was a term reserved for the Francophone white characters—I imagined that the quadroons were my ancestresses. I thought of Grandma and her two sisters, Aunt Lalie and Aunt Yvonne, as living representations of the characters Tante Josette, Tante Colette, and Tante Louisa, who represented both the privilege of white adjacency and the pride in being free women of color. I imagined myself an heir to these mythologies about mixed-race women in Louisiana. I read the novel again, dog-earing pages and talking about the novel with anyone who would listen. This was the first book that I thought, in my mere twenty-four years on this earth, represented *us.* In my young mind, this was *our people* and *our history.*

Blood Math. Lillian DeCoux. New Orleans, ca. 1908.

Anne Rice's descriptions of the characters reminded me of my mother's words, repeated to my sisters and me, as we sat on the stool in front of the big bathroom mirror of our house on Bismarck Avenue, as my mother ran the brush through my hair one hundred times, from scalp to tip, from head to waist: "You are beautiful" was my mother's mantra to my sisters and me. "You have beautiful hair," she spoke as she brushed. "They're jealous of you," she told us when we cried over lost friendships.

Her words could have been direct quotes from *The Feast of All Saints.*

Is this what we were? Sad and vapid beauties?

The symbolism directed at the liminal body and the fractions associated with race and mixed-race in the lower Mississippi River valley are powerful tools to build a work of fiction. They are also grounded in a racist calculus of hybridity, measuring the so-called Black blood, an enduring yet imprecise and slippery fiction.

*Cordon-bleu:* 1/32nd Black
*Sang-melé:* 1/16th Black
*Octoroon:* 1/8th Black
*Quadroon:* 1/4th Black
*Mulatto:* 1/2 Black
*Griffe:* 3/4 Black

Why doesn't this taxonomy look different, like this?

*Cordon-bleu:* 31/32nd white
*Sang-melé:* 15/16th white
*Octoroon:* 7/8th white
*Quadroon:* 3/4th white
*Mulatto:* 1/2 white
*Griffe:* 1/4 white

It is because, in the Americas, where racialized, unfree labor defined entire societies, blackness became the mark. In this philology of race, blackness is the stain that erases all other imaginary bloods. It is the sign of difference. Blackness is the stake on which identity pivots, the articulation of the kind of blood that determines whether a person has access to power, to resources, to rights, to full humanity. Highly charged, gendered characterizations of octoroon and quadroon women especially are defined by the imagined softened cusp of whiteness at which their bodies teeter. They are almost white; the perceived hardened edge of their blackness is barely visible at all. Anti-Black racism is clearly embedded in these imaginings. Figments of the imagination that are informed by histories of Indigenous erasure, of slavery, colonialism, and empire, octoroon and quadroon characters are largely the invention of the owning class of southern white men.

Everywhere racial slavery was practiced, the owning class defined African and African-descended women's bodies as laboring: both the physical labor that sustained the slave economy and the birthing labor that perpetuated slavery as a heritable institution.[14] Professor Christina Sharpe writes of Black women: "Reading together the Middle Passage, the coffle, and I add to the argument, the birth canal, we can see how each has functioned separately and collectively over time to dis/figure Black maternity, to turn the womb into a factory producing blackness as abjection much like the slave ship's hold and the prison."[15] Placing a dehumanizing economic value on an enslaved woman of birthing age, and her progeny, was no minor thing, as made evident in court cases in French Louisiana, in which enslaved women courageously used their voices and their testimonies not only to insist on their humanity beyond the subservience expected of them but also to command boundaries around their bodies, their partner choices, their pregnancies, and their children.[16]

And those enslaved women who gave birth to children of mixed race, especially light-skinned daughters, found, to their horror, that their girls, especially in New Orleans and Louisiana, drew special interest in the slave market. Descriptions of the bodies of light-skinned, enslaved women emphasized one particular trait: they were largely seen as "delicate." According to historian Walter Johnson, "descriptions of light-skinned slaves were projections of slaveholders' own dreamy interpretations of the meaningfulness of their skin color." Associating "lightness with feminine domesticity," slaveholders viewed domestic slaves as "intelligent," "well-bred," and "fancy."[17] As enslaved women, they were marked and monetized in these ways:

*A woman. 13 years old, Bright Color, nearly a fancy for $1135.*

*She was about thirty years old. Her color was that of a quadroon.*

*Fancy girls being sold in New Orleans for from $1000 to $3000.*

*. . . that man who bought a high priced Fancy at $1780.*[18]

"The racial gaze of the slaveholder," writes Johnson, "projected sexual meaning onto the bodies of light-skinned women." Furthermore, "these slaveholders showed that they had the power to purchase what was forbidden and the audacity to show it off."[19] This point is endorsed by historian

Alecia P. Long: "New Orleans had established an enduring reputation as a sinful, sensual, and sybaritic place before the Civil War," in part due to its status as "a center of tolerated prostitution and its position as the region's largest slave market." Visitors to New Orleans "believed the city to be wicked," yet they "were fascinated by it, simultaneously charmed and scandalized by its aura of disorder and its culture of sexual permissiveness and sensual excess."[20] One consequence of this history of slavery, sexual permissiveness, and sensual excess was "Fancy" slaves.

Francophone white men's monetized desire for women of mixed race extended beyond enslaved "Fancies" and into the populations of free women of color, those who appear throughout the fictional *The Feast of All Saints.* Most of the free quadroon women in the novel are either concubines of white men, daughters of concubines of white men, desired by white men, or sexually assaulted by white men. Historian Emily Clark explores the mythologies erected around the historical women, who were sometimes called *mûlatresses.* "Romanticized and sensationalized descriptions of New Orleans quadroons," Clark writes, framed them as women who were "almost entirely white"—"mixed-race temptress[es]" whose manufactured image obscured the hard work and the strategies of survival that they employed in the context of a society based on slave labor.[21]

Clark shares the portrayal of the idealized character of the mixed-race New Orleans woman in "The Quadroon of Orleans," an 1839 short story by Joseph Holt Ingraham. "'The *soft olive* of her complexion was *just tinged* with the *rich blood* beneath. Her profile was accurately *Grecian,* her lips a *little too full,* perhaps, but her *finely shaped mouth* lost nothing of its beauty by their richness.'" The character, named Emilie, had "large-orbed, *jet-black* eyes that seemed to float in lakes of *liquid languor,*" and her body struck an "elegant figure, a lofty carriage." Clark notes that the character in the story "diverged from European ideals of beauty *only in ways that made her more irresistible*" [emphasis in original]. Her detailed physical description is a type that is mimicked again and again. It "spins these details into a confection of exotic beauty"; she is like a delightful sweet on a plate.[22]

Searching for more examples of the quadroon character, I found the 1929 Evans Wall novel, *The No-Nation Girl.* The title character, Precieuse, lives in the feral swamps of southern Louisiana. She has eyes that are "wide and black and wondrously soft like smooth sealskin in lamplight." Reflecting the rhapsodized and racist beauty standard of the quadroon, her hair is "blue-black, lustrous, the rippling wave in it the only trace of the kink in that of her mother." Her skin is "olive," "smooth," tinged with "warm color." Precieuse's body is described in this way: "From the back of her ankles down to her heels the flesh was slightly thicker than in the average pure-blooded Caucasian. Her mother frequently told her that this was a sign of the 'n—— in her.'"[23] The novel has a tragic (and deeply racist) ending: Precieuse, the lover of a white man but who was raped by a Black man, throws herself into Suicide Basin, tortured by the thought that her unborn child would be born with dark skin.

I also read the 1928 novel *Toucoutou,* by the previously mentioned Edward Larocque Tinker. In the novel, the main character Toucoutou is the child of a white man and a Haitian octoroon, who schemes to pass her daughter off as a white child of European immigrants. Toucoutou is "tall and graceful, with lovely chestnut hair that had a natural wave"; her eyes were "a deep blue," and her skin "a smooth mat-ivory without a fault."[24] Toucoutou marries a foolish white man, who doesn't know that she is, based on dubious blood math, one-sixteenth Black; when he comes to the realization that she isn't white, it's too late: he is so enraptured by her beauty that he cannot live without her.

The novel is based on a Louisiana court case from 1859, *Anastasie Desarzant v. P. LeBlanc and E. Desmaziliere, his wife,* in which Desarzant (a free woman of mixed heritage) sued Desmaziliere (a white woman) for publicly accusing her of being a "Negress."[25] The accusation and the court case that followed are represented in the novel; so is Desarzant's, or Toucoutou's, loss of that very case. In the novel, Toucoutou is a tragic figure: after being outed as Black, she and her husband flee to Cuba where they can reconstitute their identities and where Toucoutou can flee the perceived calamity of her blackness.

Lyle Saxon's 1937 novel, *Children of Strangers,* is set in the rural northern Louisiana community of Cane River, also called Natchitoches, which is one of the oldest French settlements in the lower Mississippi River valley. Saxon's main character, Euphamie, is a woman of mixed race but "nobody, nobody in the world—unless he looked mightily close—could tell that she was a Mulatto." This inability to recognize Euphamie as a woman of color was due to the "faint row of freckles across the bridge of her nose . . . the dreaming black eyes [which] showed a thread of white beneath the pupil," and "her lips [which] were very red and not too full . . . like a Spanish girl."[26] Euphamie and her community are described as proud Mulattoes. The center of their community is the Catholic church that they themselves built.

In the novel, Euphamie has a wild affair with a red-haired white man, even though she is betrothed to her cousin Numa. The affair produces a child, Joel, whose hair is as red and whose skin is as white as his father's; he is so white, in fact, that Euphamie becomes strangely obsessed with shielding him from every harm, which eventually drives him away. Euphamie betrays the Mulatto community by selling her land to white people and then by taking a Black man as her lover. In the tragic ending, she is alone, banished from her family and her community, her beauty faded to an embarrassing, "shabby" blackness.[27]

In Euphamie, I saw the shape of "the infamous Juliette Mercier," from *The Feast of All Saints.* "A senselessly disheveled figure" who is fixated on her son, Christophe, Juliette has "beauty and money enough to make her a public offense." She is "shameful, she had no excuse" for her antisocial behavior and appearance, "her hair streaming like Ophelia." Another romanticized quadroon, Juliette has "hair of gleaming black, with skin so light she might have passed to the untutored eye, and rings on her fingers when she chose."[28]

Any reading of the works of fiction featuring quadroons and octoroons can reveal similarities among them. They are beautiful tragedies. Their beauty is framed by their almost whiteness and their barely blackness. Their eyes, lips, hair, and skin make them sexually enticing; their bodily movements make them mysterious, dramatic, drawing other characters' gaze and readers' attention. Their plot points tend to the tragic. Octoroon and quadroon characters are tormented, confused, lost, manic, sad, plagued by their blackness; some storylines end in suicide, in disappearance, in exile. These novels and the characters therein are clearly part of a larger literary genre, the *tragic Mulatto,* which was used by authors to represent the problem of the mixed-race person within the racial binary. Through these characters, authors fixate on both the body and the mind as sites of contestation over racial mixture in the United States. The tragic Mulatto is typically written as a solitary character who is alienated from others, like the main character of James

Weldon Johnson's *Autobiography of an Ex-Colored Man* (1912). They are mysterious or suspect, untrustworthy or plotting, like the character Silas Lynch in Thomas Dixon Jr.'s novel *The Clansman: A Historical Romance of the Ku Klux Klan* (1905). They compromise their relationships by passing as white, like the character Stella Vignes in Brit Bennett's *The Vanishing Half* (2020). They die violently, like the character Clare Kendry in Nella Larsen's *Passing* (1929). They suffer racism or social exclusion, like the character Phong in Nguyễn Phan Quế Mai's *Dust Child* (2023). They are confused and torn between different parts of themselves, like the character Joe Christmas in William Faulkner's *Light in August* (1932) or the title character of Ernest J. Gaines's *Catherine Carmier* (1964). And they sometimes survive a life of torment and become redeemed in the end, like the character Sarah Jane in the film *An Imitation of Life* (1959).

Although *The Feast of All Saints* might not belong within the tragic Mulatto genre, the novel contains all its elements: the mixed-race beauty, the suffering and violence associated with race, the psychological torment, and the complicated association with whiteness. As a novel set in New Orleans before the Civil War, there are added layers of historical context that are absent from other works of fiction. In the afterword of *The Feast of All Saints,* Anne Rice writes, "Aside from a few liberties with dates, every effort has been made to render the world of New Orleans' Free People of Color accurately." She acknowledges her indebtedness "to many who have written about New Orleans and the Free People of Color in the ante-bellum South, from the popular writers who have kept alive the romance and richness of those days to the scholars whose books, articles, theses, and dissertations continue to swell the growing body of work on the free Afro-American before the Civil War."[29]

As a descendant of free people of color from Louisiana, I ponder the literary tragic Mulattoes, octoroons, and quadroons. Some of the women in my ancestry were likely viewed through these lenses because they were mixed-heritage, free, Francophone women from southern Louisiana who had varying degrees of relation to white men. Some may have had a comparatively fair complexion, although that is always contestable. Encased in their bodies, evaluated according to the time and place in which they lived, they might have been subject to the sexual objectification that recurs in both fictional and historical accounts. It is a thorny consideration. How am I writing my distant ancestors and ancestresses, my great-grandmothers, my grandmothers, my mother, and the great-great men in my family line? How central is their mixedness to their life stories? Are they shaped by it, and if so, how? Which of their stories have I chosen to include in this book? Which of their photographs? How am I curating the people who came before me? Am I turning them into tropes? Am I a descendant of Fancies? Does it matter? Does it somehow reinforce the lightness of color that appears throughout so may decades of my ancestors' representations? Is *plaçage* part of my heritage? Did my ancestresses attend quadroon balls, and does that matter?

I asked my mother once, in reference to her mother, "Was Mema an octoroon?"

She laughed and then paused before answering me: "Well, not really, I don't know . . . maybe people thought of her that way. After all . . . she had blue eyes."

"Someone called me an octoroon once," my mother then shared for the first time. "A white guy said to me, 'So, you're that octoroon that I've heard about.'" Mom laughed.

Funny that he didn't say, "So, you're that Creole that I've heard about." Was this because *Creole* had been a term reserved for Francophone white people and that it didn't include people of color, like my mother, like myself? The words and works of our Creole elders argue differently, offering an alternate narrative. For example, in the 1989 television documentary *The Creole Controversy,* Tulane University archivist Ulysses Ricard explains that he grew up understanding that a "Creole is anyone who is racially mixed or who lives here in New Orleans or in southern Louisiana whose family has been here a very long time, who's descended of either a French or a Spanish family." Ricard goes on to say, "If someone would have told me twenty years ago that there was such a thing as a white Creole or a Black Creole, I would have said, 'oh, you're kidding, there is no such thing as a white Creole or a Black Creole. Creoles are only racially mixed people.'"[30]

Civil rights attorney Alexander Pierre Tureaud, whose work helped to desegregate the city of New Orleans, said in an interview, "Negroes also called themselves Creoles and others called them Creoles. In fact, in the section of the city where I lived, the Seventh Ward, we had a large number of so-called Creoles." The Seventh Ward was where my paternal grandmother grew up, in the LaCroix-Beauvais-Roux house that once stood on North Miro Street. Tureaud continued, "Their ethnic background was a mixture of French, or Spanish, or Indian or West Indian. There wasn't any challenging of anybody who called themselves Creole in those days." In reference to the authors of fiction, who labeled us octoroons, quadroons, and Mulattoes, Tureaud said, "Some of the writers have tried to differentiate between the white people who were truly the Creoles and the Negroes who were not Creoles. But the word Creole has an origin that even comes from the West Indies and it didn't necessarily mean a Caucasian mixture with any other group. It just meant a mixture of two racial groups or more."[31]

Another elder, author John O. Sarpy, insisted upon hybridity, not whiteness, as the main element of Creole. Here is his definition of Creoles, as articulated on the first page of his self-published monograph, *A Slave, A Frenchman, and the Blood of a Saint:* "those multi-racial people born in Louisiana during the 1700s and early 1800s from the union of a Black, an Indian, or mixtures thereof and one French or Spanish father," as well as "the descendants of such people." Sarpy writes, "As a result of our multiracial heritage, we strongly feel that individually [Creoles] should be able to identify with—and claim belonging to—any element of their racial makeup as they so individually choose," adding, "even if at times that may mean leaning towards identification with one element of their heritage over the other."[32]

The poet Maurice Martinez, author of the essay, "Rainbow People: Creoles of Color and the Colored-Caucasian Syndrome in New Orleans," wrote: "'Creole,' then, is a person of color, although his physical features and surname may be mistaken for 'caucasian' by an outsider. Creoles of color . . . moved with the nuances of an American black experience, yet were faced with their Europeanized features, and more important, the reality of what 'being white' meant in an oppressive society in Louisiana." Martinez explains, ". . . the term 'Creole' when used by non-whites in New Orleans refers to 'Gens de couleur'—people whose ancestry contains a descendent of Africans in the New World."[33]

Reconciling fictional works with the words and works of Creoles of color themselves, I realized that, as a diasporic person, I experienced Creole as something imaginary—as an absence. Creole was weekend visits with mixed-race elders who spoke of places I'd never seen. Creole was spoken references to people I'd never met. Creole was verbal expressions that I didn't understand or use. It was experiences that I'd never had. For me, literature filled the empty space. Mythology posed as an endearing presence. Fictional characters offered possibilities of reality. My actual friends and I represented a suburban Los Angeles ethnicity of our own, with our shared language, our shared norms and habits, our own values, symbols, signals, and ways of seeing the world.

Although my sisters and I frequently visited our extended family in the city of Los Angeles, we were largely shaped by our sheltered suburban upbringing. When my father graduated from the University of Southern California with his doctorate in biology, my parents moved "over the hill," a reference to the steep incline along the I-405 freeway that divided the city of Los Angeles from the suburbs to the north. Ours was a migration into a geography of suburban whiteness; its assemblage of social elements—modes of

Foremothers. Sisters of the Holy Family and Children. New Orleans, n.d.
Photo courtesy of Xavier University of Louisiana.

speech, ways of dress, bodily carriage, musical tastes, hobbies, cultural references, and racial (non)identity—patterned my sisters and me in ways that sometimes distanced us from our kin, real or fictive, who lived in the city.

When I reverse-migrated back to New Orleans, I came to realize that my Creoleness had been altered not only by my grandparents' decision to move to Los Angeles but also by my parents' decision to leave Los Angeles for the San Fernando Valley. I carried a secondary layer of differentiation. I also carried the works of fiction that formed a foundation for my understanding of myself and the people whom I imagined as mine. In New Orleans and in Louisiana, I stepped out of the imagined, off the page, and into the land itself. There, I found that Creole was not a white man, not a romanticized character in a book, and that we were not tragic Mulattoes, not quadroons or octoroons defined by the wildness of our hair, streaming like Ophelia, with a lavender sadness in our eyes.

# 9

# Mounds

I first came to Louisiana from the north, from the rolling green hills outside Homochitto National Forest, from the wooded trails and highways that traverse the historic lands of the Tunica, the Chitimacha, the Chickasaw, the Choctaw, and the Natchez. I came into Louisiana from the north, from the old road that linked the Cherokee, the Muscogee, and the Coushatta with the peoples, the resources, the trade goods, the tales, the foods, and the languages of the peoples of the lower Mississippi River valley. There are so many ways to come into Louisiana, so many openings into the spongy marsh, into the cypress swamps, the tributaries and the confluences, the crawfish mud piles, and the opaque waterlands of this place.

For all the times that my grandparents returned to Louisiana, all the weddings and funerals that they attended, the ordinations, the graduations, the Carnival seasons, I never joined them. When they came home to California, I received Mardi Gras beads and doubloons, the tokens thrown from parade floats. I received T-shirts with images of alligators and crawfish. I heard stories of visits with family members whom I'd never met and never would. Funny that these gifts from New Orleans were nothing more special to me than the Mandarin pajamas Grandma and Grandpa brought me from China, or the hand puppet from Italy, or the stuffed kangaroo from Australia. New Orleans was a tourist destination in the material life of my childhood, a place where gifts came from.

My arrival in New Orleans in 1994 came as a research trip. I was "an anthropologist," my fireman cousin Robert once pointed out.

In fact, I was an undergraduate student at Cal State, newly majoring in history and studying under Professor Ronald L. F. Davis, whose specialty was Civil War and Reconstruction-era Mississippi history. He invited me to travel to Mississippi to help establish a new archive, what is now the Courthouse Records Project of the Historic Natchez Foundation. Dr. Davis is tall and terribly near-sighted; we students used to gape at his very, very thick eyeglasses. When looking at faded, old historical records, he flipped his eyeglasses to rest on his forehead and held the documents very close to his face. Dr. Davis also spoke very softly, so softly that we leaned in to hear his directives, we sat close to the front of the classroom to hear his wandering lectures, we wondered why he was laughing when we knew we had missed the near-whispered joke.

During the summer of 1994, I joined a dozen history students for three months of unfolding and then reading legal documents that hadn't been opened in well over one hundred years—the ink, in some cases, having turned to black dust, insect detritus like sand tucked between the pages. Some of the documents that we read and carefully cataloged dated back to Natchez and Adams County in the early nineteenth century. For eight hours each weekday, we read legal records regarding land, marriage, commerce, personal reputation, and property, including those relating to enslaved laborers. I recall all of us young Californians being awestruck by the blunt transcripts before us: slaveholders who sued other slaveholders for work that a leased enslaved person failed to complete; slaveholders who sued slave traders for falsely advertising "able-bodied slaves" who were found to be "defective"; lending institutions that sued slaveholders for defaulting on a loan. The cruel reality of racial capitalism framed our introduction to antebellum Natchez.

A quaint, small town that sits high on the steep bluffs of the Mississippi River, Natchez is known mainly for its abundance of preserved antebellum mansions, the town dwellings of slaveholders whose farms and plantations spread out in the rich delta and bottomlands of the lower Mississippi River valley. Enslaved and free carpenters, bricklayers, and plasterers built these large dwellings whose old-fashioned names, like Stanton Hall, Longwood, Rosalie, Linden, and Melrose, draw tourists to come and reminisce about the Old South. One can visit Natchez today and take a plantation tour, learn some of the history of the family that owned each house, but learn much less about the domestic enslaved people who cleaned and maintained it. Much of Natchez culture, perhaps why it has been referred to as "the deepest South," is centered on the Lost Cause and the celebration of a certain representation of the past; that is, a past that highlights the Confederacy and an outmoded mockery of slavery.[1] Yet, Natchez is also known for revolt: at least twice in the early French colonial period, the Natchez people united with Bambara people in armed resistance against the European arrivals. One historical narrative—of a romanticized southern charm—smothers another narrative of Indigenous and African resistance.

Each morning, walking to the Historic Natchez Foundation for another long day of reading and cataloging, we inhaled the uniquely acrid smell of a paper mill, which was located in Louisiana, on the opposite side of the Mississippi River. Each evening, after we students had spent the day reading through the legal dramas of the local elite, we walked by the Big Houses that had once been theirs. Most of these mansions had been converted into historic sites, tourist attractions, bed and breakfasts, or antebellum museums. Sometimes, passing by these mansions, we caught a glimpse of a tour guide or a historical reenactor: a white woman dressed in an antebellum gown embodying the unsullied "mistress" of the house.

In the evenings, we students sometimes walked down "the hill" to stand on the shores of the Mississippi down below the city, where, more than a century before, skiffs arrived from lower Tennessee via the Homochitto River and slavers arrived from New Orleans markets. When we students worked in Natchez, there were a few local bars in that area called Under-the-Hill located at the boat landing. And the earthworks that held up the very edge of the city seemed to be falling down in crumbling pieces. Today, Under-the-Hill is a redeveloped tourist area, with a casino that draws visitors from all around, and the bluffs are supported by remarkable feats of engineering.

Some evenings, we history students walked to the edge of town to a local burger spot that was open late; I recall drinking many a vanilla milkshake there. We walked to the historic site of Fort Rosalie, a military outpost in the upper Mississippi that the Natchez destroyed in their attempts to eject the earliest French colonists. We walked through Black Natchez, whose residents observed from afar our alien presence; just our walking in the high heat of summer, even in the evening time, plus our clothing (SoCal college student casual), our backpacks weighted down with books, our body language, and our accents clearly marked us as outsiders.

Dr. Davis told us one night that we would be taking a little drive. Gathering all of us into a rented van, Dr. Davis grinned, entertained by our questioning countenances. We left town and drove along the highway; Dr. Davis remained characteristically quiet, revealing nothing. Turning onto a winding, dark country road with few markers to denote where we were, we arrived at our destination. It was off the road, unlit, rising like a massive plateau in the dark.

An Indian mound.

An earthworks construction that author Boyce Upholt irreverently writes about as "carefully arranged soils" that take the shape of "pyramids and cones and hillocks, embankments and enclosures, silhouetted effigies of animals and humans and spiritual beings."[2] Writer Kristina Kay Robinson, who as a child often visited Natchez, her father's home, offers this description: "The mound," which is the second largest in the United States, "stretching out across eight acres . . . served as both the seat of power and the spiritual center for the surrounding villages." We students stood around its base, quietly looking up at this immense earthwork rising before us. Robinson's words, published thirty years after my first encounter with the mound at Natchez, captured our reaction that night: "There is nothing much to say when you are there. All you can do is be quiet and take in the weight—the expanse—of it all."[3]

Dr. Davis gave us a brief, and characteristically quiet, lecture on the history of the Emerald Mound, which was built by the distant ancestors of the Natchez people. His information had certainly been gathered from local Natchez historians or perhaps from the archaeological findings on Mississippian prehistory, which smolder with tales of human sacrifice. These are sensationalized stories told by those who sought to establish their professional credentials and expertise in translating Native American culture into simplified Western concepts while simultaneously othering Indigenous people. Non-Indigenous misinterpretations of Indian mounds also explain why they have been marketed as tourist attractions or treated as meaningless impediments to construction.

Today, Native earthworks are generally referred to as historic sites, but Indigenous sources emphasize their character as sacred sites, as places that have always had spiritual meaning to Indigenous peoples, even if they were unable to articulate that meaning as a result of genocide and expulsion from their lands. Indigenous sources tell us that Archaic Mississippian earthworks, from the upper Mississippi to the lower Mississippi River valley, are "conduits through which Native Americans are able to channel the physical and spiritual manifestations of their beliefs."[4] Mounds were often constructed adjacent to other landscape forms like caves, mountains, crevasses, and rivers, and all are connected to each other as part of larger Indigenous cosmologies. Earthworks are sacred sites of kingship-naming ceremonies and of spiritual observances linked to the seasons, of funerary and burial rituals and practices, of birth and origination in Indigenous creation stories. They are also themselves representations of deities and their direct relationship to their human worshipers and venerators.[5]

In my Native American history and Western history courses at Cal State Northridge, I learned about the relevance of Indigenous earthworks throughout the long and deep Mississippi River valley. I knew that they had been exploited by migrants moving westward, who traversed the river to settle the western states. I knew that some had been excavated by archaeologists. I also knew that Indigenous peoples, from the Dakota peoples in the headwaters region to the Choctaw peoples in the Mississippi's delta and mouth, spoke and painted and sang and wrote their own narratives around the symbolic meanings of the mounds. Until this trip to Natchez, however, I'd never seen one with my own eyes.

And aside from my grandparents having been brought up near the Mississippi River levees and mounds, I hadn't considered my relationship to these ceremonial earthworks. Stunned that we were standing in this place, I wondered if I had some connection to the site, given that my paternal grandfather was of Mississippi Choctaw descent, that nation being among the descendants of mound builders. Even today, I can recall the lump in my throat, the tears in my eyes, and the breathless sensation of approaching the mound for the first time that summer night.

Having returned to Emerald Mound over the years, watching the sun rise and the sun set from the mound, with my offerings of red grapes and plums, eggplant, and red roses bundled at my feet, I know that these earthworks are what Diné poet Jake Skeets calls a "memory field." "Memory is a physical construction," according to Skeets, "woven in a unique matrix with land, language, and time."[6] Standing at the base of Emerald Mound, I wondered, What could be recalled from the descendants of this place, and how would they frame those recollections? The mound itself is a memory field, narrating the cycles of change in the histories of the mound builders, where "pasts, presents, and futures exist simultaneously."[7]

After Dr. Davis's brief lecture that summer night, we were reminded to honor this place with impeccable behavior. And then, we ascended the mound. Lit only by the moon, we students of history climbed to the top of what could have been a burial site, what could have been a birth site, what could have held the remains of my or anyone's distant ancestors, what could have been the feminine sacred site of my nameless Indigenous kin. When we reached the top of the mound, we sat on the grass and took in the night, the constant odor of the paper mill in the thick air around us, our sweat giving our bodies a brief chill. Dr. Davis handed out cups of sweetened lemonade.

And then he suggested that we drink a toast. We held our plastic cups up in the night air, and Dr. Davis offered that toast—to the Confederate dead. His words shocked me and the others, all of us looking at each other in the deep southern dark, wondering why we would drink to the rebels while sitting on an Indigenous ceremonial mound. Picking up my dropped jaw, I tapped my cup against that of another student, hesitating to dignify the Lost Cause on the earthworks of the Mississippian peoples. Why did he give that toast, that night, in that place? My assumption is a benign one, having known Dr. Davis to be a kind and quiet soul. He was a Mississippi historian; he might have held Confederates in a neutral place. In my memory, Dr. Davis kept judgments to himself. He may have offered the toast to shock us, to get a response. Or maybe the toast was unfinished: "Let's drink a toast to the Confederate dead," spoken aloud, in my memory; perhaps it was followed by other words spoken in a whisper so quiet no one could hear them.

Now I recall that night with a new curiosity: Might I have been as indignant had I then known the historic record of Celestin Gaudin, my great-great-grandfather, the Afro-Creole Confederate of the Pelican Battery from Darrow, Louisiana? Would I have felt another emotion, a second breath, a pause before the conclusion? Where shall I place Celestin Gaudin in the cosmos of my morality? Would he be buried in my ceremonial mound?

Dr. Davis's toast lingered with me, and I pondered the Natchez: this town named after the Native people who resisted the French, the people who have been recorded as either extinct or amalgamated into the Creek nation, "extinct" being an utter erasure from memory and feeding the harmful myth of the vanishing Indian. Erasure of the autonomous Natchez leaves not only an imagined but also a linguistic, spoken space to be filled, and that has been filled with the Confederacy and a culture that celebrates its short four-year existence. The dissonance arises here, in this contradiction: when locals speak the name "Natchez," when they say it aloud, the accent on the first syllable, they actually "activate and ruminate" on the Natchez people and their continued presence here. Geographer and artist Margaret Wickens Pearce (Potawatami Nation) reminds us, "Place names are our ancestors' speech. Place names are our identities."[8] And here at Emerald Mound (does anyone know what it was called in the original language?), here is the material, undeniable, spatiotemporal proof of the existence of those who came before, the Mississippians and their descendants. In this mound, memory is physical construction, and physical construction is memory. Regardless of the association of this town with plantation bombast, the Natchez are still here and not only in this compounded soil.

The morning after the dubious toast, I arose early and called Grandpa from the wall telephone in the kitchen of the house where we lived that summer and the next summer too, up on State Street. The wood floors of the nineteenth-century home creaked, and the windows warbled in the sun. "We visited an Indian mound," I quietly shared with him. Of course, he'd seen them in Louisiana, in places not far from his birthplace. They were strange and alluring, he shared with me, these mysterious earthworks that rose so high from the ground, that seemed to defy the very land on which they were built. Solid, flat-topped, snake-shaped, tall, profound, mountains where there were no mountains, human-made highlands in the lowlands of the Mississippi valley. In Grandpa's childhood, Indian mounds weren't tourist attractions marked by anthropological and geological signage, lined with benches or ringed with fences. They were unknown spaces out in the uncleared woods.

At Louisiana State University, students and the public are urged not to walk, slide, or sit on the two mounds located on campus. Because they are "thought to have religious and ceremonial significance," the earthworks "should be respected in the same manner as a church or cemetery."[9]

"This place is not a park," the Minnesota Dakota of the upper Mississippi want us to understand about Wakan Tipi, the sacred site near the headwaters of the river. "Our ancestors are still here."[10]

When I told Grandpa about my experience on the mound, he said, "We didn't dare walk or sit on 'em. Mama made sure of that." I couldn't help but feel terrible for climbing up the mound and sitting on the top, drinking a toast to an inglorious memory.

• • • • •

The next year, I returned to Natchez for another summer of processing court documents with Dr. Davis in his happy place, in Mississippi, with his research assistant Joyce Linda Broussard and his gaggle of students, eager for their paper taste of the Old South. The courthouse records awaited us, still folded in the tall metal drawers that were more than a century old, our handwritten notes from the previous year filed away. The heavy heat and the paper mill and the magnolias—yes, the magnolias too—anticipating our arrival.

Dr. Davis suggested something new: How about doing a research project? While you're here, use the records, visit the library, research a plantation, interview someone. I chose the last option, with an added suggestion from Dr. Davis: in 1940, there had been a terrible fire in Natchez.[11] It happened in the Rhythm Nightclub where young Black people danced to local bands and visiting ones from New Orleans, like Walter Barnes and His Royal Creolians, the band playing on the night of the fire. I began researching the terrible event while another one was buried in the back of my mind: in 1985, three weeks before my fifteenth birthday, my Aunt Lockie, Lawrencia Marie, was killed in a massive brushfire in Los Angeles. Three people died in that fire, and my mother's sister, she who earlier had been left behind in New Orleans when her parents migrated to California, was one of them. Fire remains a tender subject for me.

While my research paper from that summer of 1995 is now gone, lost to one of my many moves over the years, the methodology remained with me when I conducted research later. The first interview I conducted was with a journalist and a founder of Natchez's Black newspaper, the *Bluff City Post.* I found his office telephone number in the Yellow Pages, and I called him. Understanding that I was only there for a few weeks, he agreed to meet with me that same week to discuss the fire. I walked into his office and met his smiling face. "Are you Miss Wendy from California?" he asked me. "I thought from your voice that you were white, but now I see you're one of us!"

He warmly shared with me what he knew about the fire, which turned out to be a subject that everyone in town knew something about: more than two hundred young African Americans lost their lives as the club burned from the inside. The decorative elements hanging from the ceiling—Spanish moss treated with a flammable bug spray—had been ignited by a cigarette. Boarded-up windows blocked both escape and relief from the smoke. In the days following the fire (and immeasurable time thereafter), Black Natchezians grieved the loss of their sons and daughters, friends and fictive kin. In this very small community, the *Bluff City Post* journalist shared with me, everyone seemed to know someone who had died in the fire. Teachers lost students. Neighbors lost the young men who cut their lawn or the young women who babysat their young ones. Pastors lost parishioners. The few Black morticians struggled to handle the number of dead; segregation prohibited white morticians from assisting. The volume of human loss was overwhelming.

"How about white Natchezians?" I asked him. "How were they affected?"

He took a deep breath, smiled and laughed awkwardly, the indications of a longer and more layered history. We talked about it, nothing he said surprised me, and then I endeavored to do more research.

Thanks to connections made at the Historic Natchez Foundation, I was introduced to two elder white Natchez residents, both of whom had lived in the town their whole lives. They both agreed to speak with me—one in the living room of her very pleasant home, and the other, on the patio outside his plantation, which he had inherited from his great-greats who turned out to be not so great.

The elder white woman whom I interviewed began by asking me, "Where are you from? You don't sound like you're from the South."

"I'm from California," I shared, wondering if she was really wondering about my race. At the time, I looked much like I do now, except I was thirty years younger, with dark-brown curly hair that hung down my back. Being "from California" was enough for her to share with me some of the bitter aspects of Natchez history. That included one memory: as a little girl, she watched the Ku Klux Klan parade through the town every year on Confederate Memorial Day. "They didn't hurt anybody!" I recall her saying, as I nodded my head, forcing my face into a neutral expression and writing notes on my legal pad. When I asked her how her family responded to the Rhythm Nightclub Fire, she told me, "Our maid lost her little girl." She couldn't recall her name, but she believed her parents helped pay for the girl's casket and burial.

The second interview also began with the question, "Where are you from?" This time, I answered, "I'm Creole." Two separate foundations of my identity, offered to two elder white southerners.

Thinking that he would surely know what Creoles are—after all, Louisiana was right there, across the river—my interview subject asked, "What country is that?"

Masking my shock with a smile, I responded, "Louisiana!" adding "right across the river!"

We proceeded amicably, with this elder confirming the things the journalist shared with me in the office of the *Bluff City Post,* minus the annual KKK parade, which terrorized Black Natchezians. White Natchezians mobilized their paternalistic attitudes toward the families of their tragically deceased Black maids, nurses, porters, gardeners, and employees. As the proud product of two centuries of labor barons whose enslaved laborers made them some of the wealthiest in the United States (including the great-greats of the man before me), white Natchezians performed their empathetic grief by paying for funeral costs and donating money to Black churches. And waiting, patiently, to fill the empty spaces that their dead servants left behind.

When I shared my findings with Dr. Davis, he smiled behind his glasses. Performing whiteness in this space meant an attenuated expression of cruelty and an embellished generosity. The light-hearted way in which the first subject played down the KKK parade was an attempt to soften white southern violence; even the word "parade" evokes playfulness, celebration, music, treats, and fun for the whole family! Offering money to grieving African American families that, in 1940 especially, earned their livings mostly in service to white families, further fed the image of a paternal and friendly whiteness. And allowing African American Natchezians to erect a monument to the dead, which now sits on the bluffs of the Mississippi River, represented an ultimate act of generosity: it is a public monument to the Black people of Natchez. My position as an outsider, entering others' spaces to glean from them some understanding of race in the South, a delicate subject with which I was hardly familiar, taught me to take care with my subject position and to pay attention to how I interacted with those unfamiliar with me and those who look like me.

Having spent weeks in the research rooms, in the rented houses, on the plantation tours, in the local restaurant where we exchanged our tickets for lunch and dinner, Dr. Davis informed us that we'd be taking a trip down to New Orleans.

"Aren't you Creole?" one of the Cal State history majors asked me. "And you've never been to New Orleans?"

The loaded questions agitated the swinging door of my authenticity as a Creole. If asked, I could share my grandfather's memory of the cotton bushes on his father's land. Or my grandmother's memory of the stinking city streets across Canal Street. Or my great aunt's memory of rolling cigars in a home factory downtown. Or Uncle Aubry's memory of the Circle Food Store.

But, no, I'd never been to New Orleans.

As we drove down into Louisiana, the land flattened. Ramps and bridges rose over canals and streams, over rivers and swamps. Snow-white egrets perched in trees or stood along the side of the road, digging for food in a ditch, casually watching us speed by. I noticed advertisements for fried boudin balls, crawfish cages, alligator tail and turtle meat, Dixie Beer, fresh watermelon and strawberries, Creole tomatoes, cracklin', spray-on bed liners, and ride-on mowers. I'd never seen so many boats pulled by so many trucks, so many roadside entrepreneurs selling boiled shrimp and fresh fish.

Not long after we'd driven through Krotz Springs, a town amply decorated with Confederate flags, Dr. Davis announced that we'd be taking a little detour. We pulled off the highway and drove through the tiny town of

Livonia in Pointe Coupée Parish. Arriving at our destination, once again we came upon an Indian mound. This one, erected on Chitimacha land, rose just off the side of the road, not far from Bayou Grosse Tête. A few miles down the highway is a crescent-shaped lake called False River, where I would meet my extended cousins some years after this summer.

What is lost in the naming? Livonia Mound? What was it called a millennium ago? What was the word for this place in the language of our Chitimacha ancestors?

Trees sprung in wild angles from the top of the thirty-foot-tall conical mound, and overgrown grass covered it. A strange aberration, an unexplained growth on the earth, the mound shaped like the long body of an exclamation point, insisting that it be noticed. We walked around its base and stood silent, having nothing much to say. To my relief, there were no toasts to Confederate soldiers this time. I wondered why this mound was so steep and what its use could possibly be. Perhaps my interpretation, of use, needed correcting; maybe this was a monument of commemoration, maybe it marked a place of significance, and everyone who came around, who saw this tall thing rising on the land, would know, "This is the place." Perhaps it contained layers on layers of human remains. Remembering Grandpa's words, I was glad that we couldn't climb to the top.

Arriving in New Orleans, we history students stayed at the Hotel Monteleone, located on Royal Street in the French Quarter. I noticed young African American boys tap dancing outside the entrance, bottle tops pressed into the soles of their shoes. Embarking on our walking tour of the French Quarter, Dr. Davis shared that they've been doing this since the antebellum period.

My first visit to my ancestral city was a pilgrimage of a sort, curated by Dr. Davis. It was a site of tourism for all of us—but for me it was a meaningful homecoming to a place where I'd never been. We visited the brick-lined, arched carriageway beside the Place d'Armes Hotel, where enslaved people had once been auctioned. We walked into the Bourbon Orleans Hotel and stood in the chandeliered ballroom, where quadroon balls had supposedly once been held; it was later purchased by the Holy Family Sisters and repurposed into their convent. Of it, author Imani Perry writes, "For the Holy Family nuns, the ballroom was a symbol of domination and sin. They bought it in honor of the women who were sold in those rooms, not as slaves but nevertheless as possessions."[12]

We walked through St. Louis Cemetery No. 2, where Mother Henriette Delille and Mother Juliette Gaudin, founders of the Sisters of the Holy Family, were entombed. We also toured St. Louis Cemetery No. 1, where the tomb of Marie Laveau was decorated with bottles of liquor, real and fake flowers, cigarettes, red cloth, and paper money; a free woman of color, she was known as a notable priestess of Vodou. We ate beignets at Café du Monde and fancy food elsewhere in Jackson Square, food presented to us as "Creole" but not nearly as delicious as what my grandparents prepared in their kitchens in Los Angeles. We walked on the Mississippi River levee and looked across at the neighborhood of Algiers Point, where slavers once disembarked, emptying the suffering captives into holding stations where their bodies would be cleaned, polished, shaved, mended, and dressed for sale in markets just across the river.

Everywhere we went, I looked into the brown faces of people around me. Was that person Creole? Was this person Creole? Did that person know my family? Did anyone *see* me? Might I spot a family member, a cousin, known or unknown, an Afro-Creole or white Creole, someone black or brown or tan or bright or light? Or white? Were the descendants of Mema's father, the Grey Heron, anywhere among us? I knew his surname; might I see it, in bold on the front of a building or carved into the face of a tomb? And if so, what would I do?

Back at the Hotel Monteleone, I called my paternal grandmother, Rita Roux, from the bedside phone. Sharing with her my first visit to New Orleans, the city of her birth, she sounded unimpressed. "Mmm," Grandma said, through her perpetually pursed lips. And then: "When I was coming up, the Quarters was a slum."

I first came to Louisiana from the north, descending from the heights of the distant past, from the mounds that defied the land on which they were built, earthworks standing tall on sinking ground, acts of solid resistance against the mire, artifacts that time hadn't erased. The mound: the field of memory. I came down into Louisiana from ancient mountains where there had been no mountains at all.

# 10

# "My Father Was a French Doctor"

There are books written about my maternal great-grandfather's face, books to his narrow nose and his folded ear and his blond hair that faded to grey, books written about the lower Mississippi River valley, lands of farm and plantation, of levee and mound, of octoroon and Creole, lands that made my maternal great-grandfather a white southerner. This place is mostly water and flat land that loses small islands off its flesh every year, and miles of elevated highway crossing over swamps with fishermen in Lafitte skiffs, and dead-looking cypress trees swaying in bayous with un-American names, like Bayou de l'Outre, Bayou Nezpique, Bayou Queue de Tortue, and Bayou Lafourche. There are books written about my great-grandfather's face, sonnets to his diaphanous lashes and treatises to his widow's peak, but I have written none of them.

There are books written about my maternal great-grandfather, books written about the men who made New Orleans: the men who built the levees and the men who dug the canals, men who laid the streetcar lines, men who cleared the oaks, men who trawled shrimp and dislocated limbs, who priced the sugar cane and the cotton, men who forged the chains and men who turned the locks, men who captained the ships, men who wrote the laws and broke them, men who bought the women and broke them, men who kept the records and stamped them, men who toted the guns and shoved the heads onto spikes, men who built the jails and manned them, and men who built the hospitals and delivered the babies within them.

On the rare occasions when my maternal grandmother spoke of the Grey Heron, she said of him: "My father was a French doctor." The words are a fancy layer cake, a doberge, which sounds like *DOH-bæzh.* A marquetry of soft sponge, one layer atop another, with sweet cream between, and the icing on top, a veneer to cover the meaning beneath. How many of our Creole elders, our grandmothers and grandfathers, spoke similar words? "His father was French." "Her grandfather was French." "They all had French last names." The surname, the evidence, an enduring forelimb of our colonial patriarchs.

Ironic, then, that my grandmother carried her mother's surname Roussel. Still, it is a forefather's name, that of her mother's father Joseph Roussel, an inheritance from his father, and from father to father, reaching back two hundred years prior to my grandmother's birth: the first Roussels to enter Louisiana were men from Bretagne, from Champagne-Ardenne. (It does sound fancy, doesn't it?) Peering closely at the famous map, "Plantations on the Mississippi River, from Natchez to New Orleans, 1858," one can identify just a handful of plantations in the parishes St. James and St. John the Baptist with the name Roussel.[1] Joseph Roussel, free man of color, a descendant of one of the many planters Roussel: Was he a son of a white Roussel who gave his nonwhite child his name? Was he the descendant of a person enslaved by the Roussels, who took the surname of his "owner"? Was he a manumitted slave, who, according to the French *Code Noir,* was granted "the same rights, privileges, and immunities which are enjoyed by free-born persons"?[2] In Louisiana, all are possibilities, and the answers, speculations: the names are so ubiquitous—both the surname and the given name Joseph—that his genealogical trail becomes conjecture before 1859.

Among Creoles and non-Creoles alike, a French surname is considered a mark of a true, legitimate, and recognizable ancestral tie to colonial Louisiana. It is one's ticket to the ball. It is the prerequisite to others' indulgence, the test one must pass to access information, connections, resources. Even though I am a returnee, a person raised on the West Coast, my surname tells others that I am, at the very least, proximate. One interview subject for my doctoral dissertation, Mrs. Dorothy Dapremont Daste, very politely (and fairly) demanded my pedigree before she agreed to speak with me.

"Who are your people?" she asked me over the telephone. "Where are your people from?"

I answered, offering her my genealogy-in-brief.

"And your mother's name?" she inquired. "And where are her people from?"

After answering these questions, Mrs. Daste asked me, "And where are you from, dear?" After I offered California, she responded, "Because I couldn't tell by your voice." My list of the most recent surnames, all French except for one, and my ability to locate each surname with a recognizable place in Louisiana assured her that I was "one of us."[3]

Having a Spanish surname might reveal one's male antecedent as a Spanish colonial, or an immigrant to Louisiana from the Spanish Americas, or a Spanish slaveholder, or a freed person who took a Spanish name, all being simultaneously possible. It could also signal Isleño heritage, as the descendants of Canary Island immigrants are called here. Having a German surname requires no extravagant explanation. If you're a brown-skinned Schexnayder or a Zeringue, a Trosclair or a Haydel, we all understand. Your ancestors were those who settled the German Coast in the mid-eighteenth century, or they were those enslaved by them, or both, and you might even be the descendant of one of the sons of Ambroise Heidel. (Am I, too, one of his vast number of great-great-great-great granddaughters? Connected through LeRoux? It is an unanswered question, however unlikely.)

Having an "Anglo name," a Black Acadian professor recently shared with me, casts doubt on a person's belonging in southwest Louisiana, even if that person's family line traces back to colonial origins. When spoken, it is followed with an explanation: "But my mother's name is [insert French surname]," or "but my grandmother is a [insert French surname]." Anglo-American migrations into Louisiana, largely initiated by the Louisiana Purchase in 1803, are unfortunately blamed for bringing "the color line" to Louisiana. Anglos came from the usurped lands of Indigenous nations in the Upper South—the Carolinas, Virginia, Mississippi, Alabama, and Georgia. Largely Protestant, the new migrants to the Louisiana Territory were of Anglo, Celt, Scot, and other amalgamated ancestries, and they represented both slaveholding and non-slaveholding socioeconomic populations. Others arriving in post-Purchase Louisiana were Black, those whom historian Gwendolyn Midlo Hall referred to as "Anglo-African."[4] They were Protestant, Anglophone, free Black and multiracial people from the Eastern Seaboard and the Carolinas; some were legally free, while others were held as enslaved laborers by the migrating Anglo-Americans. Augustus Lawrence's maternal family, the Turners from Virginia, came to Louisiana as part of this wave of migration.

Even more than two centuries after this migration, the Anglo surname is still associated with their untimely arrival in Louisiana. Some histories speak of this unpleasant spatiotemporal event: the Anglo confronting a French- and Spanish-descended beige and brown sort of whiteness, that which did not speak English (nor cared to) and worshiped in the Roman Catholic faith. To add to that, they encountered beige and brown Acadians, a hybrid people of French and First Nations Mi'kmaq ancestry, whose genetic and cultural descendants are now called Cajuns.[5]Anglo-Protestant latecomers also found a confounding and multitudinous presence of persons of nonwhite status: enslaved persons of mixed ancestry, free persons of mixed ancestry, enslaved persons born on the African continent, enslaved persons born in the Louisiana territory, *le mûlatre libre* from St. Domingue, persons of Indigenous ancestry, persons of mixed African and Indigenous ancestry, and variegated people from the Spanish colonial world. Anglo-Americans must have squinted when they looked at the prism of phenotype in Louisiana, and yet, they came to impose a strict racial binary on the people of this place and are remembered for that.

The emphasis on the French surname signals a fancy Eurocentric narrative of Louisiana, a conception of the French as the root of Creole, even though there are other interpretations and uses of "French." Among the Creole migrants who settled in Houston after World War I, for example, "the term 'French' was very flexible," writes Tyina Steptoe. "It could describe people who identified as non-black," and it could refer to "black people who traced their roots to French speakers in Louisiana."[6] Centering French in narratives of self-naming is to be expected, however, as Michel-Rolph Trouillot teaches us: those who have power dominate the telling of history. "What matters most," he writes, "are the process and conditions of production of [historical] narratives," adding "the differential exercise of power . . . makes some narratives possible and silences others."[7] As the first colonizing force in the lower Mississippi River valley, the French authored our first histories, and their presence continues to shape how we name ourselves.

The first French arrived in Louisiana from opposing directions. Some came from the north, from the broad territories of New France, the upper Mississippi River valley, and the Great Lakes region. From the Illinois Country, they came down through the autonomous territories of the Miami, the Ho-Chunk, the Shawnee, the Cahokia, the Quapaw, and dozens of other Indigenous lands along the Ohio, Illinois, Arkansas, Missouri, and Mississippi Rivers. Seeking trade relationships and woodland resources, the first French who came from the north pressed themselves onto already existing Indigenous sites of trade and commerce, appropriating posts at Fort Crevecoeur in 1680, at the Arkansas Post in 1686, at Natchitoches in 1714, and at Fort Rosalie, in the lands of the Natchez people, in 1716.

Others among the first French came into Louisiana from the south, from the expansive mouth of the Mississippi River that opens into the Gulf of Mexico, which itself becomes amalgamated with the Caribbean Sea. Nearly forty years after French colonists began to build the most brutally efficient exploitation colony of St. Domingue—the modern-day Haiti—they hungrily approached the Gulf Coast. The first French touched on the coastal barrier islands there, entering the autonomous territories of the Alabama, the Chaouacha, the Tunica-Biloxi, the Coushatta, the Acolapissa, the Pascagoula, the Bayagoula, the Houma, and others. Recognizing the barrier islands as places of vast cultural and linguistic exchange, as lands of rich species diversity and seascape plenty—beyond the mangrove forests that bounded the islands was evidence of oyster and clam, of blue crab and black drum, of turtle and heron—the first French erected Fort Maurepas in 1699 and Fort Louis de la Louisiane in 1702, which was later relocated to Mobile.

"Through oral history and genealogy," interdisciplinary artist Monique Verdin (Houma Nation) shares, "we know the modern Houma trace their ancestry back to the historic Houma who lived on the blufflands near where the Red River joins the Mississippi." She continues, "They were pushed out by the Tunica and relocated near Bayou St. John in New Orleans, and back up to Ascension and St. James Parishes along the river. Through these relocations, they intermarried with other tribes in the region who were living in this era of [French and Spanish] empire: the Chitimacha, Choctaw, Biloxi, Atakapa-Ishak, Acolapissa, Oucha, Chaouacha, Bayougoula, Tchoupitoulas and perhaps other *petit nations* . . . whose names have been forgotten and erased."[8] Historians Elizabeth Ellis and Jacob F. Lee echo Verdin, demonstrating that Indigenous nations of the lower Mississippi River valley and the Gulf Coast used their power to help steer the trajectories of European colonization. Part of that history of solidarity, resistance, trade, and diplomacy among amphibious Native nations helps explain how later Indigenous peoples can identify many different tribal populations within their heritage.[9] Still, decades of French and Spanish colonization, the introduction of European epidemics, and slave raids throughout the Lower Mississippi and the Gulf South caused disruption in a region that had been highly organized long before the first French arrived.

As the men whom we imagine as our French forefathers confronted Native peoples of the Louisiana coast and the barrier islands of the Gulf of Mexico, which historian Jack E. Davis has winningly dubbed the "American Sea," our unnamed Native forefathers, in turn, confronted them. Decades of historical and demographic research have shown that autonomous, Indigenous nations of the Deep South, the Gulf Coast, and the Caribbean had long engaged in far-reaching communication and the exchange of peoples, goods, languages, and crucial information beyond their lands. The image of the unknowing and preliterate Indian, standing alone on a shore, baffled by the approach of winged ships (à la *Apocalypto*), has long been trumped by scholarship. Our Native forefathers got the memo of our French forefathers' arrival before they saw the strangers themselves: communicable disease and the rubbish of oceanic exploration preceded them. "Shipwrecks . . . gave away the presence of others," leaving "flotsam" that had been "washing onto Indian shores around the Gulf since the early days of European exploration," Davis writes.[10] Items discarded or lost by European men—textiles, decorative belongings, religious artifacts, footwear, keepsakes from home, furs, tools, ribbon, glass, and metal items—told our Native ancestors that travelers were in their midst, and so were their trade goods, and so was their litter. The discarded implements of slave trading—restraints, branding irons, seals, and manila, some of which have been exhumed by divers working with the

Slave Wrecks Project—communicated that newcomers also had the gall to bind and torture others. Colonialism was a polluting endeavor.

The first French in Louisiana comprised a population largely made up of masterless men.[11] A few were wealthy aristocrats who had acquired their status through smuggling and commerce in Canadian furs, and some practiced piracy in the Caribbean. Some were soldiers, and some were deserters. Most, however, were landless men having no title (*petit blancs*) or disposable and desperately poor French women. Their role as "founding mothers of the Gulf Coast" has received recent attention from historian Joan DeJean. "Among the founding inhabitants of settlements from Natchez to New Orleans," DeJean writes, the women who arrived in 1720 on the ship *La Mutine* "built the earliest houses . . . became property owners . . . acquired considerable estates" and "founded dynasties," whose descendants "have spread ever more widely across this country."[12]

"Genealogical histories thrive on founding figures," Philip Deloria (Yankton Dakota Nation) reminds us.[13] In our gendered colonial imagining, the father of the colony is the metropole—the center of finance, bureaucracy, and authority, in this case, France, and its monarch King Louis XIV: the Sun King, man of wig and brocade, patriarch of slipper and tights. The distant land of the periphery, the colony, is the child—Louisiana, child of Louis—and so are the lesser peoples therein, the subjects and nonsubjects, those so subaltern that they legally could possess nothing at all, including their own bodies, those so beneath that they would be viewed as perpetual nurslings. And recent scholarship adds another layer: our founding mothers are two hundred Frenchwomen who arrived here, surprisingly enough, chained in the holds of a stinking ship.

• • • • •

There are books written about the Grey Heron, and all the other herons, in the classics that made Louisiana a distinctive place. Simultaneously American and French, both southern and Caribbean, the old historical novels portray white Louisianans as another kind of white, an elevated white—a Creole white. In the words and works of George Washington Cable, of Lafcadio Hearn, of Kate Chopin, you will see him dueling under the oaks, a chivalrous character, his language formed with ease. In Walker Percy, William Faulkner, Tennessee Williams, and Robert Penn Warren, you will see him in an evening jacket drinking too many mint juleps on a covered porch, while a light-colored servant stands beside him, the flirtation between them just part of the vernacular. You will find him, too, in the works of Richard Wright, although he cuts a different image—violent, determined to hold onto his place, his cause not lost. He is there, in Ernest J. Gaines too, a country version, dustier and less couth.

There are books written about my grandmother's father. In none of them is he sorry.

In discolored monographs and dusty old encyclopedias, in expositions of the Old South and the New, in the Confederate cemetery, you will find the Grey Heron. You will find him in Ulrich B. Phillips, discredited. In E. Merton Coulter, disgraced. He is there: Can you hear him? His accented voice is singing the opera of extraction and exploitation; the lyrics are familiar enough.

The Grey Heron is also there among the white-jacketed men. Among men who found that measuring every rise and every cavity, every bump and every freckle, every bone and every tooth on the human body gave rise to their own professional clout. The length of the arms, the depth of the armpits, the height of the foot arch, the width of the nose, the heaviness and the depth of the genitals too—what a science, what a strange set of tools they built to endorse the mythology of their own superiority. You will see the Grey Heron among those who measured the circumferences of skulls and weighed the brains evacuated from them, among the men who calculated one's civilization based on the grade of hair growing from one's head, based on how plumb one's lips sat against one's face, based on the number of centimeters between one's eyes and the amount of melanin in one's irises, grey having the least, hence the most civilized. You will find his grey eyes peering into the microscope, examining the specimen taken without her consent, his mouth behind a sweaty mask, his hands gloved before the poor woman's open legs, vulnerable, her body breaking in half, in labor—and he's got the scalpel, the speculum, and the forceps. The Grey Heron is an easy one to find.

"My father was a French doctor," my grandmother, Marietta Roussel, spoke. I listened. And I found him.

With the dubious romance of blood math behind me but still with a deep curiosity about Creole history and why, in the literature, we were repeatedly denied the appellation, I moved to Baton Rouge and began graduate school at Louisiana State University. There, I studied under the inimitable southern historian Gaines M. Foster, and I made no friends. In the first year, I sat through what graduate students call the U.S. history "super-seminar," a course that assigns students at least four hundred pages of reading per week, expecting them to begin developing an expertise in U.S. historiography. It is a tremendous challenge, meant for students who do not work full-time and do not intend to do much with their lives in graduate school except read, reflect, and write. I loved the study. Every week, after the evening seminar, I went directly to Hill Memorial Library to begin reading for the next week. But socially, I was miserable. The one person I did feel a bond with was Dr. Foster.

His expertise was the White South. Dr. Foster would probably repudiate that description, but his pivotal book, *Ghosts of the Confederacy: Defeat, the Lost Cause, and the Emergence of the New South, 1865–1913,* might prove me right. He tricked his students, however; they enrolled in his New South course, perhaps thinking they'd be reading Phillips and Coulter, southern apologists, but they ended up reading African American authors. In Dr. Foster's course, I read W. E. B. Du Bois for the first time. I read Richard Wright for the first time. I read Anne Moody for the first time. What Dr. Foster taught me I still teach.

At LSU, unsure of myself as a writer, my confidence wobbly at best, friendless and far away from my family, I chose to take a written exam and to write a research paper, rather than a full-bodied thesis. I researched and wrote about New Orleans free people of color, inheritance, intergenerational wealth, and nineteenth-century articulations of the racial middle. As a graduate student who still stumbled in countless ways, I was beginning to more deeply reflect on the racial binary that we tend to unquestioningly accept in the United States. My research contributed to my changing thinking about race—it was more to me than an academic subject. The category that held the *gens de couleur libre* was real, legitimate, lived, and historical. But when articulating the connections between my historical research and my lived experience, I often struggled against the response: "They didn't want to be

Black. And neither do you." I didn't have a sufficient reply, my language still unformed. Classmates who were not from Louisiana asked me, "What is Creole?" My answer, "*Well, we're French,*" didn't help me.

I could prove it! Just look at the scaffold of surnames that upholds my Frenchness:

*Gaudin = French*

*Roussel = French*

*(La)(Le)Roux = French*

*Beauvais = French*

*LaCroix = French*

*Michel = French*

*Barbarousse = French*

*Perilliat = French*

*Hyacinth = French*

*the surname of the Grey Heron = French*

True: it was an elitist declaration. I am not French, nor have I ever been. But I knew that I wasn't a quadroon or an octoroon. I wasn't a character in an Anne Rice novel. I relied on my French patriarchs as surrogates for my inability to articulate an identity. The French patriarch—the settler and the slaveholder, romanticized in the naming—was my passageway into thinking more critically about colonialism, erasure, and fatherlessness.

• • • • •

While I was a student at LSU, my mother came for a weekend visit. She still remembers the intolerable heat that met her when she stepped off the airplane, the immediate drip from the chin and earlobes in Baton Rouge that summer. The sweltering humidity was appalling.

On that Saturday, we rented a car and headed downriver. We played tourists in the French Quarter: eating beignets and drinking café au lait at

Café du Monde; walking around Jackson Square, pausing to listen to musicians playing their brass instruments; politely passing by those offering to read our palms; purchasing a T-shirt in a shop. It was as if our ancestors hadn't walked these very streets, as if they hadn't stepped in the security of their freedom here, as if they hadn't enslaved others here or been enslaved themselves beneath these wrought-iron balconies and in the courtyards behind. We walked along the Mississippi River levee, looking across to Algiers Point, where I would live in a few years' time.

We headed toward our afternoon destination: the City Archives at the Main Branch of the New Orleans Public Library. It was the first, tender step toward looking for the Grey Heron, whose face we had never seen.

Here are the things that we knew: his full name, his occupation, and an unknown length of time spent in or around my grandmother's birthplace of Vacherie, Louisiana. We also knew that he worked in New Orleans at Mercy Hospital in 1952.

Mercy.

St. Joseph, patron saint of fathers, make him known to us.

Stepping into the air-conditioned library, we were met by the resident archivist, who suggested that we begin with the simple obituaries, which were printed and compiled in card catalogs. If we found him there, then we should find the corresponding long-form obituary in the microfilm records of the newspaper in which it originally appeared. It was the smartest advice: it was the first piece of evidence that we found. It opened the door to the rest of his history.

I loaded the microfilm rolls of the *Times-Picayune* onto the reader and scrolled until I found the publication date. I stepped aside as my mother peered at the screen. She read the words aloud.

"There he is," she said in disbelief. "That's my mother's father." A lump came to both our throats. He had been this invisible, untouchable thing, and here he was. Just a man who died of a heart attack.

This long-form obituary gave us information: his birth year and death date, his previously deceased relatives, his most recent employer, his myriad accomplishments, his burial place, and his surviving wife and sons.

"It doesn't mention that he had a daughter," my mother noted sadly.

I found the high side: "But it tells us where he worked for over thirty years." Precious information today, but especially in 1996.

My mother returned to California with the knowledge that her grandfather died when she was pregnant with my middle sister Roslyn, that he had two sons with the initials of terminal degrees behind their names. The obituary floated in her mind, awash with renewed sadness over her mother's lifelong grief. I returned to LSU with the microfilm printouts and a few handwritten notes; in 1997, I graduated with my master's degree in history.

It took another four years to uncover him.

He, in fact, was not French. He was born in 1883, in the city of New Orleans, to parents who themselves were born in the city of New Orleans and to a paternal grandfather who was born in Rouen, France. His grandfather migrated to the United States sometime before 1857, when his name appears on the Orleans Parish marriage record next to a Louisiana-born woman of Irish descent. He, the original immigrant, and his son were clerks who worked at the Louisiana Sugar and Rice Exchange. Here is a description of their profession from geographer Richard Campanella: planters from Louisiana's sugar-producing region, known as the sugar bowl, "consigned their sugar and molasses to city factors and shipped their hogsheads bound for the sugar landing" along the waterfront of the French Quarter. "There," Campanella explains, "clerks boarded the steamboats to identify which cargo were consigned to which brokers, who in turn met with prospective buyers to sample the product and agree on a price." Perched on the financial branch of Louisiana's sugar industry, their work constituted a critical element of the state's extractive and exploitative economy. As "Crescent City sugar men," the Grey Heron's elders helped establish the Louisiana Sugar Exchange and made a pretty (or ugly) penny doing it.[14]

The Grey Heron was formally educated at McDonogh Sixteen Primary School, and then at Warren Easton Secondary School, and then at Tulane University, which had been a white-only institution until 1963, the year that he died. That is, in fact, where I found his face: in the university archive, that most important of institutions, the storehouse of memory in material form, a nest of information. He is named and photographed in the *Jambalaya*, the university yearbook. In the group portrait of the medical class of 1904, I think I see him, fading out of the edge of the photograph, indistinct, almost deliberate, a blurred image. But maybe that's not him. And then, I think I see him again in another volume, twenty years later, among the graduate faculty of medicine, wearing a dark suit and a tie, made anonymous among the other herons who wear identical costume—bloodless faces sporting large mustaches and squinting their light-colored eyes in the sun.

And there is his portrait, full faced, taken for the university and tucked, unremarkably, in his faculty file, which I held, read, and photocopied. He too is unremarkable: spectacles, thin lips, the corners of his mouth turned down, a widow's peak, long ears, almost translucent eyes. The face of a bird. Can you see his face? Does it resemble your great-grandfather's face?

I made several copies of his photograph and sent them to my mother, who said she was afraid to open the envelope, to see what he looked like. What if she could see the face of her mother, Marietta, in his? What if it brought the sadness back, which she kept at bay by thinking of other things? But she opened it. "He looks like a buzzard," she said.

And there, right there in his employee file, are the answers to my grandmother's history. Beginning in 1904, he practiced obstetrics in Vacherie, the little town on the Mississippi River where my grandmother's family lived for more than two hundred years. There, he met a young white woman, and he married her in January 1905 at Our Lady of Peace Catholic Church. The Grey Heron's marriage was made possible by Louisiana miscegenation laws, which defined them as marriageable, both he and she "white" by definition.

While his wedding was taking place, Ida of the Singular Name, the One Who Coughs, was carrying my grandmother in her womb.

He later returned to New Orleans with his wife and two sons, and he established his career as a physician and an obstetrics surgeon in the city. Between the years 1910 and 1950, he worked at various hospitals, Charity and Mercy among them. At Tulane University Medical School, he taught young white doctors how to deliver babies, according to the norms of his day. Today, those practices are a subject of research in the field of the history of medicine. Today, there is an intersectional analysis of obstetrics and gynecology. Today, we recognize blatant racism and misogyny—misogynoir—in these medical practices of the past. The experimentation. The butchery. The pseudoscience madness. The analgesics withheld. The racially segregated hospital system. The collecting of biological samples without patients' permission. Being the unrecognized descendant of a white doctor from that dark place, the Jim Crow South, carries the weight of uncounted women whose bodies were treated without charity and without mercy. How would this be different, feel different, if he had acknowledged his daughter, my grandmother and muse, Marietta? If he had actually played a part in my grandmother's life? Maybe it's better that he didn't.

In his employee file, I found a list of addresses where he resided in New Orleans. Some of his homes no longer exist; like the LaCroix family home on North Roman Street, they've been bombarded and bulldozed, an inconvenient obstacle to progress. But two still stand. One is a double gallery, not very deep, which obviously housed four families: two upstairs and two downstairs. The residence of a young doctor. The second is a Greek Revival, with columns in the front, a central staircase up to the main entrance, floor-to-ceiling windows, and a circular driveway leading to secondary entrances in the back of the house. It sits high on a plateau, a ridge, from which the Grey Heron could look down on the street. The residence of an established gentleman, a professor emeritus, a retired doctor, and a father—of three.

• • • • •

There are books written about this great-grandfather of mine, books about men who shielded themselves with segregation laws, with anti-miscegenation laws and anti-cohabitation laws, anti-concubinage laws and racial integrity laws; laws that made it possible for him to father a child with a woman of color but to never be a father to that child; laws that made of him a story told before a powder-room mirror; laws that made his offspring a rumor, that made his daughters *quadroons* and *octoroons:* sexualized, romanticized, exoticized women with no claim to any paternity. Men like the Grey Heron backed those laws with pamphlets and encyclopedias and volumes that offered scientific proof that African-descended people were biologically inferior—the research, evidence, specimens, and cells gathered by doctors fancified by a fake Frenchness, gathered by the Grey Heron, whose title "doctor" cannot be removed from the context in which he lived. It has lost whatever prestige it might have once had.

Books written about the Grey Heron will name him in given and sur, but I will not. Someone will find him. Or they will find me, in the archive of their DNA, a "cousin" on a family tree made possible by the genome sequence, a technology that can be obtained for less than $100. I am the "cousin," long lost and brown-skinned. And Creole.

It isn't such a shock anymore, is it?

*Gaudin = free man of color / Afro-Creole / St. Domingue*

*Roussel = free man of color*

*(La)(Le)Roux = white French or free man of color*

*Beauvais = free man of color / racially fluid / inconsistent documentation*

*LaCroix = free man of color / racially fluid / inconsistent documentation*

*Michel = free man of color*

*Barbarousse = free man of color / Afro-Creole / St. Domingue*

*Perilliat = white French*

*Hyacinth = white French*

*The Grey Heron = white*

Can We Call Them Creoles? Children's piano recital. My father, Anthony Joseph Gaudin, in white suit (*left*), with his hand on the grand piano. Xavier University of Louisiana, ca. 1943. Photo by Arthur P. Bedou.

# 11

# Miss Audrey's World

I open my mouth, and out comes the sharp-edged, high-toned enunciation of Southern California. The honed grammar of the children of migrants shines in my voice. That must have made my grandparents happy.

"You sound like a white person." Racialization of the West Coast accent, an amused remark coming from the other end of the telephone, from a perfect stranger here in New Orleans. "I couldn't tell if you were one of us."[1]

Moving our family from Louisiana to California, from New Orleans to Los Angeles, my grandparents sought a better life for their children and their future grandchildren. That rupture separated me and other California Creoles from our culture. Even though our elders provided us with colorful and painful stories, with rich and evocative foods, with potent accents, distinctive expressions, and geographic references from our ancestral home, we were Los Angelenos. My sisters and I were Valley Girls, raised in the San Fernando Valley, where the cultural image of jaded yet privileged white kids hanging out at the mall took shape, although we didn't quite fit it.

On the weekends, we ate the Creole staples—the gumbo and jambalaya, the mirliton and boudin, the rice dressing and the gumbo z'herbes and the okra—but our daily lives were spent among non-Creoles. We had no actual Creole friends, despite a few noted attempts; outside our circle of first cousins, we had no young people who "looked like us" or whose elders looked and sounded like ours. When I met my friends' grandmothers, I thought they resembled my maternal grandmother Mema, but that may have been simply because she had blue eyes and fair skin. (Did she really look like them?) In the presence of the beloved grandmothers of my childhood friends Allyson Klein, Kelly Baxter, and Faith Haas, I detected varied accents, and I heard Yiddish expressions. I ate their handmade latkes and matzo ball soup (still a favorite of mine). When we girls opened our mouths, Allyson, Kelly, Faith, and I all sounded alike, and I suppose my grandparents would have been glad to hear it.

My voice separated me from those whom, when I returned to Louisiana in the year 2000, I imagined to be "my people." After I graduated with my master's from LSU in 1997, I enrolled in the doctoral program in history at New York University. After just one year of coursework, I took and passed my qualifying exams; after a second year in New York, I successfully completed the rest of my coursework, and I moved to New Orleans to conduct research. It was a straightforward plan: to conduct archival and field research toward the completion of my dissertation. I had no intentions beyond that. Yet, more than twenty years later, I am still here, a reverse migrant, a returnee: I now live in the city that both sets of grandparents left behind and swore they'd never reside in again. In reference to modern Vietnam, writer and interdisciplinary artist Dao Strom offers a similar sentiment: "Overseas Vietnamese come and go now; some have even returned to live here indefinitely. For many, it's no big deal anymore."[2]

Strom also points out, on returning to her native Vietnam, "One big thing is: I don't speak the language."[3] Although the principal language of Louisiana, and of Creoles in Louisiana, is English, there was no loving slack of the South in my voice. Nothing of Louisiana or New Orleans. I spoke with formality, a foreign politeness, the Gs at the ends of my gerunds closed and finished, even in casual settings, because I wasn't taught to code-switch. I failed to add honorifics to older people's names; after several times calling Miss Audrey "Audrey," another person corrected me: Hadn't I learned to speak properly in California? My voice was the voice of the migration that carried with it the baggage of the Sunset Limited, the things my people carried, the holy water and the dress patterns, the recipes and the old photos, the determination to remember Louisiana in their kitchens and in the pews of their churches, and the equal intention to allow the new to wash over them, to make of themselves a revision of what they'd been, to baptize the next generation in their new Western skin. Sun shining on the far horizon, a new day, a new beginning to a people centuries old. A new voice from a new person on the other end of the landline.

"I still live on the same street your grandmother and I were born on," Miss Audrey told me, her voice sequined with laughter, a lightness that was fully reflected in her beautiful face. Confirming what my maternal grandmother shared with me, she told me, "Come by anytime and just come to the backdoor."

Audrey Mary Garnier Nicholas Baquet, born in 1918, was one of thirteen children of D'Jalma and Florence Garnier. Eighty-two years old when I met her, she became my first friend in the city, my introduction to Creole New Orleans. She curated my field research. She represented, in my mind, what my grandmothers and my great aunts would have been like had they never left for California. Miss Audrey also opened her home to me based on one sliver of distant history: she grew up with my grandmother Rita Roux, and two of her sisters, Elsie and Sister Mary Anthony, grew up with my grandmother's sisters, Eulalie and Yvonne.

"This is my little friend Wendy." Miss Audrey introduced me to everyone we encountered. "She's Rita Roux's granddaughter, from California!" Sometimes, Miss Audrey asked others if they remembered my grandmother's family, the Rouxs, who lived down on North Miro Street, but most people had no memory of them. It was understandable: all the Rouxs had left New Orleans in the 1940s, and this was nearly sixty years later.

Many of Miss Audrey's family had also left New Orleans for California, which was "like another world," in her words; when she spoke of them, she often made a sign of the cross before her chest. I learned that she had gone to California to visit but couldn't wait to get back to her home on North Miro Street. Throughout our friendship, she inquired into my grandparents' lives and my own life, striving to understand just what was so great about California that drew so many loved ones to the West. Eager to see photos of the Gaudin house on Twelfth Avenue and my childhood home on Bismarck Avenue, Miss Audrey concluded that our lives in Los Angeles must have been rich, that the migration must have made up for all that was lost.

"So many of them left," Miss Audrey told me as we walked together through the Seventh Ward of New Orleans, sometimes holding hands, as she was a bit unsteady and the sidewalks were futile—the roots of great live oaks bulging through the slabs of concrete. That's where the Bordenaves lived, where the Broyards lived, where the Casenaves lived, Miss Audrey recited from her stunning spatial memory. Pointing: the Oliviers lived in that house, Mr. Anthony built that house with his own hands, the Aubrys lived over there. When I shared with her that Leon Aubry was my beloved uncle and godfather to my sister, she gasped (it was her fashion to gasp). That connection was stunning to her, even though we spoke several times about the settlement pattern in Los Angeles. She couldn't imagine it.

"There's where the Bourgeois family lived, but they all passed over," Miss Audrey told me, once again making a sign of the cross, an embodied ritual suggesting their death. But by that point, I knew that "passed over" referred to the death associated with becoming white. In her spoken histories and her insistence on remembering, Miss Audrey illustrated that the migration to California irreparably damaged the collective memory of this community. She found it very hard to believe that no one remembered the Rouxs. "They all gone out to *that California,*" she lamented, the western state anthropomorphized in her speech, as if it snatched people and dragged them across the desert plains.

Entire families, like the Rouxs, who left New Orleans and other Louisiana cities and regions such as Baton Rouge, Lafayette, and Lake Charles, emptied neighborhoods like this one, leaving those who did not migrate to imagine other lands, to miss those who left them behind, to strive to remain close despite the distance, to continue their lives as usual, or to wonder what could have been if they had left. Journalist Charles M. Blow, born in Louisiana in 1970, ponders the same questions in his writings. Blow's beginnings align with Miss Audrey's narrative; he described the setting of his childhood as, "a world shaped by vacancy . . . a landscape . . . specked with empty houses."[4] I, too, wondered what my life would have been like if my family had never left. Would I have grown up right here in Miss Audrey's world? Would I be a professor's daughter? Would I have learned how to swim? Would I still call myself Creole? I tried to balance in my mind both the terrible reality of exclusion that people of color experienced in 1970 Louisiana and the ways of resistance that they practiced, bringing richness, beauty, depth, stability, and meaning to their lives. We are all reminded that Jim Crow didn't define people's entire existence; segregation formed the colorless background of southern life. Marginalized people imbued the foreground with the luminous hues of family, friendship, fellowship, solidarity, and autonomy. In other words, my life might have been just fine.

Every evening of my first summer in New Orleans, Miss Audrey and I talked about her neighborhood, the Seventh Ward, and all the spaces absented of Creole families; each morning, I sat with Miss Audrey at the archive that was her kitchen table. We drank chicory coffee and ate buttermilk drops from McKenzie's Bakery while we chatted about the past. Miss Audrey was a beautiful old woman, with long hair that she brushed lightly with Vaseline and kept in an upswept style, clipped in a twist at the back of her head, which she said kept her cooler throughout the very long hot months here in Louisiana. Always smiling and laughing, she frequently apologized for her "hot kitchen," perhaps imagining that I came from a place with perfect indoor refrigeration, where there is no discomfort, no sweat. Unseen insects liked to gather in her kitchen after dark; in her characteristic sense of humor, she told me multiple times that they had to eat too. Miss Audrey's kitchen was a place of arrivals, of storytelling, of jovial contestation, of reunion. Neighbors, the parish priest, old friends, nieces and nephews, parishioners: there was always someone walking up the red steps at the back of her house and sitting in her hot kitchen. Many people came by seemingly to meet me, to see who was here from California, who was actually conducting research on Creole life—what a thought! What on earth would I want to know about *Creole?*

Miss Audrey's first son, Blainey, who lived on the other side of the double shotgun, seemed amused by my inquiries. My questions seemed obvious and pedestrian to him, yet they elicited new and fascinating information for me. Blainey's gentle demeanor, light-tan skin, wavy hair, and widow's peak reminded me vaguely of my father. Her younger son, the photographer Harold Baquet, whom Miss Audrey humorously described as "the child of my old age," came to see her often. Sunday afternoons, Miss Audrey and I walked together to her sister Miss Elsie's house on Lapeyrouse Street for more coffee and more conversation in her equally hot kitchen. Miss Elsie, the mother of nine adult children, all of them so very different from each other, could be found standing at her stove at any time of day. Multiple pots bubbled and steamed, bread in the oven, hot coffee on the counter, buttermilk drops on a covered dish on the table. I ate many bowls of gumbo and red beans and rice, and plates of fried chicken and fried fish, at Miss Elsie's loud and crowded kitchen table, while her adult children smiled, welcoming me, but hardly entertaining my Creole questions. Miss Elsie lived eight years longer than Miss Audrey, departing this earth in 2017 and 2009, respectively.

"I'm glad you're enjoying yourself with Audrey and Elsie," my grandmother said over the phone, several weeks after I'd ostensibly moved into Miss Audrey's second bedroom. "But have you visited Merce?" I admitted that I hadn't. When I mentioned to Miss Audrey that I needed to visit my grandmother's cousin Mercedes, Miss Audrey leaned into me and laughed: "Merce is your people! Oh, forgive me, I forgot!" It turned out that Miss Merce lived just one block from Miss Audrey, on North Tonti Street, and they had also known each other since childhood, but none of our evening walks went that way. "I will take you there myself!—because Merce doesn't really leave her house," Miss Audrey added, answering my unspoken question: Why hadn't Miss Merce been one of the numerous visitors who had graced Miss Audrey's kitchen table during my time with her?

A blue-eyed woman whose big smile stretched generously across her plump face, Miss Merce had a chin that protruded slightly, like my grandmother's, and her skin was just as pale as hers. She wore her silver hair cut short, and it had obviously been set by a hairdresser. A black security gate protected the front door of her cottage-style home, and she kept the blinds and curtains closed. Air conditioning plus the lack of natural light kept Miss Merce's house very cool. On the first of many visits, I observed that she and Miss Audrey lived very differently in the same neighborhood. Miss Audrey's back door remained open throughout the daylight hours, and her kitchen window remained open too, so she could sit at her kitchen table and see who was approaching her home; she also enjoyed the summer breeze. I only met one person at my cousin Miss Merce's house, and that was a relative by marriage, the master plasterer, Earl Barthé.

Rebuking me for not calling her sooner ("I'm your people, you know, not Audrey!"), Miss Merce hugged me brusquely when I stepped into her home. Having prepared a meal for me, she sat and watched me eat it. "I ate already, honey; I cooked all of this for you!" she told me with love, her smile wide and warm, her voice raspy, her accent that of my maternal grandmother. After eating, Miss Merce walked with me into her lamp-lit back room, which was where she watched TV and talked on the phone with her daughters, all of whom had left Louisiana for other states. She graciously showed me some of her photographs: herself when she was a young woman, her brother Joseph, her daughters, and her wedding photo.[5]

"That's Walter," she told me, smiling and pointing to her husband who died prematurely, leaving Miss Merce to raise three daughters on her own. Pausing at his image on the wall, Miss Merce shared, "He died and left me to raise my girls, so I went to the other side 'cause I made more money that way." My eyes widened with surprise at her admission and her comfort speaking those words. We had just met.

Miss Merce scolded me for adding "Miss" to her spoken name. "I'm family—you don't need to say 'Miss'!" she said. "That's for Audrey." But I felt very uncomfortable simply calling her Merce. The intangibles of local speech in New Orleans didn't come naturally to me.

Miss Merce was very open in our conversations. She knew that I was writing a dissertation, and she knew that the tape recorder would preserve her thoughts and memories. She spoke about her ancestry, her life, and the choices that she made, with little pause. Her mother, whose name was Margaret Rita ("Rita like your grandmother!"), married a Creole man of color named Joseph Jerome. Both families were Creole, and both families disapproved of their child's choice: Margaret's family disapproved of her marrying someone brown-skinned, and Joseph's family disapproved of him marrying someone with fair skin, blue eyes, and what Merce described as "beautiful hair," because her mother was "more Caucasian." Some members of her family married white people and virtually disappeared. Others, like Miss Merce, went to the other side solely for employment.

"Most of us didn't go to the other side for good, you know," Miss Merce explained, emphasizing an important point about the common practice of serial passing.[6] "But for those of us who could, we went for work or to sit where we want." Beginning with her first job in a laundry at the age of thirteen, Miss Merce worked as white. Three laundries employed her in a less perilous and more highly paid position as a folder. Three bag companies hired her to do machinery work, also as a presumably white person. Then she moved on to Higgins Shipyard, during World War II, to work as a riveter, a job that paid enough to support her three daughters, whom she raised as a widow. After the war, she worked as a machinist for a macaroni factory, also as a white woman. Throughout these fiscal masquerades, in which Miss Merce operationalized her phenotype for higher wages in a racialized economy, she ignored her friends on the street and on the streetcar, the same streetcar that Homer Plessy attempted to desegregate in 1892. "I did like my aunt said," Miss Merce revealed, "'you talk with your eyes and look with your mouth.'" Her skin proved to be not only the "color of freedom" but also the color of financial security. Unfortunately, it didn't make her a lot of friends.

It was clear to me, in the way she and others in Miss Audrey's world shared their practices of serial passing, that it wasn't as provocative as I had imagined it to be. With the exception of one person who refused to speak to me as soon as I said the word "passed," most people spoke very matter of factly about their experience. White southerners passed those foolish kinds of laws, Miss Merce indicated, so she broke them.

"Tell me more about your mother," I asked her in a recorded interview. Margaret Rita, like my great-grandmother Rosella Beauvais Roux, attended the St. Louis School, which was a white school at the turn of the century, when segregation laws and policies were being codified. My grandmother and she shared ancestors in the LaCroix family line. The LaCroixs had four children (one of whom, Charles Jr., was denied his inheritance in the 1898 probate case mentioned earlier): one daughter, Marie Eulalie, was my grandmother's grandmother; another daughter, Marie Eliza, was Miss Merce's grandmother. Miss Merce spoke lovingly of my family. "Rosie, your great-grandmother . . . she was a good person . . . and she believed in going to church," she told me, adding, "She believed in praying to St. Anthony." Patron saint of the lost and missing, it seemed appropriate.

When I asked Miss Merce to talk about what Creole meant to her, she told me, "Creoles is a mixture . . . Negro . . . French . . . and like me, on my daddy's side, I'm Italian." (The Italian father: a new paternity to contemplate.) Describing me, she used the word "nation." She defined the term: "It means you look like you could come from anywhere." I asked her whether she considered me to be Creole. Her answer was simple: "Well, yeah, honey, you kin to me. Your grandmother is my cousin, so we kin."

To Miss Merce, my cousin four times removed, "one of us" is a blood relation, no matter how distant.

The question occurred to me more and more as I interacted with Creole people—or people *I* thought of as Creole—both in and outside Miss Audrey's Seventh Ward world. I understood that my mere presence there—the Californian, searching for herself in New Orleans—indicated who I *was not*. Would a true Creole of Color take up our history as an academic subject of research? Would a true Creole of Color want to interview total strangers on tape about their family history? Would a true Creole of Color use the word "Creole" among people she didn't know?

"Don't you know, we don't call ourselves Creole anymore?" from a colleague.

"You're not Creole, you're from California," from the master plasterer.

"You are not Creole!" from an extended family member.

"You don't look Creole. I thought you were Indian," from a new friend.

"And what makes you Creole?" from a hesitant interviewee.

"Maybe your family is Creole, but you aren't," from an archivist.

The rolling of eyes, the sucking of teeth, the soured expressions: these were the reactions that I got when I referred to myself as Creole. I slowly became aware that there were other meanings, other implications associated with the word, and maybe that was why Miss Audrey laughed uncomfortably when I used it. In Miss Audrey's world, which I was so privileged to be invited into, I was clearly someone from somewhere else.

Miss Audrey helped to arrange a number of oral history interviews based on the subject of our conversations. She introduced me to people who were happy to talk about the old days, before the desegregation crisis sent the city into tailspins of change. She introduced me to people who wrote and self-published books and genealogies filled with long family trees and French surnames I still struggled to pronounce. She introduced me to people who were not Creoles of Color, but who lived among us and had differing observations, some positive, and others embarrassingly sad. Miss Audrey's curatorial skills were fine-tuned to a balanced view of the Seventh Ward, although most of the elders I spoke with shared stories of the very myopic world that they lived in and that my family, the Rouxes, chose to abandon.

One couple from Miss Audrey's wider world—members of my extended family whose parents left the Seventh Ward not for California but for the suburbs in New Orleans East—agreed to talk with me. Although they were incredibly generous and welcoming, they barely masked their negative opinions regarding my research. They also taught me some of the boundaries around Creole, of which I had no idea.

J. G. expressed doubt in the kindest way he could.[7] A cousin of a cousin, J. G. appeared skeptical about my research and questioned me calling myself Creole. A warm and sweet man, he and I enjoyed our conversations, even though they were sometimes difficult. He agreed to be interviewed on tape, unlike his wife T. G. who told me that she did not want to be interviewed or taped. A retired postal worker, one of the professions common among Creoles of Color and, in a larger sense, one that helped build the African American middle class, J. G. answered most of my questions with examples and stories; his responses were often followed by questions to me about my own thinking regarding race, mixture, and belonging. "Well, what do you think about that?" he turned the microphone around. "Why do you think that is?"

During our taped interview, J. G. showed me photographs of his parents, his elementary school class, and his club, a collection of men who got together to eat and drink, to fish, play cards, and to reminisce. The photos were used to illustrate many points that he made throughout our conversation.

"See my mother?" he said to me. "She wasn't Black."

Indeed, she was the daughter of a white man and a Creole woman of color, same as my grandmother Marietta Roussel. "And my father, well, you can see," he told me as he pointed out shared features between his family and mine. In the sepia faces, I was supposed to see true Creoles, people who looked like us. Observing the spectrum of characteristics among those who insisted that we look alike, I found Creole to be a vague basis of description. J. G.'s third-grade class, at Corpus Christi Elementary School, was speckled with varying shades of skin. "What would you say about this class?" he asked me, the group photo of children before us. Did he want me to say that they all looked Creole?

"It was segregated," I answered. He smiled and winked, pointing to himself in the picture, his wavy and side-parted hair recognizable even after sixty years. A characteristic of Gaudin men.

His wife T. G. questioned me with a more assertive tone. She did not believe that Creoles in California were able to replicate the old culture back home; she had been to Los Angeles many times, she told me, and she did not see a trace of Creole culture there.

Several times, T. G. shared with me stories that were, to her, unrecordable. "Turn that thing off," she gestured to the tape recorder, "so that I can tell you a story." In these unrecorded conversations and in casual talks outside the oral interview setting, I learned that she wasn't comfortable talking with me about being Creole. For her, it was an inside subject: it wasn't something for public consumption.

What I learned from J. G. and T. G., along with others from Miss Audrey's world, was that the context of recent history was much more relevant than centuries of colonialism and postcolonialism. Our multinational ancestry, hundreds of years of our proud lineage—from the African continent, from the islands of the Caribbean Sea, from our Indigenous foremothers and forefathers, from the free people of color and the histories of striving that made them free, from mixed-race women who resisted being reduced to fractions of blood, even from our European patriarchs and matriarchs—were less significant than what happened in the 1960s. They shared with me that they never used the word "Creole" in what they called "mixed company," especially when "African Americans" were within earshot, because it was insulting to those who so recently fought for equality. "Creole" conveyed a sour history of separation and a sense of superiority, so they only used it in private, with someone who was "one of us." They even advised me against using the word. "Be careful," J. G. told me, lowering his voice. "You can't use that word with everyone."

In the years since my elders left Louisiana, "Creole" had become something that shouldn't be spoken aloud. When I attempted to speak to people about being Creole, they didn't hush me; rather, they insisted that *I wasn't it.* Was this because I used the word so easily, with no sensitivity to its insulting meaning to Black people who weren't Creole? Perhaps Creoles were defined as not naïve, as people who knew better; I was so very naïve and didn't know any better. Maybe their admonishments could be interpreted as "You aren't Creole; if you were, you wouldn't be talking about it so freely."

In response to J. G., I insisted, "But I am Creole, why shouldn't I be able to tell people? I don't think it makes me better than anyone."

"You can 'be Creole' because you're from California," J. G. answered. "You can 'be Creole' . . . you can be a Buddhist or whatever you want to be . . . because you weren't here when everything changed. Your perspective, your way of thinking, it's different."

When everything changed.

A reference not to the eighteenth or the nineteenth century but to the civil rights movement, to the reckoning of decades of racism, violence, and exclusion preceded by hundreds of years of enslavement and Black people's resistance to it. The narratives of those in Miss Audrey's world, those who lived through this period, conveyed to me that we Californians, we migrants, we who escaped, were framed by a construct of force and freedom. We were forced to leave a place in which we couldn't be free. Those who were left behind were forced to engage in racial justice activism that cost people their homes, their income, their freedom, their bodily integrity, their lives—the force of the White South a wall to be torn down. In the West, we migrants were free to define ourselves however we pleased, free to think differently, free to cross over into whiteness, free to use the word "Creole" without the worry of offending others. Those who remained behind, who lived through the civil rights movement, were forced to reckon with the elitism in their own selves and their own communities, forced to silence the Creole name, forced to quiet their identity lest it insinuate their superiority, their uppity association with Frenchness—their fathers, French doctors?—their ancestors, *gens de couleur libre*? The movement for Black liberation forced a public dialogue that challenged the pigmentocracy in New Orleans. And we Californians had freed ourselves from all of it.

Were those whom I encountered in my research forced to revisit a painful history? Forced to confront the freedom of the Californian, who can so easily exist in this world, as a self-defined Creole? She, who was free to flaunt that privilege?

Historian Adam Fairclough explains the change that my extended family member J. G. pointed to: "'Black Power,'" writes Fairclough, "challenged the very concept of 'Creoleness.' It even sometimes implied that the old 'lighter is better' standard should be replaced by a 'blacker is better' ideal." In defiance of political moderation represented by the early years of civil rights activism, "Black Power now challenged light-skinned Creoles to abandon their alleged social exclusivism once and for all and to identify with the black struggle unambiguously."[8] The movement to dismantle Jim Crow and desegregate Louisiana aimed a focused critique at Creoles of Color, who were often seen as contemptible people who perpetuated racism by keeping their social and familial circles narrow and light, by failing to speak and act in concert with the larger African-descended population, by passing as white when it was convenient (and possible) for them, and, I dare say, by leaving the suffering of segregation behind for the shiny shores of the Pacific.

Author Imani Perry learned some of this history from her mother. "She did tell me about the cruel Whiteness of power in 1960s New Orleans," she writes. "She told me about how Black power took hold and straight-haired Creoles teased their hair in an imitation of nappiness, claiming blackness more aggressively than their jealously protected genealogies ever said or believed they should."[9]

In the words of my distant cousin J. G., who pointed out that my thinking was different and that I didn't understand why using the word "Creole" was problematic: "We became Black in the Sixties. There's no need for Creole anymore." J. G.'s friend, Lawrence Winnier, shared the same, in a recorded interview at his home in New Orleans. "Creole has had its day," he told me. "It's history, it's not a part of living today. It's not necessary anymore."[10]

I pushed J. G. further. "So, when we talk about Creole today, right now. If there's no need for Creole anymore, what are we talking about?"

He paused before offering an answer to my question: "Creole is this conversation, what we're doing right now. Remembering the past. Remembering where we came from, how we lived, who our people were."

It's a strange contemplation, to be a relic of the past. "If the past is another country, then I am its citizen," writes Saidiya Hartman. "I am the relic of an experience most preferred not to remember, as if the sheer will to forget could settle or decide the matter of history."[11]

Am I a relic of the Creole lineage? What makes me Creole? The yearning for shared memory? The rejection of the will to forget? The desire for connection with my ancestral home, a world of the past that Miss Audrey could recite, could map out from memory, even when it had been emptied, so profoundly, of her own people? Are we still here in the sacred sites of history? And if we cannot name ourselves, then who are we?

# 12

# Topophilia

Lake of rains. Plain of rains. Sky of rains.

Sodden.

This is flat land. This is uninterrupted horizon, all the clouds visible from start to stop, resembling Arabic script, the curled rise and the fancy puff and the long line. This is the savanna of swamp and slough. The concave places collect rain, and the convex areas are up in pine country, the levees engineered by free men and erected by those in chains. This is the exposed limb of Turtle Island, the curved edge of a massive stolen continent. This is the epitome of the Global South: sun darkened and silt rich, ancient as bone, and born again just yesterday. Bought and sold, traded, bought and sold. Perpetually giving to the Global North until there's nothing left to give. Older than writing. Wet with monsoons whose names are chanted like prayers, sung like dirges: Laura, Ida, Katrina.

This land is a great trickster: its moss that is not really moss, its grassy green fields obscuring water underneath, its False River that is really a lake, its dead-looking cypress not at all dead, its Black Catholics and "white slaves," its Houma, its Caddo, its Creoles, its Isleños. The Mississippi River's edge shifts with each wave of ecological disaster, the solid and steady place where you once stood ten years gone.

The land is flat here, so the rain spills in every direction, boundless.

Rain collects itself in any unwitting crevice. Rain in ditches with summertime wild grasses. Rain in deer blinds. Rain in rabbit traps. Rain in sugar cauldrons. Rain in buckets inside the house. Rain on pelts hanging from tin-can roofs. Rain on the nightshade. Rain in the ferry captain's hat. Rain in the beds of rusted trucks. Rain in the tackle. Rain in the bellies of trawlers and pirogues. Rain in sucked-out crawfish heads. Rain in the crawfish pot.

Rain makes a labyrinth of this place—funny that someone once thought they could impose a line here. Funny how the earth soaked their carpets, funny how the storms corroded their metals, funny how the Mississippi River ran their boats away, with biting shrimp and ancient gators, with tangled webs of grasses, with unfriendly banks, mighty breath and surge. Funny how this land laughs at lines, this place where everything sinks and slants downward, where everything has the posture of an abandoned child. The room that was added to the back of the house is lower than all the others, and the floor in the kitchen slouches; the wooden planks nailed to the sides of houses begin on one plane and end on another, several centimeters lower. Roads crumble, sink, burp, gurgle, fill with water. Even tombs are sinking: the beloved ancestors who were entombed on the bottom are submerging, the names on their resting places meeting the earth and then disappearing. Lines transform into ringlets, waves turning starboard and port, diving deep and rising skyward. Here, we play directional symphonies and arrange ourselves in bends. Here, we make deities of our waters, delicacies of our cane syrup, oracles of our mother's hair.

These are the Lowlands of the Catastrophic Storm.

• • • • •

The *Plaquemines Pride* ferry launch is tucked into a sharp curl in the Mississippi River, near one of a chain of Becnel's farm stands where you can buy sprouted vegetable plants and young trees, frozen crawfish boudin, persimmon and satsumas, Creole Rose rice, five-dollar cracklin', and Ponchatoula strawberries. The word "Ponchatoula" likely comes from the Choctaw meaning flowing hair, in reference to the Ponchatoula River, which sounds like *PAWN-shuh-TOO-luh*.

Anthony, my guide into lower Louisiana, released his jaw when the ferry's horn called—horns and ships and ferries and skiffs having been a regular part of his life since he was born into this watery place. Raised in a wobbly house, its unused front door confronting the river's levee and the crooked back door opening onto the endless wetlands to the east of Pointe-à-la-Hache, Anthony shucked oysters as soon as his child's fingers could pry open the stubborn shell. He shot BBs into squirrel and killdeer, into robin, crane, marsh hen, wild duck, pooldoo, and heron. He skinned coon and rabbit, muskrat and nutria; he scaled largemouth bass and black buffalo under live oak and bald cypress, caressed by the velveteen tresses of Spanish moss and bourbon and beer, all of it supplementing the base diet of the unschooled bayou: assorted shellfish and waterfowl for days.

"That white man is staring at us," I said to Anthony, the watery drone of the *Plaquemines Pride* urging a rise in the volume of my voice. The ferry crosses the Mississippi at one of the many bends where passing cargo ships disappear into a line of trees, leaving behind their wake, which causes the ferry to surge upward and tilt gracefully from side to side. A musty smell came off the brown water. Plaquemines, the name of a parish in southernmost Louisiana, where the land meets the Gulf, is not to be confused with Plaquemine, a small city in Iberville Parish, but the names of both likely were derived from the Indigenous Atakapa word *piakimin,* meaning "persimmon." Take care with your pronunciation: one sounds like *PLACK-uh-mins* and the other *PLACK-min.*

"That's not a white man," Anthony flashed a tobacco smile, laughing at my most recent faux pas. "That's my cousin."

The ferry bumped against the riverworks, and a man in greasy boots and gold incisors walked nonchalantly to the edge, easily tossing the thick braid of rope around a bollard. Habit permeated the boat: motorists knew how to navigate, how to arrange themselves effortlessly like dominoes. Friends and familiars called out to each other, "All right," as they exited the ferry, driving up onto the levee and down to the highway below—the *all* fallen down and stretched out, the *right* rising up, as if the English language had the tones of the Vietnamese, the relaxed accent of the South defying the stiff standards of the North.

His neck and arms sunburned a dark orange, skin scarred by nearly five decades of manual labor, sweat grasping feather-light hair underneath an old cap, amber-dollop eyes, and slightly bowed legs, Anthony waved at his cousin as both of our vehicles turned toward Pointe-à-la-Hache, his arm hanging out the window as he drove. As you read, say it aloud: *PREENT-laash,* that first syllable squeezed from the back of your throat, not an open-throated *point* but a tight-throated *preent,* like the call of a bird who only knows the skies above Plaquemines Parish.

With Mother Mississippi on our right and rural settlements on our left, we wound our way into lower Louisiana, passing tiny communities that exist on a strip of land less than a mile wide, sandwiched between the river and the wetlands beyond. Dalcour. Mary Plantation, its fluted columns and wraparound porch, its outdoor staircase and concrete statuary, its discourteous signage as a "plantation wedding venue." Woodlawn. Wills Point. Poverty Point. We turn off Highway 39 onto Highway 15. Phoenix, where Anthony attended a segregated school, receiving what he called "daily ass whippins on accounta my color." Myrtle Grove, where I attended a Creole boucherie, the day-long butchering of a hog. Davant. Perez Road, named after the virulently racist Isleño, Leander Perez, an arch-segregationist who served as Plaquemines Parish district attorney during the middle of the twentieth century. St. Thomas Catholic Church, where Anthony's mother cooked for the parish priest. Houses on slabs, trailers on beams. Front steps and front doors faced the River Road, trucks and boats parked on wet and muddy lawns, omnipresent statues of the Virgin Mary offering protection, the burial grounds in the marsh beyond, piles of brick and concrete, crumbling and sunken into the ground.

I spotted a baby alligator dead in the road.

Anthony turned the wheel slightly to avoid hitting a turtle. "They make a good stew," he commented. "You got caouane in California?" which sounded like *Cal-i-FAW-nya.*

We and the rain arrived simultaneously in Pointe-à-la-Hache. It came like a hillslide in this place of no hills. We saw it coming from miles away: on this side of the river, the east side, the sky was the bluest blue, an oceanic blue that eats little pieces of you; on the other side of the river, the west side, a pewter wall of rain, looking as if it had been painted in one broad and beautiful stroke from the top of the sky down to the ground. And it came. Rain in my eyes, rain in my mouth, fish-smelling rain, rain that fell like fire, rain that kissed our faces and later broke our hearts.

Rain, the waters of women blossoming
Rain, the knives of the storm clouds
Rain, the whispers of the saints
Rain, the silhouettes of invisible men
Rain, the veves of the Creole people

Out here, the rain comes and comes, the line between land and water smeared.

Anthony's mother Dolores offered me a towel when I entered her home through the bent back door that opened directly into her kitchen, my hair dripping on her buckled linoleum floor. Her skin was the color of boiled rice water, and it hung from her limbs like fins. My instruments, tape recorder and notepad, were tucked comfortably and dry in my backpack. My accent, as Californian as a surfboard, did not impede my duty to eat every dish of everything that was laid out on her modest kitchen table.

Stewed rabbit. Stuffed mirliton. Dirty rice. Oyster dressing.

Dolores was one of ten girls, all born at home to a mother who spoke no English, who had no formal schooling, there having been no school out on the bayou. All of them were born in a lantern-lit clapboard house out on stilts over the wetlands near Encalade. On one bank of the river, it sounds like *ANK-uh-lard,* and on the other, *ONK-uh-laid.* I found her mother, Esmeralda Barthelemy, in the 1910 census for Plaquemines Parish, she "keeping house," and her father, Georges, "fishing." They and their children, like my family then and before then, living up and down the river, on land as low as this and higher still, classified by the census taker as *Mu*: Mulatto.

As the oldest sister, Dolores, whose name, she told me, "means suffering, whatcha think about that," watched as her mother married all of her young sisters off to fishermen—

thorn-skinned
storm-thrushed
water-cut
hook-thumbed
loose-toothed
100-proof

moon-gazed
scale-shellacked
fist-smacked

Her sisters were adolescents; the fishermen were not.

In this Creole aquatic, young girls were fished like croaker and drum.

As soon as Dolores's sisters could "keep house," the fishermen floated in, quiet as a germ, some docking their boats and some staying down there in the water. They came looking with rubber boots and overalls, with their fishing poles and shrimp nets and crab traps and oyster sacks: all the instruments to make a catch. Before each man, her mother dangled a daughter.

When her day came, Dolores's fisherman stank of liquor and loam. Scum under his fingernails, leathered necklaces of skin around his collar. The teeth of a sheepshead in his mouth. "I didn't hardly seen him at all," Dolores told me as she watched me eat her peppered food that set my mouth on fire. "He stayed on the boat til it was time to make another baby." Another baby. And another baby. Out on the water near Encalade, they had no power, no water pipes, sometimes no milk and no food. Dolores gave birth to four of her five children in that house on weak stilts, her husband a phantom on the dark water. Her fifth child, Anthony, was born to another man years after she left her first husband; Anthony was the one born on the land.

Anthony's mother and her nine sisters had no ball at the Autocrat at which to choose their man: no jeweled masks, no layered gowns with tulle slips. Their grandmothers' grandmothers had no genteel manner, no French schools, no classic literature. No quadrille. Nothing that the Creole girls in New Orleans might have had. They had nothing. Nothing but the storms rolling in, and the rains hanging from the sky, auspicious as an ocean dream.

• • • • •

"A Creole was never a slave," Winnie Ancar told me, the hair on his upper lip stiff and yellowing grey; his balding head hairless, save the ring of what my mother would call "strings" that dangled around the edge. Even though he had so little hair, it looked like it needed a trim. His skin, beautiful, sun darkened, pulled tight. "Let me ask you," he pointed at me, his finger bent at a raw angle, which actually pointed off to the side of me, "have you found the slave in your family?"[1]

When you say his name aloud, it sounds like *WHY-NEE,* accent on both syllables.

It was three years before Hurricane Katrina made landfall twenty-one miles from his family home in Diamond, Louisiana.

Anthony sat at the table across from me, saying nothing.

Downriver from Ironton, upriver from Potash and Port Sulphur, Diamond signifies the industry that lines the Mississippi River in this deepest part of southern Louisiana. In 2004, one year before Hurricane Katrina, a resident of Diamond, Margie Eugene-Richard, won the prestigious Goldman Environmental Prize for her work. According to the Goldman Environmental Foundation, "Margie Richard secured [an] agreement from Shell Chemical to reduce its toxic emissions by 30 percent, contribute $5 million to a community development fund, and finance relocation of her Old Diamond neighbors in Louisiana." Even before the catastrophic storm, the area was, "plagued with reportedly high rates of cancer, birth defects and other serious health ailments," which devastated this small community of "1,500 residents who lived on the four square blocks sandwiched between the Shell plant and a Motiva oil refinery owned by a Shell subsidiary."[2] Richard, which sounds like *REE-shard* when you read it aloud, is noted not only for her work in Plaquemines Parish but also for being the first African American winner of the Goldman Environmental Prize.

Diamond, the mineral hope of beauty, was lined with cemeteries along Diamond Road—Mange Cemetery, Feets Cemetery, St. Paulinus Cemetery, Diamond Cemetery: the small community looks east and sees the levee of the Mississippi River and looks west to the flat bottomlands of lower Louisiana. Indigenous trade, French intrusions, African marronage, and Filipino fishing vessels shaped this area in earlier centuries, and the high rises of industry shape it now. The tallest things around, factories grey the sky during the daytime and twinkle like worrisome diamonds at night. And Winnie, a cousin of a cousin of Anthony, had never lived anywhere else.

The bayou, and a life of fishing, shrimping, farming oysters, repairing nets, setting hooks, and crouching in boats, had forced his body into a curl, a bend, a fiddlehead. Somehow, he looked both fragile and very strong at the same time, his teeth, his finger joints and nails, his neck, his eyes, all weathered; his hands and arms riven with veins; his muscles looking meaty, but his carriage betrayed him as an old man.

"No, I have not found 'the slave' in my family," I admitted, holding back the feeling that it was an unfair question to ask, but Anthony had warned me. Baffled at why I would want to come down the bayou to talk to people about "their identity"—he said the words with sardonic laughter—he still carried me here. To this matte trailer in Diamond, Louisiana.

I could identify the slaveholders in my family, the free men and free women of color; but these are the people whose histories are considered valuable, noteworthy, their surname, a form of legitimacy. If we are descended from the first Africans who came into Louisiana—the Bambara, the Wolof, the Mandinga, the Ewe, the Fon, the Yoruba, the Koromanti peoples—we are descended from those whose first vision of this place was framed by the lower deck of a slaver, whose first actions were to resist the violence that was perpetrated against their bodies. When the first captives came into Louisiana, they likely encountered African men who were masterless laborers on ships flying European flags, as well as free African and African-descended persons who had migrated north to Louisiana from the Spanish colonies to the south—we could be descended from them as well. Some of the earliest arrivals had never been enslaved; characterized differently by historians, they might be called "Atlantic Creoles." Multilingual and skilled in trade and diplomacy, Atlantic Creoles were among the first African peoples to engage in cross-oceanic trade. They, too, could be our ancestors.[3]

I answered him: "But that doesn't mean that some of us don't have enslaved ancestors. Records aren't easy to locate." Our Fon forefathers, our Bambara foremothers are there. Forgotten or erased in the dominant narratives of history, their names are lost, but they are there, nonetheless. "But if Creoles were never slaves, then how would you define Creole?" I looked to Anthony, who'd lit a cigarette and blown the smoke out the window. Utter disinterest.

"Some of their daddies was white, like mine," he told me. "French."

"Your father was French?" I asked him, pushing gently, the meaning of "French," a nondescript composite of French speaking, French surnamed, of French ancestry, or ethnic white. His accent called my grandfather back to me.

"Yeah, he was French! Didn't speak no English."

"So," I pushed a little harder, "he *spoke* French, or he *was* French?"

"Mmmmhm," his lips closed.

"And this is what we come from," speaking directly to me, he encircled me within his idea of "our people." "We speak French. We practice the Catholic religion. Creole is French and Spanish . . . not supposed to be any Colored in it. But there is," he said. "Creole is a mix."

"And we look like us."

He gestured toward himself. And to Anthony. And then, he gestured toward me.

• • • • •

The ferry motor rumbled. Wind, water, birdsongs. Patron saints quiet from exhaustion.

And the treehouses rose in the distance.

I stood on the edge of the Pointe-à-la-Hache ferry, the river blowing its pallid spit into my face. This time, and the times leading up to this one, I felt more at home on the ferry, my body ready for the surge, the occasional bounce, the massive ships that dwarfed us as we crossed from one side of Mother Mississippi to the other. Every time I cross the Mississippi River on one ferry or another, moving from one side of the river to the other, from east to west to east, I feel more at home here in Louisiana. A little bit more accustomed to the habits of the ferry crossings, a little bit more relaxed in my interactions with others, a little bit more embodied in my Creoleness, but always a product of the California migration. The deeper I descend into Louisiana, from Acadiana in the southwest to Plaquemines Parish, the more I understand this place and my life here as an insider–outsider. I and other returnees to Louisiana straddle the fence of the past and the present. I wish us all a home in our ancestors' lands.

Most of my visits to Plaquemines Parish are now on my own, as my friends and fictive kin have since left this earth or migrated to the North, another Great Migration: this time, a flight from natural disaster. I come here, and sometimes I drive to the end of the line, the end of Highway 23 where a sign reads, "WELCOME You have reached the Southernmost Point in Louisiana. Gateway to the Gulf." Here is the imagined entryway of our ancestors, or at least a semblance of it, since the Mississippi River has been reshaped and moved in the hundreds of years since. I see that we California Creoles are bitemporal in our diaspora: we are attached to our people buried in these water/lands, and attached, too, to our smartphones, our Google maps, which show us the little blue dot, our position on the brown-grey river or the levees that lie in intimacy beside it, lest we lose our way in a landscape that isn't truly ours. I have developed a love for this open space, and for these narrow strips of land between the river and the wetlands, and for the ferry itself, an affection for the wordless efficiency of the ferry men, who answer my bubbly "Good morning!" with "Fare."

From the ferry launch, I could see the burned-out shell of the Plaquemines Parish courthouse, the tiny post office, and a large, elevated, white house with columns and a long front porch. Had it once been a Big House? Or had someone modeled their house after that antebellum horror, a common practice here in Louisiana and elsewhere in the South: the monied imagine their houses are grand plantation estates, adorned with columns and wraparound porches, with "lawn jockeys," waiting at the ready, and sugar cauldrons haunting. (And what would chattel slavery look like in this watery, desolate place?) There were fewer cars, fewer trucks, and fewer boats than on the *Plaquemines Pride*, the Pointe-à-la-Hache ferry being much farther away from New Orleans, much farther south toward the Gulf of Mexico. This is the last ferry crossing the Mississippi River, the southernmost path from levee to levee.

Heading down to the ferry, on the west side of the river, there was Diamond, where I interviewed several men in their trailers and fishing camps. There was Happy Jack, where Anthony's uncle taught him how to fight. There was Grand Bayou, where I went swimming while Anthony rowed the skiff. Empire. Port Sulfur. And Buras, where Hurricane Katrina came into Louisiana on August 29, 2005.

These are the Lowlands of the Catastrophic Storm.

It has been said: New Orleans was hit hard. So many suffered, particularly older folks, disabled and hospitalized folks, incarcerated people, those of lower socioeconomic status, those without the means to evacuate, those considered "critical personnel," young and helpless children, and those who may have lived through previous hurricanes that weren't so bad so they decided to stay and "ride it out." The deaths due to drowning, evacuation, police violence, suicide, neglect, so-called mercy killings, and unknown causes are losses that the living will continue to grieve. The destruction of the Ninth Ward levees will go down as a most pernicious, reckless, and devastating event, as memorialized in numerous books and films. S. Leo Chiang's *A Village Called Versailles* focuses on the Vietnamese American community in New Orleans and that population's activism around environmental racism in the post-Katrina landscape of New Orleans East. Monique Verdin's *My Louisiana Love* addresses the wider catastrophes of Hurricane Katrina followed by Hurricane Rita, which hit the Gulf Coast two and a half weeks apart. Verdin's work focuses on lower Louisiana and the Indigenous populations there, especially members of the Houma Nation who, despite "inheriting a dying delta," strive to persist on their traditional lands.[4]

Although Hurricane Katrina devastated the entire Gulf Coast, much of Katrina's narrative centers New Orleans, and some of the most moving writings about Katrina have come from New Orleans writers. Reflecting on that time, Kristina Kay Robinson writes, "I am one of the lucky ones. One of the luckiest. I am home. I am sane. I am alive to speak for myself. I mourn for those lost and struggle with the gratitude and guilt of being spared."[5] Robinson and other writers consider the meanings of persisting, of remembering, of surviving in the new New Orleans, where Mardi Gras parades still roll, where gumbo still simmers in the pot, where universities still teach and archives still remember, where newcomers still arrive, where displaced folks are still gone, where tourism still exploits the outlandish elements of our culture, and where police violence still escalates.

Of the "rapidly gentrifying Fifth Ward/Mid-City neighborhood" of New Orleans, Robinson writes, "I am always ridden by the recollections of what was there before Katrina. All over the city are the places that no longer exist, the dimension of my childhood, adolescence, and early adulthood, the evidence of which has been mostly washed away."[6] Of post-Katrina Gulfport, Natasha Trethewey writes, "The fears for the future, expressed by the people I spoke with on the coast, are driven by the very real landscape of ruin and by environmental and economic realities associated with development, but they are driven by nostalgia too." She adds, "When we begin to imagine a future in which the places of our past no longer exist, we see *ruin*."[7]

"We are black and alive, still," Robinson declares, "This is the truth, despite what the pictures say."[8]

But what do the pictures say of Plaquemines Parish, where Katrina made landfall?

And did the land fall.

The photos of Plaquemines Parish show that very little, including industry, survived this catastrophe. Evacuations of the lower parishes were mostly effective in mitigating the human cost of the hurricane. Indigenous communities in the lower parishes, including the Houma and the Isle de Jean Charles band of the Biloxi-Chitimacha-Choctaw, had already been experiencing evacuation and forced migration inland due to land loss from sea-level rise associated with climate chaos, industry in lower Louisiana and in the Gulf, and saltwater intrusion that has caused widespread erosion. Louisiana's wetlands are not surviving, and those decaying limbs of our ecological body are leaving us increasingly vulnerable to the next catastrophic storm.

"All we had was our color," Anthony told me as we drove through Plaquemines Parish after the storm, ruin all around us. "Now we got less than that."

With Mother Mississippi on our left and mostly empty settlements on our right, we drove from the Pointe-à-la-Hache ferry up toward New Orleans. Passing through communities absented of people, I saw eerie front steps leading to concrete slabs where homes once sat. I saw occasional road signs blown at odd angles, but most roads were made anonymous by the storm; one had to know what was once there to know where they were. I saw abandoned homes that survived the storm, overgrown with grass and weeds, windows broken and roofs sunken in, homes occupied by wild beings, homes that once stood sturdy now slouched in new woods. I saw trees still cracked forward at the trunk, electrical poles still stiffly surrendered to the wind, leaning at peculiar angles. I saw the Virgin Mary standing watch on many lawns, with nothing behind her but tall grasses and rainwater, and purple and white and yellow wildflowers growing however they pleased, in need of no saintly protection. I spotted Saint Martin de Porres in a similar stance: absent a church building, the cemetery barely visible in the bright-green landscape of new growth, he, like Mary, appeared to be waiting for new arrivals, waiting to protect those brave enough to live here once again.

It took three months for Dolores to find what was left of her house. Most of it had landed up on the levee near Davant, its roof completely collapsed onto its walls; the rest of it was presumably in pieces among the ruins or had floated down the river and rolled into the Gulf. It had already been a weak one, Dolores's house: the floor at the base of the toilet splintered, and the wall behind the bathtub soft to the touch. The windowsills hung at strange angles, and the light bulbs in the kitchen flickered. In an ordinary storm, her walls heaved and recovered, some of them papered with the *Plaquemines Gazette,* which reminded me of the walls of sharecroppers' cabins that I'd seen on a research trip with Dr. Davis. It had already been feeble and sad, Dolores told me, "'cause my second husband didn't give a damn about me and my children." This man, who built houses during the day and drank in the barroom at night, who broke her jaw and dislocated her shoulder, who had the nerve to punch her in front of her three sons, in front of Anthony, and dared them to do anything about it. Dolores's no-good second husband left her with a limp house in a storm.

Somehow Dolores found some of her angels. Before the storm, painted and embroidered, porcelain and glass, wooden and ceramic; bought at the Family Dollar or gifted from Rome, pink-hued plastic and golden angels with white hands and rosebud mouths sat on every surface in her home. Holiday cards with angels, propped on the crumbling mantlepiece; angel magnets on the icebox. Of all her beloved angels, the only ones Dolores found in the hurricanic rubble were the ones given to her by the priest at St. Thomas Catholic Church, the priest who heard her weekly confession.

Hurricane Katrina brought ruin to everyone in Plaquemines Parish, including the folks whose homes and camps Anthony brought me to in the years before the storm. Miss Mildred filled a bag of pecans that she gathered from her front lawn and made them into a pie while we talked about her mother; her house had been washed away, and only parts of the metal roof remained. Miss Gertrude and I spent hours looking at photographs of all fifteen of her grandchildren, all having moved to New Orleans; luckily, she took her photos with her when she evacuated because they would've been gone, along with everything else she owned, all of it, snatched by the flood. She spent the rest of her life in the city. Miss Agnes, a cousin of Dolores, spoke to me very freely about her life as a fisherman's wife but then refused to answer any more questions after I told her that I wasn't Catholic; the front steps of her home and her concrete statue of Mary were all that were left. Her family installed a trailer on her land almost nine months after Katrina, and one of her grandsons agreed to live there with her; within three months of living in relative isolation, they gave up and moved to Algiers. Paul, a former fisherman, thirty years my senior, leaned into me, close enough for me to smell his breath, and asked me if I was married; his camp had been destroyed by the storm. No surprise: I remember being nervous walking on the floorboards, the waters of Encalade foaming and brown beneath my feet. Martin, who was named after De Porres, told me that Creoles were "those of us who sat in the middle of the church, not in the back and not in the front." The foundation and several walls of his brick home survived the wind, but standing water rotted much of what was left.

And Fredrick, who lived out on Grand Bayou, wondered why on earth I would swim in those waters, among the mottled ducks and the biting shrimp, and the beloved frogs who sat in meditation along the edge—my favorite animals—and the froggers who caught them for the meat in their legs. Fredrick, about whom Anthony told me: "Don't say nothin' about him being black," despite his deeply beautiful, dark brown skin, which he attributed to his Indian grandmother. Nothing was left of his camp, and he died shortly after that terrible summer ended.

Miss Dolores moved in with her son Anthony for some years after the storm. Then she moved to Houston, where she died in the spare room in her daughter's house.

Of those who refuse to abandon Plaquemines Parish, those whose ancestors are buried here, newcomers who have come to love it here, those who are younger and see this place as a new beginning, or those who grow rich from the industries that kill the people here, there is no other option for them but to rise. Knowing that living on the land is a tenuous promise—future storms could wash it all away once more—they now live high among the trees. They levitate, in perpetual evacuation from the land below. Old plantation estates and brand-new houses and double-wide trailers now stand up on eight-foot, fifteen-foot, twenty-foot stilts and higher. Trucks and boats are parked under the new dwellings; massive staircases and residential home elevators carry the people of Plaquemines Parish up into the trees.

I call them treehouses.

"An inability to manage stairs does not prevent one from living safely or living in Coastal Louisiana," writes Lucile Guidry for the LSU Ag Center. "Options such as ramps, platform lifts, elevators, stair lifts and sloping fill can help residents live above the water safely in their elevated homes."[9] Even St. Thomas Catholic Church reestablished itself up among the trees, on stilts, too high for the elders to climb.

Those who live in the treehouses play the numbers of depth and resistance. Will the stilts sink? Is the land firm enough to hold them afloat? Those who remain in Plaquemines Parish gamble and risk their safety, the steadfastness of their possessions, the quickness of their ability to escape in time. They put all their money on calculations of base flood elevation and ground elevation. They roll the dice against wind speed—their floating houses will not flood, but tornadoes are now more common in southern Louisiana. The live oaks that have survived the catastrophic storms, the trees with their massive limbs and trunks, they envision as saints. Instead of riding the Sunset Limited westward, they ascend in true Catholic form, their robes and habits the veils of Spanish moss. They seek the protection of human engineering, of concrete and steel, of the shoring company, but not what lies flush on the earth.

Saint Medard, protect them.

Oya, blow what threatens them away.

# 13

# Another Country

"The monk," I said quietly. "He is like me? He is mixed like me?" I used the impolite Vietnamese because that's all I knew. "Mỹ lai," I said, the tones becoming more at home in my mouth, but still, my language is the language of someone from somewhere else. A direct translation: American mixed.

"Khong, khong," she said. "No, no, he is not like you, not like you." I wonder whether she means that I am not a remnant of the war; instead, I am a remnant of colonialism and slavery, of Indigenous and African and European, not of Vietnamese and European and American. Can the proper pronouns be switched out, rotated: Indigenous for Vietnamese? African for what? Is American the same as European?

"No, no," she said, "no, not like you," and then she returned her attention to the chanting and said nothing more.

• • • • •

"Vạn Hạnh, your hair is too short." He was speaking to me using one of my names, in my native tongue, his shaved head blocking the sun, a blurred halo hovering there. The ceremony has ended, so his orange robe would soon be removed and carefully folded according to tradition, and he would be dressed in the same temple clothes as I was then dressed. "You look like nun. Not woman."

A plate of rice, vegetables, and tofu in my right hand, chopsticks in my left, my áo tràng (the grey ceremonial robe that is worn by lay Buddhists) draped unceremoniously over my shoulder, I looked up at him. Quietly correcting him, knowing that I had permission to add the article, I said, "A nun. A woman." I wasn't bothered by the observation, although my mother still hadn't forgiven me for cutting off all of what she called my "long, beautiful hair."

It was a Sunday afternoon in New Orleans, and I was where I had been on most Sunday afternoons in the years just after Hurricane Katrina: sitting in the sun, on a concrete bench behind Chùa Bồ Đề, a Vietnamese Buddhist temple on the west bank of the Mississippi River, where New Orleans spills into St. Bernard Parish to the southeast and Plaquemines Parish to the southwest. I had driven by the temple on many occasions on various treks to conduct oral history research in Diamond, Davant, Grand Bayou, Encalade, and Pointe à-la-Hache. Before the hurricane, I had glanced at the magenta temple, which arose under a bridge that crossed over the Intracoastal Canal, but I'd never ventured there. After Katrina and after my return to the city, I developed an interest in practicing meditation. I had never been a devout Catholic, and sitting meditation seemed like an effective way to process the grief and change taking place in my ancestral and adopted city.

In the words of Kristina Kay Robinson, I was one of the lucky ones: a friend insisted that my son Aubry and I join her family in evacuating the city. She saved us from the chaos and the suffering of those who didn't or couldn't leave. That temporary stay on the north side of Lake Pontchartrain led to Aubry and me flying to California and staying with family for several months. When we came back, our house was exactly how we left it, except for the new, empty refrigerator, which the landlord had replaced before our return.

My family assigned my post-Katrina interest to my personality. Seeing me as "different," as the only member of our immediate family to return to Louisiana not just to visit but also to live, they didn't delve too deeply or make any efforts to understand why I would choose Buddhist meditation as my practice. I could say that my father planted the seed: when he chose to study biology at the University of Southern California, he also began to doubt his Catholic upbringing. As his parents became more involved in Holy Name of Jesus Church in Los Angeles, Dad's life became more engrained in science: an altar boy turned herpetologist. As children, my sisters and I attended Mass every Sunday morning, and we each completed religious education classes, becoming confirmed as Catholics, but Dad was clearly fulfilling an obligation in our religious education. He never felt the same attachment to the Catholic Church that my mother did.

"Aren't you a Creole?" my mother asked me. "Didn't you go to New Orleans to learn about being Creole?" Yes, I did. "What does that have to do with Buddhism? Or Vietnam! Shouldn't you be going to Mass?"

It was a reasonable question. And to many in my circle of friends and acquaintances, this shift may have seemed strange. But the quiet and stillness of Buddhist practice spoke to me; so, too, did the ethical principles of Buddhist teachings. Uninterested in salvation or sin, I wanted to fully engage with my human experience and step outside the binaries that I perceived in my Catholic rearing. I didn't realize what else would open to me when I joined the community at Chùa Bồ Đề.

• • • • •

I had just driven up from the *Plaquemines Pride* ferry stop. On a whim, I decided to park in the lot at Chùa Bồ Đề and to take a look around. From the building behind the main temple, a man came out to greet me. He sported a shaved head and wore a white undershirt and thin pants. Coming out to the balcony, he waved at me; not knowing whether he spoke English and not wanting to shout, I gestured to him with my hand: a key turning a lock and then pointing to the temple. (Can you open the door?) He came down, opened the door, and I entered. Thanking him and walking into the empty building, I asked him, "Do any monks live here?" He smiled and said, "I am a monk."

Within a few weeks of meeting Thầy, we had become good friends. We shared lunch together in the temple kitchen, we took walks on the Mississippi River levee, and he began teaching me how to pronounce the five tones of the Vietnamese language: *sắc, huyền, hỏi, ngã,* and *nặng*. Ever the good student, I practiced them every day. The multiple *Us*: u and ư. The many *Os*: o, ô, and ơ. The words that begin with ng. The difference between tr and ch sounds. I aimed to become proficient in Tụng Kinh, the Vietnamese style of Buddhist devotional chanting. In the summer, we chanted as termites flew into the temple, surrendering their wings to our robes. In the fall, we chanted through sunny days and cool breezes. In the winter, we chanted in gloves and scarves, my extra-thick, tan-colored socks exactly matching those on

Thầy's feet (a gift from me). On Friday nights, we chanted Buddhist sutras; on Saturday nights, we practiced silent meditation and cleaned the temple; on Sundays, we had service and lunch. I appeared at the temple for Tụng Kinh so regularly that when I didn't show up, people asked, "Where is the foreigner?"

After attending service at the temple for two years, learning how to chant the Buddhist sutras in Vietnamese, and studying the precepts, or vows, of lay Buddhists, I decided to complete my first ordination. All the elders in the temple were present as I recited the precepts in my shaky Vietnamese; they watched as I received my áo tràng, my layperson's robe. When the ceremony was complete, Thầy smiled at me proudly. "Vạn Hạnh is the Dharma name chosen for you," he told me in so many words. "It means 'Ten Thousand Good Actions.' It can also mean 'Innumerable Virtues.'" I repeated my name. "Vạn Hạnh," the back of my throat tightening slightly to pronounce the nặng tone correctly. The temple elders applauded. One woman exclaimed, "You're the first foreigner to take the precepts in this temple!"

On many days at the temple in New Orleans or at Chùa Tam Bảo, the temple in Baton Rouge, Vietnamese practitioners smiled and asked me, "Are you Vietnamese?"

At first, I wondered whether they were teasing me, or if they were asking me, "Why are you here?" I clearly was not Vietnamese—I didn't speak the language, I only understood some customs by learning them in the temple, I was not visibly Southeast Asian. I didn't understand how to address others in the respectful ways of Vietnamese (always, a gentle assumption of age in reference to mine). I also made many cultural faux pas, marking me clearly as *người nước ngoài:* someone from somewhere else.

After some time, I learned how to answer them: "Tôi là Người Mỹ" (I'm an American).

"Are you sure you're not Vietnamese?"

I began wondering where this question came from. Until a brown-skinned woman with long, curly hair appeared at Chùa Bồ Đề one Sunday morning. Approaching each other, we both stared for a moment, smiling widely, and we greeted each other in the way of the temple, bowing and speaking the name of the Pure Land Buddha, "A Di Đà Phật." An older Vietnamese woman grasped her arm; she, too, looked at me, curiosity written on her face. I made the presumption that the brown-skinned woman was biracial and that the older woman was her mother.

On another visit to the temple, this time at Chùa Tam Bảo, I encountered a man whom I would have assumed to be African American. Once again, we looked closely at each other in a friendly way. I approached him and spoke to him in English; he answered me in Vietnamese. I smiled and laughed, indicating that I couldn't understand. Later, I asked the temple monk about him. "He is a member of this temple, Vạn Hạnh," the abbot told me with a quiet and gentle voice. "He is *Người lai*. That means a mixed person. His father was an American soldier, and his mother a Vietnamese woman. He has had a very difficult life."

I then understood the inquiries directed to me. "Are you Vietnamese?" meant, "Are you *Người lai*, a mixed person?" More specifically, it meant, "Are you *Mỹ lai*, a mixed person with an American father and a Vietnamese mother?"

People of mixed heritage in Southeast Asia are most recently a product of the U.S. war with Vietnam, which began with diplomacy and intervention in 1955 and ended with withdrawal and defeat in 1975. During those twenty years, U.S. soldiers fathered an unknown number of children with Vietnamese women; some of those children traveled to the United States as part of a family unit, but most were left behind in Vietnam after 1975. Children with distinctly "Western" features—blue eyes, a long nose, blond or brown hair, or kinky or coily hair—were marked as children of the enemy, thus treated as outsiders in their mother country.[1] Some years after the U.S. withdrawal, Congress passed legislation to support the migration of Amerasians from Vietnam to the United States; one of those acts was called the Amerasian Homecoming Act of 1987.[2] The many inquiries that I received in the temple were framed in that history, which was mostly unknown to me.

However, Vietnam and Southeast Asia have a longer history of *métissage,* the French word for racial and cultural mixture, reaching back to the second wave of French colonialism in the nineteenth century. Spanning from the 1850s until the 1970s, the struggle to claim and control natural resources and the establishment of global empires brought the old European colonizers—Spain, Great Britain, France, Portugal, and the Netherlands—and other nation-states (Germany, Belgium, Italy, and the United States) into Africa and Asia. Southeast Asia drew the attention of the French, who saw Vietnam as an expansion of their trade in southern China. Beginning with the port city of Đà Nẵng in 1847 (which France later renamed "Tourane"), France established colonial territories and protectorates throughout Vietnam, Cambodia, and Laos. As French priests, traders, colonial authorities, and citizens settled in Vietnam, a cultural syncretism arose there. The French introduced Roman Catholicism to what had been a predominantly Buddhist culture. French judges ruled over French colonial courts, where French colonial laws were applied to Vietnamese people who, when they broke those laws, were incarcerated in colonial jails and prisons. The French also imposed their language on the Vietnamese. After some time, as in every European colony in the world, a *métis,* or mixed, population emerged. Con Lai, or children of mixed ancestry, born of the imbalance of power between French men and Vietnamese women, introduced complexities absent in earlier histories of mixture between Chinese men and Vietnamese women.

Writings from nineteenth-century Vietnam reveal many of the same strains that we see in the literatures of the colonial Caribbean. Métissage is not simply a recognition of the mixture of cultures and peoples due to colonization. It is a gendered reading of colonialism, in which European men assume roles of power in the periphery or the colony, while Indigenous and African women are politically disempowered; yet their perceived sexuality is formidable. In the colonial framework, white European men, like our French patriarchs, were government officials, judges and lawyers, prison wardens, bankers and tradesmen, headmasters of schools, planters, physicians, and religious men (like the father of the unnamed biracial narrator of Viet Thanh Nguyen's novels, *The Sympathizer* and *The Committed*). They are imagined as men of power who are simultaneously weakened by the irresistible temptations of colonized, non-European women, who are either overtaken by European men or who target European men with their own weapon, their sexuality. In Mexico, the empowered and seduced European men are Spaniards, and the disempowered temptresses are Indigenous women. In Brazil, it is Portuguese men who are helplessly drawn into sexual congress with African women and mulattas, seen as seductresses. In Louisiana, it is the French men who cannot resist quadroons.[3]

In so-called Indochine Française, French men, who held all the positions of authority, from the governor general to the colonel, from the archbishop to the warden to the headmaster, were imagined as vulnerable to so-called *Congaie,* a Francophone cognate of the Vietnamese *con gaí,* meaning unmarried girl. *Congaie* were represented as inferior, of "low origin," but as sexually irresistible to French men who, in turn, were portrayed as far away from home and alienated from French women, who were largely few and far between in colonial Vietnam. But not all the French men who engaged in sexual encounters with Vietnamese women were white. As the Vietnamese resistance to the French grew in the 1910s, 1920s, and 1930s, the French conscripted African men from Senegal and Algeria, at the time considered part of French West Africa, to fight in Vietnam. Thus, some métis people in colonial Vietnam were colonized on both sides: the maternal, Vietnamese; the paternal, West or North African—both areas part of the French colonial world.[4]

These complicated versions of métissage in Vietnam fit within the larger framework of racial and cultural amalgamation in colonial worlds. In this way, then, Con Lai of French Vietnam and Mỹ lai of the American War are siblings to mixed-heritage Creoles. This history helped me understand Vietnamese Buddhists' grappling with my presence in the temple. Somehow, I must have fit this calculus—otherwise, why would I be there among them?

• • • • •

From the back seat of the spotless, air-conditioned Honda Accord that drove me through Quảng Nam Province and into the village of Quế Sơn, I watched nimble and fine, brown-skinned people on motorbikes, wearing slip-off sandals and plastic flip-flops and rice-water boots on their feet as they maneuvered around winding dirt roads and mountains. A wide, generous sky met rice fields that danced gently in the wind, and houses straddled generations: nineteenth-century tile roofs and twenty-first-century tile porches. Some houses, I noticed, resembled the shotgun house of Louisiana: elevated, with a front gallery, long and narrow, the front door parallel to the back door.

Down the road, skinny boys led water buffalo by a rope, stray dogs lingered, and the brightest green I'd ever seen met my near-sighted eyes. It was the green of life that will not be destroyed, not by fire or fuel, not by poison or terror, not by grenade or landmine; it was the green of life that will not be destroyed by loss of memory or history, the fullest green of life that will not now and not ever be put out. I wondered if my world-traveling grandparents had been to Vietnam on any of their trips around the globe; if so, they would have been astonished at the pure and bright beauty of this green.

I came to this place in Quảng Nam Province, in the middle of Vietnam, with no reason or endeavor other than to experience life in a Buddhist temple in Vietnam. I yearned to see the length of the country by train and to spend some time in the Central Highlands where Thầy was from. I also thought perhaps I'd have an opportunity to investigate Vietnam's Con Lai population, remnants of so-called French Indochina and the subsequent American war, whom I now see as within a global framework of colonial and postcolonial fictive kinship. If Creole is seen as solely an element of the African diaspora or solely a population belonging to the Americas, then there is no connection to Vietnamese Con Lai; if Creole is seen as a syncretic population born of French colonialism, then Con Lai are kin to us.

In Quảng Nam Province, I was hosted by Miss Năm, whose home faced an aquatic rice field and the electronic pulse of karaoke that blared from the house across the field every evening. Her home felt more like a pagoda than a residence: the first room that I entered dwarfed me with tall statues of the Pure Land Buddhas, photographs of her deceased parents, and offerings of fresh fruit, sweets, and incense. In a series of harmonious movements, I bowed to the altar and to the holy trinity of the Pure Land: to *A Di Đà,* Buddha of Infinite Light, to *Quan Âm,* the Hearer of the Cries of the World, and to *Địa Tạng Vương,* Earth Store Bodhisattva. The statue of *Quan Âm* gave me pause, because I wondered whether she was the Virgin Mary. The images are remarkably similar: the lit halo around the head, the long veil that draped the head and body like a robe, the peaceful expression on the face, the long line of the body, the light-colored skin.

I bowed deeply and slowly to the photograph of her barely middle-aged father, whose life ended at the blunted, hollow mouth of a gun held by one of my countrymen; his violent death left her mother to raise her daughter on her own, a hard life in this land of fathers and men. And Miss Năm, watching me take my respectful bows, opened her home, her ancestor altar, her windows, her doors, her guestroom, her warm and fine face to me, to my English language, my strange and dangerous tongue.

Miss Năm's welcome was food and there was lots of it; we ate at a circular metal table unfolded and erected in front of the Pure Land Buddhas and the ancestor altar, where Miss Năm placed little bowls of rice and saucers of fried tofu. We sat on plastic stools with thin bracings where I rested my bare feet, and I ate as Miss Năm watched me, chopsticks in my left hand, little bowl nestled in my right, saying *delicious!* in the common language of the grinning and nodding face, because I didn't know how to say it in Vietnamese. Our clothing dried quickly in this very hot weather, hers a polyester set, the shirt matching the pants, a pattern of light-colored flowers, and mine, light-grey, thin temple clothes. There was rice and đậu hũ (dry tofu), fruit and rau muống (water spinach) and fresh yogurt, a combination I came to expect when eating in the home of a Buddhist.

I noticed that Miss Năm didn't ask me what I was. She didn't ask me to explain my skin color, my hair, my facial features. What she knew was that I was an American friend. Would she have asked any questions had she learned my surname Gaudin, the imprint of France on my being? My Buddhist name gave one thing away: that I was a foreigner with a given Vietnamese name.

While we were eating, Miss Năm's friend, Miss Nuôi, arrived with smiling eyes that didn't leave my face. I returned the expression, my joy at being here in the Central Highlands overpowering the humidity and resulting constant sweat. The heat was not unlike the heat that met me in my home, in Louisiana, where so many Vietnamese refugees settled and remade their lives in our rivers that had become their rivers, in our bayous that had also become theirs. That narrative, often symbolized by the terrible ocean migrations from postwar Vietnam, sometimes reminded me of African-descended diasporas across the sea. The descriptions of the vessels, the suffering, the sickness and death, the fear, the prayers, the utter helplessness in the face of humanity and nature itself, bound our peoples to each other in my mind. The diaspora too: making a replica of the old home in the new: Louisiana for my temple family, and Los Angeles for mine. And some say the ocean migrations built the foundation for Vietnamese survival during Hurricane Katrina.

Miss Nuôi, who brought with her white corn that was cooked inside the husk, wore a blazer over her clothes—a blazer in this 99° heat. She served herself some food and, while eating it, talked about me to Miss Năm. I noticed that Miss Năm had a calm demeanor in true Buddhist fashion, as if this meal were no different from any other meal, while Miss Nuôi ate her food excitably, sometimes laughing dizzily in my direction. Offering me a cob of corn, she watched as I meticulously plucked each strand of silk from the cob. "It's all right for Older Sister to eat," she said, about me, in Vietnamese. "*Nó sẽ giúp chị ngủ ngon.*" It will help her sleep.

After we ate, I helped carry the bowls and spoons and chopsticks to the three-walled kitchen, and we unfolded the stools and the circular table and stored them. Not allowing me to help her wash the dishes, Miss Năm said something to me in Vietnamese. Patiently, she gestured toward the porch, and I realized that she was telling me to go, to walk, to relax; I was her guest. Outside, the wind entangled the trees—a cooling monsoon—and, like a Marian apparition, my light-colored clothes blowing around my body, my utter joy singing in the air around me, I stood on the road and glowed.

• • • • •

It was dusk and a dog was barking—at me. The people who lived in Quế Sơn slowed down, turned their heads, and stared at me as they walked or bicycled or motorbiked by. Some stared in disbelief or shock, some with obvious unease. The dog barked in my direction, telling the people who lived in this village, "She is someone from somewhere else."

There were two plastic stools in the front courtyard of a house with a sloping, tiled roof. I occupied one stool, and another woman occupied the other, and the dog occupied himself with barking. The woman appeared to be twenty years my senior. We smiled at each other, neither of us conversant in the other's language but both occupying a contained space, alone and without a translator. She went inside the house and came out with a water bottle, which she handed to me with a slight bow. "*Cám ơn, Cô,*" I said to her politely. Thank you, Auntie.

The dog barked and two people approached the courtyard but didn't enter it. I bowed my head to them, and Cô said something to them that I understood because they were words that I'd heard countless times in association with me. Foreigner. American. Buddhist. No, she cannot speak Vietnamese.

A few minutes later, Miss Nuôi arrived at what I then learned was her house, bringing my friend Thuận, who ate with us and translated the long list of questions asked about me. Where does she come from? Is she married? Why is she here? How old is she? Why is she wearing those clothes? Is she a nun? Nothing about my race. Miss Nuôi's home resembled the colonial-style homes of Hội An, where I had spent a few days walking through streets that reminded me of New Orleans.

A young woman with a child walked into the courtyard. Self-conscious of my accent, I hesitatingly said, "*Xin chào, Em,*" addressing her as Little Sister, and her face read curiosity. "*Xin chào, Chị,*" her voice hesitating too, saying, "Hello, Older Sister," her face working hard to fix the dissonance of the scene. She spoke to me, but I couldn't understand what she said. My Vietnamese was very limited; I could say and understand the names of fruits and vegetables and dishes we ate in the temple, Buddhist expressions and temple references (statue, cushion, incense, meditation), cleaning actions (mop, clean, cook), and elementary conversational things. Shaking my head and making the universal nonverbal expression that said *I'm sorry, I don't understand you,* I smiled, looking at the young woman's face, her eyes and nose, her jawline, the light color of her hair.

My friend Thuận told me that there were many Con Lai people in this region. American soldiers had bombed Quảng Nam Province for years, and when they weren't dropping bombs, they were using their English language, their U.S. dollars, their unusual phenotypes to assail the women. There was Operation Suwanee and Operation Mississippi. Operation Shasta and Operation Kansas. Operation Allegheny, Operation Teton, Operation Mecon, Operation Big Lodge, and Operation Arcadia. All these American-named acts of military violence on Vietnamese people, their daughters giving birth to children whose fathers were dropping these bombs.

We ate in the courtyard while termites swarmed the lights above us. I carefully swatted them from my food while smiling at the neighbors who came and stood by the table to watch me eat. "Look how the foreigner uses her chopsticks," they said, "with her left hand." I looked at Cô while she told us about her experience of the American war: she hid in tunnels with her father, as the cacophony of American bombs fireworked above. Having lost interest in me, the barking dog took to slumbering across the road. Miss

Nuôi smiled widely: I was her guest, and she would be remembered for this night, she who had a foreigner for dinner in her little courtyard in Quế Sơn.

"*Tôi xin lôi*," I said to Cô, using the wrong words for this kind of apology. Guilt filled my belly along with the rice noodles, green salad, and my favorite, rau muống. I'm sorry my countrymen did these things to you and your community.

"It's all right, Little Sister," she said in Vietnamese, "it's all right." And I wondered if she said, "*I survived*," but I wouldn't have understood those words if she had.

• • • • •

"The monk," I whispered, "he is like me? He is mixed like me?" I used the impolite Vietnamese because that's all I knew. "Mỹ lai," I said: a Vietnamese who has an American parent.

We were in a temple for Sunday morning service, somewhere in Quảng Nam Province. I wore the grey robe of the lay Buddhist, and my hair was shorn down nearly to my scalp, to my mother's horror, a blasphemy to the Louisiana Creole: *a woman's hair is her beauty*. As I had learned in the temple in New Orleans, I was able to follow the chanting service. The people stared at me as my mouth moved with theirs; they must have wondered, "Who is this foreigner?"

The monk was familiar to me. His body was draped and layered in the golden robes of a Thích Thầy, what I understood to be a venerable master. Marking his body as untouchable, protected by more than two hundred vows that are recited together according to the lunar calendar, the long patchwork robes accentuated his body as unusually tall. Were his robes made for him? Or did the sewing of robes change after the American war, when taller-bodied Con Lai people became monks and nuns? When I went to the market in Hồ Chí Minh City to purchase my own temple clothes, the women there always expressed shock at how unusually large and tall my body was; I purchased the largest size available.

I noticed the squared monk's jaw and his freckled nose, which was long and angled down, one among many attributes he was teased for as a child: postwar Vietnamese call Western-faced people "long nose." His eyelashes and eyebrows were almost blond, and his hands were remarkably large. I watched him as he lit the large stick of incense, as he placed it in the brass pot at the center of the altar, as he bowed from the waist slowly; my stare followed him as he descended onto his knees elegantly, without the help of his hands or arms, as he bent forward, curling his body until his face was on the floor—a prostration. He smoothly rose back onto his feet, bowed again, and then was on his knees again, fluidly, face on the floor. My eyes followed him as he did this a third time, finishing a ritual that he had probably performed since he was a child, a little freckled boy whose grandfather or whose father came here to Vietnam to dominate or to kill other fathers.

There are books written about him and others like him. Books written about his skin and hair, his eyes and his lips, his nose and long legs—all the pieces of him that made up a body of difference. There are books written about him and his mother; she—an exotic woman of the East, her long hair like a black river, her small body barely that of a woman, the words coming from her mouth, whispered, light, like drifting opium smoke—is someone's misty dream. She slides from innocent to vulnerable to available; in her silken clothes, she flows into a man's arms, and in the image, he is not Vietnamese. In motion, she is fluid, her limbs and core in one flowing movement, carried by her embroidered ankle-length áo dài and the silk pants beneath, or she is toughened, rugged, barefoot, and still desirable. She is a bar girl, pushed into selling her body for sex, and her daughters will not write these books about her, but her granddaughters will. There are books written about his mother: she is a fisherman's daughter, she is the first-born daughter, she is the daughter of a French diplomat, she is the daughter of a duck farmer, she is the daughter of a soldier, she is the daughter who becomes a victim of war—and she is a mother who gives birth to a tragedy. For the child is a tragedy too: an orphan, left behind, given away, the child is a stain that tells the world: my mother gave herself to the enemy, even if there'd been no consent. If the child is Black, it's even worse.[5]

Is there a Vietnamese word for quadroon?

There are books written about this man and his mother, books that make them symbols of what happens under colonialism and in war, but I have written none of them. He is called a child of the dirt. Fatherless: his patriarch is / in another country.

My friend answers my inquiry, very quietly. "Yes, he is like you. Mix, right?"

I nod yes.

"Of course!" my friend says, "But he is Vietnamese. Just Vietnamese."

Blood math seemed to appear once again, here, in Central Vietnam. The one drop of Vietnamese blood formidable enough to erase the American.

Pat Robertson, the evangelical Christian who once suggested God was punishing Americans with Hurricane Katrina, says a "pact to the devil" brought on the devastating earthquake in Haiti.

—CNN.com, "Haiti Earthquake," January 13, 2010

*Everything here feels delicate.*
*Even the barbed wire twisted like strands of DNA*
*along the tops of the high walls surrounding the homes of the rich.*
*We are the same color, he said,*

*gesturing to me, indelicately, as he navigated his Range Rover*
*around giant concrete slabs lying at odd angles in the streets*
*and people shouting in a cacophony of sound,*
*in Kreyol, the language of Black liberation.*

*Funny, I thought he was darker than me.*

*Approaching his house in the hills above Port-au-Prince,*
*my host waved to the man standing under the bougainvillea,*
*little pink petals fluttered in the wind around his head*
*and an AR-something slung across his back.*

*The armed guard: a sighting as ubiquitous*
*as the thorned bushes whose flowers looked*
*as delicate as the wings of a bright-colored moth,*
*of a butterfly.*

*I'd never been to Haiti before the quake.*

*It was just like this, he lied, you didn't miss anything,*
*but I knew that I had missed everything*
*the moment his maid handed me a decanter of clean water*
*to keep by the bathroom sink.*

*He meant we are the same people, he and I. Our limbs,*
*unbroken by the revolution in tectonic plates.*
*His maid limped in from the kitchen*
*and watched me from the corner while I ate.*

# 14

# Time Is a Wheel

"Anyone who comes here comes too late, after a climax of which little has been preserved, yet early enough to dare imagine what it might have been."[1] I carried these words of anthropologist and historian Michel-Rolph Trouillot in my backpack as I arrived in Haiti nearly two hundred years after my family fled this country. My tattered and annotated copy of *Silencing the Past: Power and the Production of History* has accompanied me from graduate school in Baton Rouge to New York to New Orleans and, finally, to Port-au-Prince. Guided by Trouillot's efforts to recenter Haiti in narratives of the Americas, I arrived a few months after the earthquake of 2010. Too late yet early enough.

I had never been to the St. Domingue of my ancestors. That place only exists now in the past, in literature and archives and museums, in the ruins of someone's unsound empire, in the memory fields that beg us to remember. There are plenty of historical monographs that address the violent exploitation and world-shaping role of enslaved laborers in St. Domingue. There are what remains of sugar and coffee plantations and French colonial forts, some of them still blackened by cannon fire, aimed out at the sea or the imagined enemy beyond the nearest mountain range. There are revolutionary-era sites too. Although some of them stand out for their size or expanse or magnificence, like the ruins of Sans Souci, or the abandoned fortress of La Citadelle Laferrière, or the Palais de la Belle Rivière, or La Crête À Pierrot, there are numerous less-known places—some of them elaborate stone foundations, some with staircases and doorways and window openings, some with wells and chimneys, some with fractions of walls, their jagged angles revealing their collapse.[2] Some are protected places; others are used by goats and cattle, by roaming dogs and playful children. St. Domingue, the old colony challenged in word and deed by our patriarchs of the Black republic of Haiti. St. Domingue, the sugar machine set afire by those whose names were never recorded in written history, those counted in ledgers and plantation diaries, those whose identities we will never know.

I imagine that when Haiti became an independent country on January 1, 1804, bells rang all over the countryside. The same bells that once called the laborers to the fields, to the cauldrons, to the wharves, to the marketplaces, to the Big Houses, signifying the calendar minutia of the workday, thenceforward rang out to the people a celebration of freedom. I imagine the blowing of conch shells, the beating of drums, the clapping of hands, laughter, and embrace: the colonial St. Domingue was no more! I can see brown bodies, standing on the shores looking north and south out to sea, looking west to Cuba and Jamaica, looking east to the Spanish-held Santo Domingo, declaring that if liberation happened here, it could happen out there, beyond. Haiti is the first nation in the Americas to abolish slavery. The first Black republic in world history. The second (non-Indigenous) independent nation in the West. An example of what enslaved people could accomplish, their bodies laboring toward the end goal of their own freedom. Did my ancestors hear those bells ringing, the conch shell howling, the drumbeats, and the clapping of hands echoing from mountain to mountain, from one coast to another? Did Barbarousse and Gaudin and Rousseau and La/LeRoux celebrate? Did they buzz with excitement? Or did they—as it appears—run for their lives?

On that rocky and mountainous land, on what had been the lands of Taino and other Indigenous peoples of the Caribbean and circum-Caribbean, Haiti began its independence with autocracy. Having overcome enslavement, abuse, exploitation, and extraction, Haiti's first independent leader, Jean-Jacques Dessalines, declared himself "Emperor for Life," perhaps in imitation of what colonial St. Domingue had always experienced: European monarchs who ruled, unquestioned, forever. Four years after its Independence Day, in 1808, the same year that Mother Juliette Gaudin was born in Cuban exile, Dessalines was assassinated, and Haiti split in two: the north ruled by Henri Christophe, who was largely responsible for the construction of many fortresses and palaces throughout the country, and the south ruled by Alexandre Pétion, a leader of the *gens de couleur*, also called the free Mulattoes, who had lived in exile in France for some years during the revolution.

Pétion supported the Mulatto side during the War of the Knives, which was taking place at the time of my Haitian ancestor Amédée Barbarousse's birth. Interestingly, Pétion's spirit was known to have visited a séance table of the Cercle Harmonique, a collection of Afro-Creole men who practiced Spiritualism in antebellum and postbellum New Orleans. As explained by historian Emily Suzanne Clark, Pétion's depiction as a "'Mulatto legend' in contemporary nineteenth-century histories of Haiti might explain" why his spirit appeared before the Cercle Harmonique. However, other Haitian revolutionaries joined Pétion around the Cercle's table, especially those who supported republicanism, democracy, "full political participation and equal citizenship," and ideals of nationality and fraternity that disputed the hierarchical tensions between Mulattoes and Black Haitians. "One of the Haitian Revolution's main points of inspiration for members of the Cercle Harmonique," Clark writes, "was that race did not dictate the value of a people."[3]

After Pétion's death (from yellow fever, in 1818) and Christophe's death (by suicide, in 1820), Jean-Pierre Boyer, a member of the Mulatto bloc, reunified the country. In the decades following, Haitian people saw their government held by a series of autocrats and dictators, of violent regimes and U.S. occupations, by rotating Black and Mulatto factions.

On my own departure for Haiti, after I'd received my tetanus, hepatitis A, and malaria vaccinations, a Creole friend advised, "Be careful in Haiti. It's a dangerous place for a woman like you." A woman like me? I didn't ask for an elaboration. I haven't forgotten the advice.

• • • • •

Flying over and into the city of Port-au-Prince, located just fifteen miles from the epicenter of the 2010 earthquake, I witnessed what many scholars, writers, journalists, and travelers also saw: the anguished and steadfast Haitian people living however they could, however they must. I saw brown hillsides crowded with solid and makeshift homes; waterproof tents; public art; spacious homes behind barbed-wire fences; abundant bougainvillea in red, pink, and magenta; and impossibly small gardens (but we know that nothing is impossible in Haiti). I saw violently deconstructed, concrete edifices in enormous, jagged rubbish piles in the streets, and colorful tap-taps picking up brave passengers. I saw foreigners with cameras, light-blue-clad UN peacekeepers, non-Haitian and non-Black businessmen in suits frantically grabbing at the opportunities opened up by catastrophe, and the Black Haitian unsuited entrepreneurs of persistent informal economies, selling pharmaceuticals, bandages, salt, SIM cards, batteries, toothbrushes, toothpicks, tools, twist ties, fingernail clippers, water, writing utensils, folded-up ponchos, socks and underwear, keychains, and countless other items in little plastic bags that became litter in the already heavily littered streets.

I traveled to Haiti with colleagues from Xavier University of Louisiana, the only historically Catholic and historically Black college in the United States. Our aim was to establish a partnership with a Catholic and Black university in Haiti, the Université Notre Dame d'Haïti. Based on my travels to Vietnam and my background as a history professor at Xavier, its then-president, Dr. Norman C. Francis, asked me to help support and develop the partnership. The first few trips included a pharmacy professor, an education professor, a New Orleans architect who would advise on buildings and structural renovations, the director of Xavier's international programs, sometimes Dr. Francis, and me.

Dr. Norman C. Francis is among a handful of Creoles of Color who were what Kim Lacy Rogers calls "racial diplomats," political moderates who "interacted well with white men of power, and personally demonstrated that blacks deserved the rights guaranteed to them by the constitution."[4] Francis stands alongside Ernest "Dutch" Morial, the first Black U.S. attorney in Louisiana and New Orleans's first Black mayor; Alexander P. Tureaud, whose work as an attorney helped end school segregation in Louisiana; and Dr. Leonard Burns, the first Black member of the Louisiana Tourist Commission who led successful boycotts of segregated Mardi Gras parades and city institutions, such as the Municipal Auditorium. Francis, who grew up in the Acadiana region of Louisiana, integrated Loyola University in New Orleans and became the first layperson and the first Black person to serve as president of Xavier University of Louisiana. A recipient of the Presidential Medal of Freedom, Francis was also the longest-serving university president in the

United States, serving in that role for forty-seven years. A kind man who led Xavier through the very difficult years after Hurricane Katrina, Francis is also now commemorated in New Orleans in at least one deeply satisfying way: Jefferson Davis Parkway, a major thoroughfare in the city that bordered one side of the historically Black university, is now Dr. Norman C. Francis Parkway.

A short time before I was to give a colloquium on my research in one of Xavier's lecture halls, I saw Dr. Francis walking down the sidewalk toward his car; never having had a single conversation with him, I introduced myself to him and extended an invitation to my lecture. I told him, "I'll be speaking about my research among Creoles here in New Orleans, Dr. Francis. Maybe you'd be interested in the subject?" I hoped that he would, even though I'd never (and still have never) heard him refer to himself or his family as Creole. All his racial justice work, his role as president of an HBCU and of the United Negro College Fund, pointed to his identity as an African American. Might he, like so many of us, see himself as both? Was Creole an irrelevant category to him? It would make sense: he is a product of the civil rights generation, thus embracing blackness as a personal source of pride. J. G.'s words ring true: "We became Black in the Sixties. There's no need for Creole anymore."

Shocking me, Dr. Francis took me up on my invitation. I remember watching him enter the lecture hall; my nervousness worsened. Other professors greeted him, surprised to see him there. Was my research legitimate? Was it academic enough? Would I alienate those in the audience who were tired of hearing about Creoles? Would I alienate Dr. Francis? Would my work be interpreted as anti-Black? At the end of my talk, the multiracial audience offered positive feedback and insightful questions; Dr. Francis left at the start of the Q&A, so I never could gauge his response.

Our stays in Port-au-Prince followed a pattern. We landed at the busy airport and found our hosts, typically a group of smiling priests in shirtsleeves and Roman collars. We embraced the members of the friendly group and proceeded to a hotel: the Karibe, the Kinam, the Oloffson. Then a driver ferried us to a restaurant; my photos of those years show us sitting at neat tables set up for tourists, with gates around the periphery keeping the local people out, protecting the diners within, and producing a flimsy imaginary of disconnectedness. We ate fruit juices and fish and rice. I recall someone asking about the safety of eating meat, another asking about eating lettuce, another holding back the question: Can the people in this neighborhood eat the food that is served in this place? Can we give our food away? At the end of our meals, we were escorted through the gates, where we passed people walking and standing in the streets. I know that I wasn't the only person who felt awful in those moments.

Photographs of Port-au-Prince show not only the devastation associated with the earthquake but also the dehumanization felt by Haitian people whose images were taken without their permission, at a terrible and vulnerable time in their lives. "Photographers played a huge role in informing the world of the extent of human suffering taking place in Haiti," writes Carmelo Larose. "No matter how grim," Larose adds, "the work of photographers served to underscore the urgency of what was being reported in the news and emphasized getting across reality as fact."[5] However, those of us who were working in Haiti after the earthquake and taking photographs of what we saw along the way were not adding to global knowledge about what had taken place there. We were also not disaster tourists, like those who toured the Lower Ninth Ward in the months after Hurricane Katrina. We were both struck by the sheer collapse of this city and hopeful that our planned work would make a difference, at least in higher education.

From the backseat of the vans and trucks that carried us from airport to hotel to restaurant to university, that carried us through Haiti's *terre glissée,* or the slippery ground, we directed our cameras to the suffering passing us by, to the tents where people slept, to people conducting business in the streets, to people sleeping on the dusty sidewalks or among the rubble of great architecture. Until we were directed to stop. Of course, we immediately obeyed.

• • • • •

We were northerners on yet another flight, this time within Haiti, and we buzzed with a palpable anxiety. We were used to airplanes, we well-traveled academics, but not this one: a very, very small propeller airplane in a land foreign to us. We needed to move and stretch. Accustomed to distance between us but having so little space, we rubbed and tapped and rested against others whom we might not define as one of us. The aisle was so narrow that the fluff of our arms almost touched across that space; perhaps my memory is shrinking the width of the plane. There was one row of seats on each side. *Tortug Air* was painted on the exterior: *tortuga,* the Spanish for turtle and the name of an island off the coast of Haiti. Were there ten seats? Twelve? There were so few passengers that I could learn all their names. There was a woman in a pink sweater, even in this tungsten heat. There was another woman with an overflowing, flowered carry-on bag that she carried in her lap. This time, our president Dr. Francis, was not with us. The pharmacy professor sat in the seat in front of me; she was thin limbed and beautifully Black, her long hair spilling over the seat. The education professor, who advised me to invest in a suit, sat at the front of the plane. I suspected that she was an old-school Creole of Color, but she never used the word; when I told her about my research, she just nodded her head and remained silent. The New Orleans architect proved to be a warm presence, his dimpled smile catching and keeping my attention. In the rectory of the church where we were staying in Port-au-Prince, he told me that he couldn't drink, and I knew what he meant—that if he were to drink, his plane would fall from his sky.

We learned that the pilot was Dominican, although it sounded to me like he was speaking Catalan. He rushed onto the plane after we had all boarded, finishing his loud telephone conversation as a man in street clothes pulled the hatch shut.

The fields around the runway were riddled with the random refuse of previous flights, including some planes like this one, nestled silently in overgrown grass; it wasn't a comforting sight. Goats and other grazing animals sauntered by, and people in carts drawn by mules passed without turning their heads.

The small plane taxied clumsily. Were there potholes on this lane? Were the roads sinking—subsiding—here, as in New Orleans? How long before the runway turned to weeds?

The plane was so much louder than the large one that brought us here, so I turned up the volume on a Fiona Apple song. That way, I could focus on her lyrics, the worries of her life and not mine, floating precariously over brown mountains and Black people looking up at the buzzing overhead. We bumped and shook and dipped. Bumped, shook, dipped. Quickly leaving the air above the capital, we observed the land below us becoming brown, absent of trees, even absent of the dull grey of concrete. A few waterways, like in New Orleans, were also brown, their reflections of light above, muted. Tones of brown appeared to represent rises and falls in the landscape. The darker browns, low and wet places, saturated, and the lighter browns, high and dry places, thirsty. All of it—mountains and valleys—largely denuded of green. I looked for the green of knife-sharp sugarcane leaves; I looked for the green of coffee bushes. I saw very little green of new vegetation, of chlorophyll, of new life on the branch or the stalk. A sudden drop of the plane sent my heart pounding in my chest—"I want to live," I said quietly to myself, "I want to live, to survive; I want the land and the people to live, to survive, to be surrounded by the brightest green of life that will not ever surrender." A deep drop of a large jet over the Amazon once sent my heart pounding like this, but I remember thinking that time, "If we keep falling, the dense mattress of the rainforest will soften our landing." This time, I just wished for green down below.

But from the skies over Haiti, as we flew due north, we could spot the blue dots amid the brown down below, like the markers of place on our Google maps: that's where the people were, under those blue tarps. Human life huddled under plastic salvation, in tents that offered no security nor privacy, tents that made all people, especially women and the young, vulnerable to unrestrained men. Would Haitians one day build treehouses?

What were these mountains called in the language of the Taino? Is it true that "Ayiti" is the Taino word for "mountains"? That when we utter the name of the nation, we are speaking the Taino into being? Haiti, an Indigenous tautology, a memory in the naming. The Haitian American writer Edwidge Danticat pointed out that naming also arises in the history of the quake. "We have a lot of names for hurricanes, and we have experience with hurricanes," she says, "but earthquakes we don't name, so people would say . . . 'bagay la,' you know, 'the thing.' A lot of people in Haiti also call it 'gudugudu,'" she says, an onomatopoeia that represents the sound of an earthquake shaking. "There was poetry in the rubble," Danticat reminds us, in the efforts to name something to remember it.[6]

On the shortest flight I've ever taken, shorter than the drive from New Orleans to Acadiana, the tortuga made a bumpy rise and a bumpy descent into Port-de-Paix, a city on the northernmost coast of Haiti. Port-de-Paix: port of peace. (Why isn't this place better known to us from the North?) We—the pharmacy professor, the education professor, the warm New Orleans architect, and I—exited the plane onto the runway. The airport looked like a small business office; the runway, a wild place with a strip through it, split by a narrow line of order. I unfolded my fingers, whose nails left imprints in my palms, as my hands had been in tight fists through the last moments of the flight. The pilot hopped out of the plane, briefly acknowledged us, and walked off for a cigarette.

A priest who resembled Dr. Francis greeted us and led us to his church, the Cathédrale Notre Dame de l'Immaculée Conception. Scaffolding had been erected in front of the gorgeous structure; however, renovations did not lessen the beauty of the church. I snapped photos of the stained glass, the ceiling decorated with fleur de lis, the superb brickwork along the side of the church, the shiny pews, the altar, and the dome above it. In coming days, we would meet with other Religious and university administrators at the Port-de-Paix campus of Université Notre Dame d'Haïti. Despite our efforts, we would not fulfill our mission of establishing a partnership. All our meetings with officials, with eager students, and with professors; all the drafts of the university agreements, the revised budgets, our trips to Haiti, and our Haitian partners' trips to New Orleans ended only with smiling faces, handshakes, pleasant photographs, and these memories.

In Port-de-Paix, we slept in simple guestrooms of the very large rectory, where three stories of balconies wrapped around the building. In the morning, those who served the priests brought us French bread and eggs and Haitian coffee with Haitian sugar. I thought, What a figurative breakfast.

Haitian history, right there before us, to consume.

• • • • •

Don't go to Haiti unless you have a driver. I was told, it is one of the essentials when traveling to that country. Every time I arrived in Haiti, either as part of a delegation from my university or on my own, I had a driver. Once it was a businessman who, along with his wife, hosted me in their protected home in the hills above the capital. It was unexpectedly posh: a grand piano in the living room, what appeared to be marble floors, original oil paintings stacked from eye level to the very high ceilings, sculptures on pedestals, multiple balconies overlooking the city down below. White furnishings. An armed guard at the gate. And a housekeeper in the kitchen, who prepared for me plantains, shrimp stew, steamed fish, poul ak nwa (stewed chicken served over rice), and a luxurious version of beans called sòs pwa nwa. When I asked her if she wanted to join me at the table, gesturing "join me" since I knew no French or Kreyol, she declined; instead, she sat in the kitchen and waited for me to finish eating.

Another time, my driver was a young priest, a novice, from a church I cannot recall in Port-au-Prince: he had deep dimples and deep-set eyes. He drove a truck and maneuvered it with the expertise of a taxi driver. On another visit, it was a librarian and translator from the université who drove a Mercedes SUV. That was not a comfortable ride—passing by the hundreds of people recovering alongside the road from the capital airport, the countless tents in grey and blue. I felt awful, zooming by at a deliberate speed in a luxury automobile (my first time in a Mercedes). On another occasion, our delegation was driven in a small, lightweight van, and we all tossed around the bucket seats, holding on to each other, a strange and unexpected intimacy for a group of university professors and administrators.

A foreigner cannot exist in Haiti without a driver who can maneuver the pavement and the dirt roads, the mountains and the monuments. We were chauffeured around La Neg Mawon, a monument to the Black Maroons whose actions helped make the St. Domingue Revolution possible. We were driven around the Bicentennial Monument, a tower erected to celebrate Haiti's two hundredth year of independence from France. We were carried to the white National Palace, its dome collapsed on its side, and the pink and white Cathédrale Notre-Dame de l'Assomption, which had been hollowed out by the earthquake. My photos show an airy frame, giant flower-shaped holes that once held stained glass, collapsed walls, hills of debris, and Haitian people sleeping on the concrete ground within. Our drivers swept us into sites and then quickly carried us off.

*Should I be afraid?* The question flitted through my mind, a flying insect. But I wasn't. Maybe because I was on the passenger side, and this time, Monsignor Pierre-Andre Pierre, then-rector of Université Notre Dame d'Haïti, was driving. In his rugged four-door truck, we left Port-au-Prince for Les Cayes, then Jacmel, and then back to the capital. Monsignor Pierre coolly mastered the truck along the very edge of the highway, along the very edge of a steep drop into what, to me, looked like emptiness. In the distant past, Maroons, or escaped enslaved laborers, found long-term refuge in these very mountains, lit only by celestial bodies and their luminous insistence on freedom.

The deep dark of rural Haiti enveloped us as we drove at night. I knew that we were traveling through mountains, the rising, falling, and curving road ahead of us lit up by the truck's headlights, the dirt and gravel roads kicking up brown dust that looked like hovering mosquitoes. There seemed to be no nighttime electricity in the area. Off in the distance, I saw sporadic, glimmering lamps. Pedestrians startled me, suddenly appearing on the night road with wobbling flashlights or sharp lights from cellphones.

Monsignor Pierre's truck made a knocking sound, and he smiled in my direction. Embarrassed? Expected? Worried? Just another day on the uneven and unpredictable Haitian roads? Instructing me to remain in the truck, he pulled over onto the thinnest of shoulders, got out, opened the hood, and peered at the truck's machinery with the light of his cellphone. I waited, looking out into the mountainous abyss. After a brief phone call, we drove very slowly down into the nearest town and spent the night with a generous parishioner, who had guest rooms set up on opposite sides of her house for the monsignor and me. There was no electricity that evening, but a large candlelit dinner awaited us when we arrived. I comfortably joked with the monsignor about his having a romantic dinner with an American woman; we laughed as we ate, his warm and deep voice, his candid smile giving me ease. I trusted him, as well as my surroundings on this night, completely. As I had multiple times, I apologized for not speaking a single word in Kreyol or French, both languages having been lost in my family; Grandpa was the last to speak any form of our patriarchal language. After several trips to Haiti, I learned to say "hello," "thank you," and "come again?"

The next morning, while a man repaired the truck, I took a photograph of Monsignor Pierre in his monochrome black attire, standing under a cascading wall of pink bougainvillea. I took another photograph of him taking a photograph of the woman who cleaned the house, her smile shy, as she stood under the same blossoming flowers. We drove into La Vallée-de-Jacmel, a city whose architecture, design, and decorative elements closely resembled those in New Orleans. A family hosted us on their immaculate outdoor patio, lined with banana trees and deep-red flowering vines, and floored with freshly swept linoleum; the photographs that I took from their home show partly deforested hillsides, few green spaces interrupted with stretches of brown, and the seaside city of Jacmel in the distance. Domestic servants offered us fresh fruit, mayi moulen (a cornmeal porridge) with smoked herring, and nonalcoholic Haitian gold juice. Other priests from Université Notre Dame d'Haïti joined us, all of them jovial, friendly, warm, their skin colors varying from mine to the monsignor's and lighter and darker still, skin color seeming to have no apparent significance among these beautiful brothers and men.

Instead of Monsignor Pierre, a young man drove me to the Jacmel campus of the local university. When we arrived, he practiced his English with me. What did I think about Haiti? How many times had I visited? From where in the United States had I come? I smiled, answering his questions.

"I'm not very comfortable sitting here talking to you," he confessed, grinning, after a few moments of silence had passed between us.

"Why?" I asked him. "Because I'm North American?" It had occurred to me that I might have been seen as an unwelcome presence, as a foreign body, with my doctor honorific, having been driven around Haiti, chauffeured, often in the back of a vehicle.

"Because you're Mulatto, madam, and I don't interact with many Mulattoes," he said, very politely.

Come again?

Taken aback by his frank statement, I answered, "I'm not Mulatto. I'm Creole."

He then asked me, "What is Creole?" Since the term had been used on that very island years before the nation of Haiti even existed, as long ago as seventeenth-century St. Domingue, I knew his question was a friendly challenge. Certainly, he knew the term, but he wanted to know what it meant to me. I offered him what I'd learned from my grandparents' mouths, from the mouths of their peers, from the mouths of aunts and great-aunts, and from my parents' mouths, who learned what Creole was (and was not) from those who came before them.

"A Creole is a person whose ancestors originated in Louisiana when it was a French colony," I answered him, adding, "Creoles are of mixed heritage."

"*Mulatto,*" he replied, giving me the gift of a chuckle.

"No, I'm not Mulatto," I told him again. I never used that term to describe myself. Remnants of my childhood friend Cindy: "Isn't that what they say," she said after my parents' separation, "that mixed couples don't last?" It left a bitter taste in my mouth. So, too, did the "tragic Mulatto" characters, the psychically lost, the tortured, the doomed. But I also believed that, in Haiti, "Mulatto" represented something that I didn't embrace. It was the separatist stance, the differentiation on the clear basis of not-blackness. It was synonymous with the Brown philosophy of the Dominican Republic, just across the border, where Haitian nationals and Dominican-born Haitians lived (and continue to live) as a stateless and loathed minority. I wanted to hold two things in the same hand. Yes, Haitian Mulattoes and mixed-race people in other Caribbean nations had a different historical experience: that cannot be ignored or denied. However, the application of the label "Mulatto" to me, in this island nation, was incorrect; it linked me with a history that was not mine.

Ignoring my protestation, he answered, "Black men here do not associate with Mulatto women," adding, "it's very strange."

Was this the warning that my Creole friend gave me prior to my departure for Haiti? That I would be perceived as a Mulatto? That I would be a woman traveling in a place perceived as "dangerous"? Or that my presence, my body, and how it would be read in Haiti might be dangerous to others?

Or would it be perceived as familiar? Many of the priests and nuns whom I engaged with in Haiti, either in the many spotless rectories where I stayed as a guest or at the universities that I visited, recognized my surname and welcomed me with warm and beautiful smiles. "You have been to the village of Gaudin?" one young nun asked me, her skin a deep and perfect brown; at the time, I didn't know there was such a place. I still haven't visited it. Somehow, I hadn't expected my surname to be a mark of belonging in this place. Did Gaudin hold any local meaning? I imagined an expansive version of my experience with Miss Audrey, walking through the Seventh Ward where my grandmother had grown up, and no one remembering the

Roux family. Walking here, in Haiti, were there any Gaudins left and anyone who would remember them? Hundreds of years is a long time.

And were they worthy of remembering?

Did these nuns in Port-au-Prince know about Mother Juliette?

Introducing myself to my new Haitian friends, who knew my name, I used its Louisiana pronunciation: *GO-dæ,* the *n* at the end silent. "*Gaudin,*" my listener repeated, and I nodded my head. Hearing the pronunciation of my surname in a Haitian person's voice, I couldn't help but feel it was a more authentic sound. A genuine representation. A real existence. The way that we had said our name as children, the California pronunciation—*go-DAN,* hard *N*—rang in my ears. Hearing my name spoken back to me, in this Francophone place, this diasporic place, this Indigenous place devastated by colonization, this Black place, I felt the warmth of postcolonial, fictive kinship. Perhaps seeking to affirm a global recognition between us, we of circum-Caribbean brown skin, many of the people who spoke my surname asked me, "Your family is Haitian?"

As if Haitian were a time and not a place, as if Haiti were an event in the timeline of my family's history, my return, the completion of a circle, I nodded my head and offered the only answer that I knew to be true: "A very long time ago."

This is the way home feels to me.
Does it feel this way to you?

—VANESSA A. BEE

The Gaudin Girls in Easter Suits. Leslie, Roslyn, and Wendy Gaudin. Northridge, California, ca. 1974.

# Conclusion

Of all the times my mother has come back to Louisiana, and of all the times my father, my sisters, my cousins, and my nieces have visited, no one has come for Carnival, for Jazz Fest, for the French Quarter Festival, or all the other festivals that southern Louisiana is known for. My first residence in New Orleans, a bottom-floor apartment in a double gallery on Laurel Street, faced a staging spot for uptown Mardi Gras parades that began on Napoleon Avenue and rolled up toward St. Charles Avenue, where they turned and continued toward Canal Street and the French Quarter. Hours before the krewes began rolling, their marchers lined up on my street; I walked among the marching bands, dancing krewes, and costumed riders on horseback, and I took photographs. Riding my bike up Napoleon Avenue and watching the very beginning of the parade, I turned and rode back home to Laurel Street before the crowds gathered. As close as I was to the routes of Mardi Gras parades, no one in my family came.

It is a strange experience, being a newcomer in a city of traditional celebrations, of collective history that my distant family once partook in. New Orleans is largely known for Carnival, the annual pre-Lenten, Latinate celebration encompassing parades, balls, street parties, krewes, and family gatherings. Tourists from everywhere in the world come here for it; locals participate in any number of ways. Afro-Creoles, African Americans, and other people of color mask as Indians, as Babydolls, as skeletons in the Skull and Bone Gang; queer friends march in the Krewe of Red Beans and Rice, and Vietnamese American friends now march in the new Krewe of Mung Beans;

costumed dogs and their humans parade in the Krewe of Barkus. New Orleans Creoles hold their annual balls; in Acadiana, Creoles and Cajuns enjoy Zydecos and the Courir de Mardi Gras. I remain on the outside, an observer and never a participant, my California distance activated. Masking, parading, and engaging in seasonal celebrations must have played a part in my ancestors' lives; in an old photo, my father stands as a little boy in a Mardi Gras suit that his mother sewed. But for what occasion? For which parade? No one knows, and my father doesn't recall. The photo is emblematic of the Creole diaspora. It has shifted from lived experience to distant memory, a subject for someone to ponder and write about, to speculate on, a thing that connects the past to the present, the details lost forever.

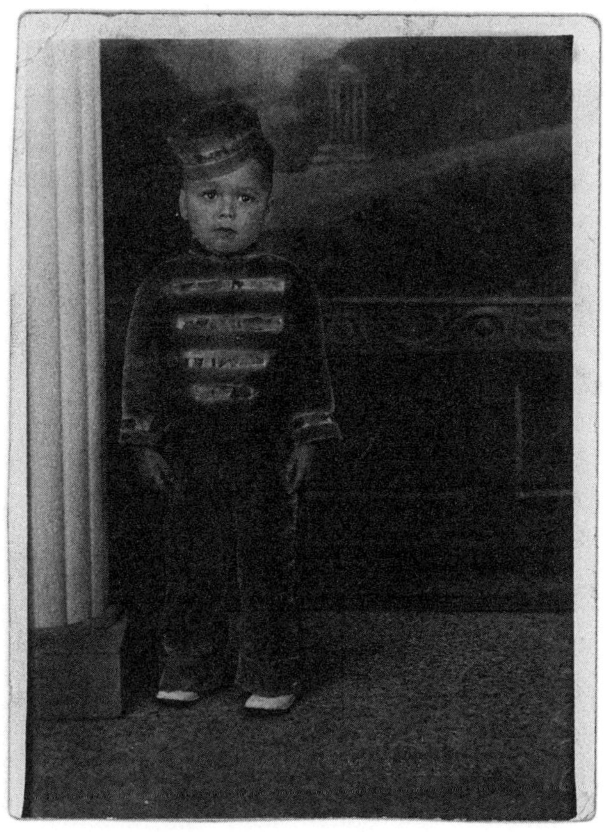

Past and Future Tense. Anthony Joseph Gaudin.
New Orleans, ca. 1943. Photo by Florestine Perrault Collins.

Some years after I moved to New Orleans, my mother came back to visit during my academic spring break. As always, we indulged in the usual New Orleans fare: we walked through the French Quarter, visited shops that cater to tourists, rode the nearby ferries, ate beignets, walked along the Mississippi River, and Mom enjoyed fresh crab and boiled crawfish, two sticky crustaceans that I still do not care to wrestle with. We spent some time at Xavier, where I introduced Mom to Dr. Francis, which illustrates how small Xavier is and how personalized his presidency was. Mom also visited my Louisiana History class, where she sat quietly, beaming with pride, in the back of the classroom. All three of her daughters are educators. Mom would have been a stellar piano teacher and choral director if she'd been encouraged in that direction. Her musical skills have passed down to her children and her grandchildren, even though she never became an educator by profession.

During that visit with my mother, we departed New Orleans and drove up to Vacherie, the birthplace of her mother, her mother's mother, and several generations of Roussels dating back to an immigrant beginning about which we can only speculate. We explored the town, focusing our eyes on the oldest-looking dwellings adjacent to the sprawling sugarcane fields. *Could that have been where she lived?* we asked each other, not knowing the exact location of Marietta's childhood home, not knowing whether the structure still stood. Here in Louisiana, the impermanence caused by nature's travails, not to mention the destruction of homes to make way for industry, could have torn the home from the land long ago. *A child in these lands: What did she see?* we two asked ourselves, asked each other. *Where did she walk? What did she touch?* My mother regrets her parents' unwillingness to share more of their history with her; in me, she sees the opposite energy.

For my mother marks a tectonic shift in her family's history. Born in Los Angeles in 1939, she was the first in her family, at least since the Louisiana Purchase, to be born outside Louisiana. Her siblings *remembered* New Orleans; even if their memories were amorphous (her brother's vague memory of departing on the Sunset Limited) or painful (her sister's memory of her parents' departure, without her, on the same train), at least they had *memories.* My mother comes to Louisiana with a deeply emotional yearning for it; when Mom comes to see me, she comes to a place she feels attached to, even though she has not lived here a day in her life. She comes here to *make memories* where she has none.

I seek the same. Although this may not be my home for the rest of my life, it is the home that I've chosen for more than twenty years. I acknowledge my subject position as a diasporic returnee; I am not a native of New Orleans. I cannot speak from the position of a native of this city. This is an important point, because the voices of newcomers are too often prioritized above those of native people. Some, like me, who migrated to this city, are speaking of New Orleans as *their city,* a claim that is contested by those who have been here for generations and never left. Many newer settlers are benefiting from their zip code, from their recent time here, from new money, from their references and local knowledge, while native New Orleanians are being left out. While I write this, at the dignified Latter Memorial Library, I emphasize my subject position as a *returnee,* not as a native; indeed, when my grandfathers lived in this city, they would have been barred from this library due to their color—one of the many reasons why they left.

Holding two things in the same hand, Louisiana is my ancestral inheritance and my chosen, adopted home; when my mother comes to visit, she too feels this is a kind of home, a place where she feels she belongs. Our Creoleness is a strong rope that ties us to the bollard that is Louisiana.

In Vacherie, my mother and I stood before Our Lady of Peace Catholic Church. Because it was locked and no priest (or monk) appeared to escort us inside, we were left to wander around the church grounds and the parish graveyard. There, we read the stiff tombs, the French names no longer automatically racialized as white, feeling either fanciful or oppressive in our West Coast mouths. Detiveaux. Bethancourt. Duplantier. Melançon. LaGarde. Oubre.

"Roussel!" my mother gasped, the emotion unfound in our English language: a meeting of overwhelming joy, unexpected discovery, and unresolvable sadness. (What is the word for that?) Several headstones spoke to my mother: we are here. After a few minutes of searching, we found the grave of her Aunt Ella, whom she recalls meeting as a little girl. "My family!" she said, an audible lump in her throat. A reunion decades too late but early enough.

Departing the cemetery, Mom and I drove toward the levee and stopped at B&C Seafood for a late lunch. While we ate, I made a promise. "I will find out more about her history, Mom," I told her. "And I will write about her."

From there, Mom and I drove to the Mississippi River levee, near the Laura Creole Plantation; we parked my car, walked up the levee and down the batture to the river's edge. Unsure of her footing, she still walked down to the water. I followed her with my camera.

Standing by the river, she turned, and I snapped her photo. "I'm walking where my mother walked," she told me. "My mother stood right here and put her feet in this water."

Her mother and the mothers before her once stood in this spot, their histories stretching and curling around the archives that illuminate some of their history and the mythologies that continue to exoticize them, the blood mathematics that threatens to quantify them, the racial compulsions that pushed them to opposing poles of their heredity, and the monographs that tell a fuller story of their lives. Trampled by settlers and slave traders; trafficked on the Atlantic Ocean, the Caribbean Sea, and the Gulf of Mexico; ferried on the Mississippi River; and floated on the railroad tracks that carried the Sunset Limited westward, our ancestors are shaped by their choices and nonchoices, their actions and inactions, their resistance, their assimilation, their movement from farm to city, from South to West, from city to suburb. And now from West to South, me: a future ancestor about whom my descendants might someday write.

"I will write about her," I told my mother, specifically in reference to her mother, but I also vowed to someday write about all the mothers and fathers, grands and greats, whose histories I could grasp, whose stories might contribute to larger narratives about Creole Louisiana, about New Orleans, about the South and the migration West. Some members of my family are excited by this endeavor, seeing it as a manifestation of their kin's writerly life, their sibling's or cousin's deep interest in our shared Creole heritage. Some younger relatives text or call me from California with questions about their history, asking me, "What is Creole?" My own son asks me the same when his peers press him to better define his ethnicity; he struggles to answer the question. My family members push me forward, encourage the research, share what they know; as historian Joan DeJean wrote of her own experience, "I somehow became the last French speaker in a long line. This explains why, as my parents' generation aged, family members begged me to hold onto every reminder of earlier generations. No one else could read the letters and other records of our past."[1] While my grandparents were the last in our family to speak French, I still hold the family documents of the earlier generations; I translate their historical meaning to our present-day understanding; I imagine what filled the empty spaces.

Others in my extended family are hesitant. Why must you write about us? Can't you just write a novel? Can you change our names? Alter some of the less savory details? Leave our side of the family out? Some contest my interpretations or remember things differently. Some very clearly see our family, and see themselves, as Black—that this is Black history and Creoles of Color belong under that umbrella. Others are unshakable in their understanding of our family and themselves as multiracial, as people whose cultural identification and affinity were always more tangible than the racial category that was attached to them; these kin speak of blackness as something we are adjacent to, as a space we can enter and depart as we please. There is no final either / or here. We Creoles are like everyone else: we are spacious beings, and we can encompass many experiences. We are many things.

What is written here is both deeply personal and universal. It isn't just my story, and it isn't only the story of Marietta Roussel, Rita Elizabeth Roux, Augustus Lawrence Burns, and John Norah Gaudin. It is a story about how we are connected to history, how we hold the stories of our ancestors, and how we can understand the effects of migration on the generations who live with its inheritance. It is about reckoning with the actions of our great-grandmothers and great-grandfathers and grappling with how those actions (or inactions) shape those of us living today. This book is also about memory: Who is remembered and how? Why do we remember the things that we do, in the ways that we do, and why do we forget? Here, I want to highlight the personal works of Viet Thanh Nguyen, Martha Hodes, Ruth Behar, Imani Perry, and Grace Elizabeth Hale, five academics from different fields who have written personal histories that helped me imagine how to straddle my field and my family's history.

Finally, this book is about one family's life as Louisiana Creoles. It does not represent all of Creole history, nor does it represent all the experiences of the Creole diaspora to California. Like any other ethnic group or racial population, our experiences differ vastly, and no one family story is everyone's story. There is no singular story, no metanarrative. In my family's history, there is the downtown New Orleans Creole, the uptown New Orleans Creole, the Creole from the west bank of the River Parishes, and the Creole from the east bank of the River Parishes. Here, I am reminded of a Vietnamese friend's story, which was shared with me while riding together on a bus in Bảo Lộc, Vietnam: "My mother was from the North, she migrated to the Middle and met my father. They got married and had my older brother, then they migrated to the South, where I was born. So, I am all of Vietnam: North, Middle, and South." I am very fortunate in that my Creole story is not representative of only one neighborhood, one parish, or one ward of New Orleans. All four of my grandparents represent four directions of Creole geography; in my son's paternal history, he contains Cane River Creoles in the north of the state and Plaquemines Parish Creoles in the deepest south. In him, there is an even more expansive Creole heredity. What this means to me is that he, and so many others like him—Creoles of Color from Lafayette, from Lake Charles, from Baton Rouge—contain many different versions of what Creole is. Not to mention the many Latin American and Caribbean interpretations of Creole. Any attempt to define Creole in a narrow and simple way is futile.

In the book's introduction, I wrote that a student asked me once, "Of course, you're Creole, Dr. G., but what are you *really*?" Throughout my family's history, we are Afro-Creole, Creole, Black, white, mixed, and racially fluid. We are stories of wealth and privilege, poverty and loss, migration and nativity. We are perceived as light, dark, brown, yellow, red, bright, white, black, mixed, and neither. We are Indigenous; we are diasporic. We are narratives of enslavement and freedom, of leaving and returning. In the end, the answer to the question is here, right here in the pages of this book.

# ACKNOWLEDGMENTS

My work would not exist without the work of Michel-Rolph Trouillot and other literary, theoretical, artistic, and academic ancestors. I mention just a few of the many, many persons and entities who made this, my first book, possible. Ronald L. F. Davis, Gaines M. Foster, Sybil Kein, Walter Johnson, Martha Hodes, and Robin D. G. Kelley led, inspired, and guided me at different times throughout my formal education. The folks at the Historic Natchez Foundation trained me in the delicate work of southern history. Elizabeth Y. Hammer, Elizabeth Manley, and other valued colleagues in the Xavier University Faculty Writing Group supported me. The *North American Review* gave me my first true publication. A Studio in the Woods gave me my first writing residency. The Faculty Resource Network at New York University gave me my first scholarly residency. Monson Arts Residency, in Monson, Maine, gave me a month of writing and revising, with a background of lakes, mountains, and one sweet day of snow.

Viet Thanh Nguyen, Natasha Trethewey, Edwidge Danticat, Maryse Condé, Dao Strom, Austin Clarke, Jesmyn Ward, Louise Erdrich, Marlon James, Quan Barry, Ocean Vuong, Ernest Gaines, and Joseph Boyden taught and continue to teach me that the past is always deeply present in the written word. Thank goodness that this world has been gifted the works of these, and so many other, authors. Likewise, the works of Gwendolyn Midlo Hall, Monique Verdin, Fatima Shaik, Peggy Pascoe, Christina Sharpe, Ruth Behar, Jessica Marie Johnson, Sylviane Djiouf, C.L.R. James, Shirley Elizabeth Thompson, Angel Adams Parham, Dionne Brand, Julius T. Scott, Lawrence Powell, Rodolphe Lucien Desdunes, Sophie White, Naomi Zack, Alecia P. Long, Saidiya Hartman, Michael Tisserand, Jack E. Davis, Nikky Finney, Bliss Broyard, Kristina Kay Robinson, Kim Vaz-Deville, and Emily Suzanne Clark. Thank you, Elizabeth Moore Rhodes and the Louisiana Creole Research Association for seeing me and valuing my work. Thank you, Greg Osborn, for being such a help early in my years of research. Thank you to Mark Broyard and Roger Guenveur Smith for memorializing the Creole Mafia. Thank you to Jessica Marie Johnson, Eva Semien Baham, Laura Rosanne Adderley, and Chenise Calhoun for community. Thank you, Billy Sothern and Anthony Roque, for giving me very different gifts in this life; I'm sorry that neither of you lived to see this book to completion. Thank you to the Chauvin family, the Broussard family, the Barthelemy family, the Duplessis family, and the Garnier family for opening your arms to me and for easing my work throughout the years.

Thank you, Aunt Rosie and Aunt Sandy, for entrusting me with the Gaudin family documents and beloved historical objects. Thank you, Audrey Garnier Baquet, Elsie Garnier Dannel, and Mercedes Prograis Barthe for holding my hand and leading me into a past that you all knew so well. Thank you, Uncle Jules, Aunt Theda, and Mary Lee Broussard for your elder voices of experience. Thank you, Vincent Roux and Bailey Duhé, for your own important work. Thank you to my writing partner, Arden Eli Hill, for reading every word and every chapter in each stage of this book; thank you, too, for asking me one day, "Have you read Natasha Tretheway?" Thank you to my loving friends, Bart Everson and Mel Michelle Lewis, for faithfully reading and lovingly critiquing many of these chapters. Thank you, Nguyễn Thái Thuận and Trần Khánh Nhi, for guiding my steps in Vietnam, from Hồ Chí Minh City in the South to Hà Nội in the North. Thank you, Corine Brown, for teaching me to trust my vision. Thank you, Jenny Keegan, for inviting this manuscript, supporting me throughout the process, and waiting patiently for every revision. Thank you to the editorial team at Louisiana State University Press. Thank you to the anonymous readers for giving me feedback that enormously strengthened this book.

DJ Joe Kay, Soulection Radio, Ryuichi Sakamoto, Steve Roach, Brian Eno, and Harold Budd serenaded me through every word on every page. Richard Collins, Michaela O'Connor Bono, Thích Đồng Lưu, Thích Đạo Quảng, and the sisters at Chùa Phước Viên taught me to sit and to trust the dharma. Kandis Marie Pierre loved me without condition and cheered for me every step of the way. My mother and my father, Eleanor Burns and Anthony Gaudin, gave me everything that they possibly could in this life.

My long line of ancestors—those who would recognize me and those who wouldn't, those who gave their names to their progeny and those who didn't, those who made it into the historical record and those who didn't—sit at my altar and receive my daily gratitude for the innumerable virtues offered to me. And my beloved son, Aubry Norah Roque, is every beautiful thing that I wish for the future.

# NOTES

## 2. A BLOND ROUX IS THE LIGHTEST ONE

1. "What is Bulbancha?" https://www.betterfutureprogram.org/bulbancha.html#:~:text=As%20Potawatomi%20geographer%20and%20Mississippi,names%20are%20our%20ancestors'%20speech.

2. Some quotes throughout are attributed to recorded interviews with Rita Roux Gaudin (1995, 1999, 2000, 2001). Others are from unrecorded conversations.

3. Jessica Marie Johnson, *Wicked Flesh: Black Women, Intimacy, and Freedom in the Atlantic World* (Philadelphia: University of Pennsylvania Press, 2020), 171–72.

4. Clint Smith, *How the Word Is Passed: A Reckoning with the History of Slavery across America* (New York: Little, Brown and Co., 2021), 61–62.

5. Parish Court Cases, No 7120–7187, Orleans Parish, Louisiana, 1813–1851.

6. For more on race and status in colonial St. Domingue, see John D. Garrigus, *Before Haiti: Race and Citizenship in French Saint-Domingue* (New York: Palgrave McMillan, 2006). For a more expansive view of race, hybridity, and status in the Caribbean, see Tessa Murphy, *The Creole Archipelago: Race and Borders in the Colonial Caribbean* (Philadelphia: University of Pennsylvania Press, 2021).

7. For more on the linkages between the Caribbean and colonized New Orleans, see Cécile Vidal, *Caribbean New Orleans: Empire, Race, and the Making of a Slave Society* (Chapel Hill: University of North Carolina, 2019).

8. Rashauna Johnson, *Slavery's Metropolis: Unfree Labor in New Orleans during the Age of Revolutions* (Cambridge: Cambridge University Press, 2016), 1–23.

9. Johnson, *Slavery's Metropolis*, 109.

10. For more on the racial politics and solidarity among Creoles of Color in New Orleans, see Fatima Shaik, *Economy Hall: The Hidden History of a Free Black Brotherhood* (New Orleans: Historic New Orleans Collection, 2021).

11. Louisiana District and Probate Courts, Orleans Parish, Case Papers 1880–1929, Civil District Court Case Papers, No 56833–57025, 1898.

12. New Orleans, Louisiana Birth Records Index, 1790–1899, vol. 23, p. 425

13. Steve Luxenberg, *Separate: The Story of* Plessy v. Ferguson, *and America's Journey from Slavery to Segregation* (New York: W. W. Norton), 489.

## 3. SUN FIRE LEO

1. For more on the history of Robert Charles and racial violence in New Orleans at the turn of the century, see William Ivy Hair, *Carnival of Fury: Robert Charles and the New Orleans Race Riot of 1900* (Baton Rouge: Louisiana State University Press, 2008).

2. Bruce Raeburn, "Kid Ory," *64 Parishes*, November 25, 2022, https://64parishes.org/entry/kid-ory.

3. Jack Kelly, "The Rise and Fall of the Sleeping Car King," *Smithsonian Magazine*, January 11, 2019, https://www.smithsonianmag.com/history/rise-fall-sleeping-car-king-180971240/.

4. Larry Tye, *Rising from the Rails: Pullman Porters and the Making of the Black Middle Class* (New York: Henry Holt, 2004), 86.

5. Tye, *Rising from the Rails*, 93.

6. Tye, *Rising from the Rails*, 77.

## 4. HOLY NAME

1. Some quotes throughout are attributed to recorded interviews with John Norah Gaudin (1995, 2001). Others are from unrecorded conversations.

2. Verdin writes about the land, language, race, memory, culture, and migration, among other things, in her beautiful text: Monique Verdin, *Return to Yakni Chitto: Houma Migrations* (New Orleans: University of New Orleans Press, 2020).

3. Verdin, *Return to Yakni Chitto*, 8.

4. Frank Deloria, "When Tribal Nations Expel Their Black Members," *New Yorker*, July 18, 2022, https://www.newyorker.com/magazine/2022/07/25/when-tribal-nations-expel-their-black-members-caleb-gayle-we-refuse-to-forget-alaina-e-roberts-ive-been-here-all-the-while.

5. Mel Michelle Lewis, "Erosion," in *Biomythography Bayou* (Lewisburg, PA: Bucknell University Press, 2025), 111–16.

6. "Widow's Application for Pension," Louisiana State Archives, Louisiana Confederate Pensions, 1898–1950.

7. "Widow's Application for Pension."

8. "5th Louisiana Field Battery," Wikipedia, the Free Encyclopedia, Wikimedia Foundation, April 17, 2024, https://en.wikipedia.org/wiki/5th_Louisiana_Field_Battery.

9. "1910 Census Instructions to Enumerators," United States Census Bureau, October 8, 2021, https://www.census.gov/programs-surveys/decennial-census/technical-documentation/questionnaires/1910/1910-instructions.html#:~:text=For%20census%20purposes%2C%20the%20term,110.

10. "Soldier's Application for Pension," Louisiana State Archives, Louisiana Confederate Pensions, 1898–1950.

11. Shaik, *Economy Hall*, 65.

12. Caroline Randall Williams, "You Want a Confederate Monument? My Body Is a Confederate Monument," *New York Times*, June 26, 2020, https://www.nytimes.com/2020/06/26/opinion/confederate-monuments-racism.html.

13. "Soldier's Application for Pension," 1898–1950.

14. "Widow's Application for Pension.".

15. Sister Mary Bernard Deggs, *No Cross, No Crown: Black Nuns in Nineteenth-Century New Orleans* (Bloomington: Indiana University Press, 2002), 5–6.

## 5. SUNSET LIMITED

1. John Warner Smith, "Bucket," *About Place Journal, 1963–2013: A Civil Rights Retrospective,* https://aboutplacejournal.org/issues/civil-rights/future-past/john-smith-3/. Smith read "Bucket" at the Opelousas Museum and Interpretive Center on December 6, 2023; I was present at the reading.

2. For more on how World War II shaped Washington State, see James R. Warren, *The War Years: A Chronicle of Washington State in World War II* (Seattle: University of Washington Press, 2001).

3. "Camp Hayden: Port Angeles, Washington," *Atlas Obscura,* August 15, 2022, https://www.atlasobscura.com/places/camp-hayden-abandoned-wwii-bunker.

4. John Norah Gaudin, interview by author, February 25, 1995, Los Angeles.

5. Earl Barthé quoted in Jonn Ethan Hankins and Steven Maklansky, *Raised to the Trade: Creole Building Arts of New Orleans* (New Orleans: Historic New Orleans Collection, 2002), 119.

6. Gaudin, interview.

7. Mark Broyard, "To Miss New Orleans: How a Transplanted Creole Community Made LA Home," *LAist,* June 9, 2023, https://laist.com/news/essays/to-miss-new-orleans-how-a-transplanted-creole-community-made-la-home.

8. Broyard, "To Miss New Orleans."

9. Bernard Brulé quoted in Elizabeth Mullener, "California Creole" (part 2), *Dixie,* May 20, 1984, 12.

10. Leonard Tureaud quoted in Mullener, "California Creole" (part 2), 20.

11. Rita Roux Gaudin, interview by author, June 18, 1999, Los Angeles.

12. S. Sukardi, "The Birth and Death of a Name," Autostraddle, May 26, 2021, https://www.autostraddle.com/the-birth-and-death-of-a-name/.

13. For more about racism in California, see Aparajita Nanda, *Black California: A Literary Anthology* (Berkeley: Heyday Books, 2011).

14. Marie Leday quoted in Ginger Thompson, "Spicy Parties Set Tone for Creoles' Life in Southland," *Los Angeles Times,* February 5, 1989, 5.

15. Broyard, "To Miss New Orleans."

16. "Hi Y'all," *Bayou Talk,* October 1987, 1.

17. "Autocrat West," *Bayou Talk,* October 1988, 6.

18. "Jolly Jokers," *Bayou Talk,* October 1988

19. "Bon Ton Social Club," *Bayou Talk,* October 1988.

20. Tyina Steptoe, "When Louisiana Creoles Arrived in Texas, Were They Black or White?" Zocalo Public Square, December 15, 2015, https://www.zocalopublicsquare.org/2015/12/15/when-louisiana-creoles-arrived-in-texas-were-they-black-or-white/ideas/nexus/.

21. Broyard, "To Miss New Orleans."

22. Kim Lacy Rogers, *Righteous Lives: Narratives of the New Orleans Civil Rights Movement* (New York: NYU Press, 1993), 5–6.

23. For more on George Herriman, see Michael Tisserand, *Krazy: George Herriman, A Life in Black and White* (New York: Harper, 2016). For more on whiteness and ethnicity, see Matthew Frye Jacobson, *Whiteness of a Different Color* (Cambridge, MA: Harvard University Press, 1999).

24. Natasha Trethewey, "Letter Home," *Bellocq's Ophelia* (Minneapolis: Graywolf Press, 2002), 7.

25. Audrey Garnier Baquet, interview by author, June 25, 1999, New Orleans.

26. Audrey Garnier Baquet, interview.

27. Allyson Hobbs, *A Chosen Exile: A History of Racial Passing in American Life* (Cambridge, MA: Harvard University Press, 2016), 28.

28. For more on the civil rights movement in Louisiana, see Adam Fairclough, *Race and Democracy: The Civil Rights Struggle in Louisiana, 1915–1972* (Athens: University of Georgia Press, 1995); Kim Lacy Rogers, *Righteous Lives: Narratives of the New Orleans Civil Rights Movement* (New York: NYU Press, 1995); Lee Sartain, *Invisible Activists: Women of the Louisiana NAACP and the Struggle for Civil Rights, 1915–1945* (Baton Rouge: Louisiana State University Press, 2007).

29. All Delery quotes throughout are attributed to Ferdinand Delery Jr. Interview by author, March 6, 2002, New Orleans.

30. Harold Baquet quoted in Lynell George, "Who's Your People? Mixing with the Creoles of L.A.," *LA Weekly*, November 13–19, 1992, 27.

## 6. TAXONOMY

1. For a history of the San Fernando Valley, see Laura A. Barraclough, *Making the San Fernando Valley: Rural Landscapes, Urban Development, and White Privilege* (Athens: University of Georgia Press, 2011).

2. For more on Jewish settlement patterns in Los Angeles, see Jonathan L. Friedmann, *Jewish Los Angeles* (Charleston: Arcadia Publishing, 2020).

3. Viet Thanh Nguyen, *A Man of Two Faces* (New York: Grove Press), 260–61.

4. Being the child of a scientist helped me see that scientific inquiry was part of my, and our, heredity. This is beautifully written about in Chanda Prescod-Weinstein, *The Disordered Cosmos: A Journey into Dark Matter, Spacetime, and Dreams Deferred* (New York: Bold Type Books, 2021).

5. For more on the histories of free men of color in Louisiana, see Sybil Kein, *Creole: The History and Legacy of Louisiana's Free People of Color* (Baton Rouge: Louisiana State University Press, 2000).

6. Natasha Trethewey, *The House of Being* (New Haven: Yale University Press, 2024), 19.

## 7. THE HABIT AND THE GHOST SHIRT

1. Marie Fazio, "From Sacred to Secular: What Happens When a Catholic Church Shuts Down?" *Chicago Tribune,* June 28, 2019, https://www.chicagotribune.com/2019/06/28/from-sacred-to-secular-what-happens-when-a-catholic-church-shuts-down/.

2. All quotes attributed to Eleanor Marietta Burns (Gaudin) are taken from unrecorded conversations.

3. Sandy Banks, "Pioneers of LAUSD Desegregation," *Los Angeles Times,* February 11, 2012, https://www.latimes.com/local/la-xpm-2012-feb-11-la-me-banks-20120211-story.html.

4. Nguyen *A Man of Two Faces,* 275.

5. Luxenberg, *Separate,* 406.

## 8. A WORK OF FICTION

1. For more on New Orleans and Louisiana literature, see T. R. Johnson, *New Orleans: A Literary History* (New York: Cambridge University Press, 2019); Mathe Allain, *Louisiana Literature and Literary Figures* (Lafayette: University of Louisiana Press, 2004).

2. I want to note here that there is a large body of Caribbean literature that also represents "Creole" in different ways. Depending on the nationality and the cultural definitions of these terms, some authors distinguish white Creoles from Creoles of Color, other authors only use Creole to describe a person of European ancestry, and still others recognize Creole as a language that is not necessarily tied to any race or color.

3. Lafcadio Hearn, "Los Criollos," quoted in Frederick Starr, *Inventing New Orleans: Writings of Lafcadio Hearn* (Oxford: University of Mississippi Press, 2001), 31.

4. Alice Dunbar-Nelson quoted in Kein, *Creole,* 8–9.

5. Edward Laroque Tinker, *Toucoutou* (New York: Dodd, Mead, and Co., 1928), 8.

6. Allison Davis and John Dollard, *Children of Bondage: The Personality Development of Negro Youth in the Urban South* (New York: Harper and Row, 1940), 127.

7. Lyle Saxon, *Gumbo Ya-Ya* (Boston: Houghton Mifflin, 1945), 139.

8. Saxon, *Gumbo Ya-Ya,* 158.

9. Anne Rice, *The Feast of All Saints* (New York: Ballantine Books, 1991), back of paperback edition.

10. Rice, *Feast of All Saints,* 11–12.

11. Rice, *Feast of All Saints* 14.

12. Rice, *Feast of All Saints* 13.

13. For different interpretations of quadroon balls and *plaçage,* see Kenneth Aslakon, "The 'Quadroon-Plaçage Myth of Antebellum New Orleans: Anglo-American (Mis)interpretations of a French-Caribbean Phenomenon," *Journal of Social History* 45, no. 3 (Spring 2012), 709–34; Monique Guillory, "Under One Roof: The Sins and Sanctity of the New Orleans Quadroon Balls," in *Race Consciousness: Reinterpretations for the New Century* (New York: NYU Press, 1997), 67–92.

14. For histories of enslaved women, see Stephanie M. H. Camp, *Closer to Freedom: Enslaved Women and Everyday Resistance in the Plantation South* (Chapel Hill: University of North Carolina Press, 2004); Alexandra J. Finley, *The Intimate Economy: Enslaved Women, Work, and America's Domestic Slave Trade* (Chapel Hill: University of North Carolina Press, 2020); Marisa J. Fuentes, *Dispossessed Lives: Enslaved Women and the Archive* (Philadelphia: University of Pennsylvania Press, 2018).

15. Christina Sharpe, *In the Wake: On Blackness and Being* (Durham, NC: Duke University Press, 2016), 74.

16. Sophie White, *Voices of the Enslaved: Love, Labor, and Longing in French Louisiana* (Chapel Hill: University of North Carolina Press, 2019).

17. For more about the history of slave trading in the city of New Orleans, see Walter Johnson, *Soul by Soul: Life inside the Antebellum Slave Market* (Cambridge, MA: Harvard University Press, 1999).

18. Johnson, *Soul by Soul,* 152–58.

19. Johnson, *Soul by Soul,* 157–58.

20. Alecia P. Long, *The Great Southern Babylon: Sex, Race, and Respectability in New Orleans, 1865–1920* (Baton Rouge: Louisiana State University Press, 2004), 2. For more about the monetization of enslaved Black women and girls, including those called "Fancies," see Emily A. Owens, *Consent in the Presence of Force: Sexual Violence and Black Women's Survival in Antebellum New Orleans* (Chapel Hill: University of North Carolina Press, 2023).

21. Emily Clark, *The Strange History of the American Quadroon: Free Women of Color in the Revolutionary Atlantic World* (Chapel Hill: University of North Carolina Press, 2015), 66–70.

22. Clark, *Strange History,* 136–37.

23. Evans Wall, *The No-Nation Girl* (New York: Century Co., 1929), 12, 16.

24. Tinker, *Toucoutou,* 87.

25. For discussion of the so-called Toucoutou case, see Shirley Elizabeth Thompson, *Exiles at Home: The Struggle to Become American in Creole New Orleans* (Cambridge, MA: Harvard University Press, 2009).

26. Lyle Saxon, *Children of Strangers* (Boston: Houghton Mifflin, 1937), 6.

27. Saxon, *Children of Strangers,* 294.

28. Rice, *Feast of All Saints,* 15.

29. Rice, *Feast of All Saints* 571.

30. Ulysses Ricard, quoted in *The Creole Controversy,* produced by Karen Snyder for WYES-TV, 1989, videocassette.

31. Alexander Pierre Tureaud, interview by Joseph Logsdon, A. P. Tureaud Collection, University of New Orleans, Special Collections, acquisition #164, box #1, 13–14, 17–18.

32. John O. Sarpy, *A Slave, a Frenchman, and the Blood of a Saint: A Story of the Cane River Creoles and the Introduction of the Sarpys into the Metoyer Family Line* (Shreveport, LA: Sarpy Publishing, 2001), 63.

33. Maurice Martinez, "Rainbow People: Creoles of Color and the Colored-Caucasian Syndrome in New Orleans," in *Perspectives on Ethnicity in New Orleans* (New Orleans: Committee on Ethnicity in New Orleans, 1980), 48.

## 9. MOUNDS

1. Richard Grant, *The Deepest South of All: True Stories from Natchez, Mississippi* (New York: Simon & Schuster, 2020).

2. Boyce Upholt, "Monuments upon the Tumultuous Earth," *Emergence Magazine*, March 23, 2023, https://emergencemagazine.org/essay/monuments-upon-the-tumultuous-earth/.

3. Kristina Kay Robinson, "Letter From New Orleans: Never Can Say Goodbye," *Burnaway*, December 22, 2023, https://burnaway.org/magazine/letter-from-new-orleans-never-can-say-goodbye/.

4. Roxanne Gould and Jim Rock, "Wakan Tipi and Indian Mounds Park: Reclaiming an Indigenous Feminine Sacred Site," *AlterNative: An International Journal of Indigenous Peoples* 12 (3): 224–235, 2016.

5. Gould and Rock, "Wakan Tipi and Indian Mounds Park," 224–35.

6. Jake Skeets, "The Memory Field: Musings on the Diné Perspective of Time, Memory, and Land," *Emergence Magazine*, October 14, 2020, https://emergencemagazine.org/essay/the-memory-field/.

7. Skeets, "The Memory Field."

8. Margaret Wickens Pearce, quoted in "What Is Bulbancha?"

9. LSU Campus Mounds, https://www.lsu.edu/mounds/index.php.

10. Gould and Rock, "Wakan Tipi and Indian Mounds Park."

11. For more on the history of the Rhythm Nightclub Fire, see Karen L. Cox, "'The Rhythm Club Is on Fire!' Tragedy Devastated Young Black Natchez in 1940," *Mississippi Free Press*, April 21, 2023, https://www.mississippifreepress.org/32719/rhythm-night-club-fire-natchez-1940.

12. Imani Perry, *South to America: A Journey below the Mason-Dixon to Understand the Soul of a Nation* (New York: Harper Collins, 2022), 322.

## 10. "MY FATHER WAS A FRENCH DOCTOR"

1. For more on the histories and the historiography of plantations along the Lower Mississippi River, see Laura Kilcer VanHuss, ed., *Charting the Plantation Landscape from Natchez to New Orleans* (Baton Rouge: Louisiana State University Press, 2021); "Plantations on the Mississippi River, from Natchez to New Orleans, 1858," https://www.loc.gov/item/78692178.

2. Joseph Meredith Toner Collection, Historical Collections of Louisiana: Embracing Translations of Many Rare and Valuable Documents Relating to the Natural, Civil and Political History of That State, edited B. F. by French (New York: Wiley and Putnam; etc., et-53, 1846), www.loc.gov/item/02002986/. Code 59 is quoted here.

3. Dorothy Dapremont Daste, interview by author, July 20, 1999, New Orleans.

4. For more on histories of Francophone and Anglophone populations in colonial Louisiana, see Gwendolyn Midlo Hall, *Africans in Colonial Louisiana: The Development of Afro-Creole Culture in the Eighteenth Century* (Baton Rouge: Louisiana State University Press, 1995).

5. For histories of Cajuns, see Shane K. Bernard, *The Cajuns: Americanization of a People* (Jackson: University Press of Mississippi, 2003); Maria Hebert-Leiter, *Becoming Cajun,*

*Becoming American: The Acadian in American Literature from Longfellow to James Lee Burke* (Baton Rouge: Louisiana State University Press, 2009).

6. Steptoe, "When Louisiana Creoles Arrived in Texas, Were They Black or White?"

7. Michel-Rolph Trouillot, *Silencing the Past: Power and the Production of History* (Boston: Beacon Press, 1995), 25.

8. Verdin, *Return to Yakni Chitto,* 7.

9. For Indigenous histories of the Deep South and the Gulf Coast, see Elizabeth N. Ellis, *The Great Power of Small Nations: Indigenous Diplomacy in the Gulf South* (Philadelphia: University of Pennsylvania Press, 2022); Jacob F. Lee, *Masters of the Middle Waters: Indian Nations and Colonial Ambitions along the Mississippi* (Cambridge, MA: Belknap Press, 2019); Tim Alan Garrison and Greg O'Brien, *The Native South: New Histories and Enduring Legacies* (Lincoln: University of Nebraska Press, 2017).

10. Jack E. Davis, *The Gulf: The Making of an American Sea* (New York: Liveright, 2017), 52.

11. For histories of French colonials and their interactions with Indigenous peoples in Louisiana, see Sophie White, *Wild Frenchmen and Frenchified Indians: Material Culture and Race in Colonial Louisiana* (Philadelphia: University of Pennsylvania Press, 2012).

12. Joan DeJean, *Mutinous Women: How French Convicts Became Founding Mothers of the Gulf Coast* (New York: Basic Books, 2022), 3.

13. Deloria, "When Tribal Nations Expel Their Black Members."

14. Richard Campanella, "The Louisiana Sugar & Rice Exchange, 1884–1963," Preservation Resource Center of New Orleans, February 11, 2018, https://prcno.org/louisiana-sugar-rice-exchange-1884-1963/.

## 11. MISS AUDREY'S WORLD

1. Some quotes are attributed to Audrey Garnier Baquet, interview by author, June 25, 1999, New Orleans. Others were remembered and taken from unrecorded conversations with Baquet, 1999–2003.

2. Dao Strom, "Dao Strom: From the Other Shore," *diaCRITICS,* July 7, 2014, https://dvan.org/2014/07/dao-strom-shore/?mc_cid=9299bd22f1&mc_eid=b156ef4b9b.

3. Strom, "Dao Strom: From the Other Shore."

4. Hope Wakube, "Charles Blow's 'The Devil You Know' Is a Black Power Manifesto for Our Time," Review of *The Devil You Know: A Black Power Manifesto,*" NPR, January 26, 2021, https://www.npr.org/2021/01/26/960665185/charles-blow-s-the-devil-you-know-is-a-black-power-manifesto-for-our-time.

5. Some quotes are attributed to Mercedes Prograis Barthe, interview by author, June 28, 1999, New Orleans. Others were remembered and taken from unrecorded conversations with Barthe, 1999–2003.

6. For more on different forms of racial passing, see Hobbs, *A Chosen Exile.*

7. Some quotes attributed to J. G., interview by author, March 1, 2002, New Orleans. Others were remembered and taken from unrecorded conversations with J. G. and T. G., 2001–2003.

8. Adam Fairclough, *Race and Democracy: The Civil Rights Struggle in Louisiana, 1915–1972* (Athens: University of Georgia Press, 1999) 383.

9. Perry, *South to America,* 331.

10. Lawrence Winnier, interview by author, March 11, 2002, New Orleans.

11. Saidiya Hartman, "A Journal along the Atlantic Slave Route: An Essay," *Narrative,* Winter 2007, https://www.narrativemagazine.com/issues/winter-2007/nonfiction/journey-along-atlantic-slave-route-saidiya-hartman.

## 12. TOPOPHILIA

1.Winnie Ancar, interview by author, June 12, 2002, Diamond, Louisiana.

2. "2004 Goldman Prize Winner Margie Richard," Goldman Environmental Foundation, https://www.goldmanprize.org/recipient/margie-richard/#:~:text=Richard%2C%20whose%20campaign%20has%20been,win%20the%20Goldman%20Environmental%20Prize..

3. For more on Atlantic Creoles, see Jane G. Landers, *Atlantic Creoles in the Age of Revolutions* (Cambridge, MA: Harvard University Press, 2010).

4. Monique Verdin quoted in *My Louisiana Love,* directed by Sharon Linezo Hong. Vision Maker Media, 2012.

5. Kristina Kay Robinson, "Ten Years Since: A Meditation on New Orleans," *The Nation,* August 13, 2015, https://www.thenation.com/article/archive/ten-years-since-a-meditation-on-new-orleans/.

6. Robinson, "Ten Years Since."

7. Natasha Trethewey, *Beyond Katrina: A Meditation on the Mississippi Gulf Coast* (Athens: University of Georgia Press, 2010), 63.

8. Robinson, "Ten Years Since."

9. Lucile Guidry, "Accessing an Elevated Home Using Elevators and Lifts," LSU Ag Center, https://www.lsuagcenter.com/topics/family_home/home/design_construction/construction/foundation%20floors%20roof%20walls/foundation%20floors/elevated%20first%20floor/accessing-an-elevated-home-using-elevators-and-lifts.

## 13. ANOTHER COUNTRY

1. For more on the experiences of Amerasians in Vietnam, see Robert S. McKelvey, *The Dust of Life: America's Children Abandoned in Vietnam* (Seattle: University of Washington Press, 1999).

2. For more on the migration of Vietnamese Amerasians to the United States, see Thomas A. Bass, *Vietnamerica: The War Comes Home* (New York: Soho Press, 2003).

3. For more on the gendered colonial imagination, see Suzanne Bost, *Mulattas and Mestizas: Representing Mixed Identities in the Americas, 1850–2000* (Athens: University of Georgia Press, 2003) and Marilyn Grace Miller, *Rise and Fall of the Cosmic Race: The Cult of Mestizaje in Latin America* (Austin: University of Texas Press, 2009).

4. For more on mixed-race Franco-Vietnamese, see Emmanuelle Saada, *Empire's Children: Race, Filiation, and Citizenship in the French Colonies* (Chicago: University of Chicago Press, 2011); Milkie Vu, "'Ménages irréguliers': Interracial Liaisons in Colonial Indochina, 1905–1938." *History of the Family* 23, no. 1 (2017): 154–74.

5. For histories of Amerasian children and their mothers, see Steven DeBonis, *Children of the Enemy: Oral Histories of Vietnamese Amerasians and Their Mothers* (Jefferson, NC: McFarland and Co.).

## 14. TIME IS A WHEEL

1. Trouillot, *Silencing the Past,* 33.

2. For more on St. Domingue and Haitian historical sites, see Mapping Haitian History, https://www.mappinghaitianhistory.com/.

3. Clark, *A Luminous Brotherhood,* 173–74.

4. Rogers, *Righteous Lives,* 8.

5. Carmelo Larose, "Documenting Haiti after the Earthquake," *DOCUMENT Journal,* February 7, 2018, https://www.documentjournal.com/2018/02/documenting-haiti-earthquake/.

6. "Edwidge Danticat, 2010," *Literary Arts,* April 22, 2010, https://literary-arts.org/archive/edwidge-danticat/.

## CONCLUSION

1. DeJean, *Mutinous Women,* 368.

# BIBLIOGRAPHY


Bass, Thomas A. *Vietnamerica: The War Comes Home.* New York: Soho Press, 2003.

Bates, Beth Tompkins. *Pullman Porters and the Rise of Protest Politics in Black America, 1925–1945.* Chapel Hill: University of North Carolina Press, 2001.

Behar, Ruth. *An Island Called Home: Returning to Jewish Cuba.* New Brunswick, NJ: Rutgers University Press, 2007.

———. *Traveling Heavy: A Memoir in between Journeys.* Durham, NC: Duke University Press, 2014.

Bell, Caryn Cossé. *Revolution, Romanticism, and the Afro-Creole Protest Tradition in Louisiana, 1718–1868.* Baton Rouge: Louisiana State University Press, 1997.

Bost, Suzanne. *Mulattas and Mestizas: Representing Mixed Identities in the Americas, 1850–2000.* Athens: University of Georgia Press, 2003.

Brand, Dionne. *A Map to the Door of No Return: Notes to Belonging.* Toronto: Vintage Canada, 2023 (reprint).

Broyard, Bliss. *One Drop: My Father's Hidden Life—A Story of Race and Family Secrets.* New York: Back Bay Books, 2008.

Clark, Emily. *A Luminous Brotherhood: Afro-Creole Spiritualism in Nineteenth-Century New Orleans.* Chapel Hill: University of North Carolina Press, 2016.

———. *The Strange History of the American Quadroon: Free Women of Color in the Revolutionary Atlantic World.* Chapel Hill: University of North Carolina Press, 2013.

Danticat, Edwidge. *The Butterfly's Way: Voices from the Haitian Dyaspora in the United States.* New York: Soho Press, 2001.

Daut, Marlene L. *Tropics of Haiti: Race and the Literary History of the Haitian Revolution in the Atlantic World, 1789–1865.* Liverpool: Liverpool University Press, 2015.

Davis, Jack E. *The Gulf: The Making of an American Sea.* New York: Liveright, 2017.

———. *Race against Time: Culture and Separation in Natchez since 1930.* Baton Rouge: Louisiana State University Press, 2004.

DeBonis, Steven. *Children of the Enemy: Oral Histories of Vietnamese Amerasians and Their Mothers.* Jefferson, NC: McFarland and Co., 2013.

Deggs, Sister Mary Bernard. *No Cross, No Crown: Black Nuns in Nineteenth-Century New Orleans.* Bloomington: Indiana University Press, 2002.

DeJean, Joan. *Mutinous Women: How French Convicts Became Founding Mothers of the Gulf Coast.* New York: Basic Books, 2022.

Edwards, Erika Denise. *Hiding in Plain Sight: Black Women, the Law, and the Making of a White Argentine Republic.* Tuscaloosa: University of Alabama Press, 2021.

Ellis, Elizabeth N. *The Great Power of Small Nations: Indigenous Diplomacy in the Gulf South.* Philadelphia: University of Pennsylvania Press, 2022.

Fairclough, Adam. *Race and Democracy: The Civil Rights Struggle in Louisiana, 1915–1972.* Athens: University of Georgia Press, 2008.

Farmer, Paul. *Haiti after the Earthquake.* New York: PublicAffairs, 2011.

Fuentes, Marisa J. *Dispossessed Lives: Enslaved Women, Violence, and the Archive.* Philadelphia: University of Pennsylvania Press, 2016.

Gaines, Ernest J. *Catherine Carmier.* New York: Vintage Press, 1964.

Garrigus, John D. *Before Haiti: Race and Citizenship in French Saint-Domingue.* New York: Palgrave McMillan, 2006.

Grant, Richard. *The Deepest South of All: True Stories from Natchez, Mississippi.* New York: Simon & Schuster, 2020.

Hale, Grace Elizabeth. *In the Pines: A Lynching, a Lie, a Reckoning.* New York: Little, Brown, and Co., 2023.

Hall, Gwendolyn Midlo. *Africans in Colonial Louisiana: The Development of Afro-Creole Culture in the Eighteenth Century.* Baton Rouge: Louisiana State University Press, 1995.

Hankins, Jonn Ethan, and Steven Maklansky. *Raised to the Trade: Creole Building Arts of New Orleans.* New Orleans: Historic New Orleans Collection, 2002.

Hartman, Saidiya. *Lose Your Mother: A Journey along the Atlantic Slave Route.* New York: Farrar, Straus and Giroux, 2008.

Hill, Arden Eli. *Bloodwater Parish.* Cincinnati: Seven Kitchens Press, 2022.

Hoang, Carina. *Boat People: Personal Stories from the Vietnamese Exodus, 1975–1996.* New York: Beaufort Books, 2013.

Hobbs, Allyson. *A Chosen Exile: A History of Racial Passing in American Life.* Cambridge, MA: Harvard University Press, 2016.

Hodes, Martha. *My Hijacking: A Personal History of Forgetting and Remembering.* New York: HarperCollins, 2023.

Johnson, Jessica Marie. *Wicked Flesh: Black Women, Intimacy, and Freedom in the Atlantic World.* Philadelphia: University of Pennsylvania Press, 2020.

Johnson, Rashauna. *Slavery's Metropolis: Unfree Labor in New Orleans during the Revolutions.* Cambridge: Cambridge University Press, 2016.

Johnson, Walter. *Soul by Soul: Life inside the Antebellum Slave Market.* Cambridge, MA: Harvard University Press, 2001.

Andrew Jolivette. *Louisiana Creoles: Cultural Recovery and Mixed-Race Native American Identity.* New York: Lexington Books, 2007.

Joseph, Ralina L. *Transcending Blackness: From the New Millennium Mulatta to the Exceptional Multiracial.* Durham, NC: Duke University Press, 2012.

Kein, Sybil. *Creole: The History and Legacy of Louisiana's Free People of Color.* Baton Rouge: Louisiana State University Press, 2000.

Lam, Andrew. *Perfume Dreams: Reflections on the Vietnamese Diaspora.* Berkeley: Heyday Press, 2019.

Landers, Jane G. *Atlantic Creoles in the Age of Revolutions.* Cambridge, MA: Harvard University Press, 2010.

Lee, Jacob F. *Masters of the Middle Waters: Indian Nations and Colonial Ambitions along the Mississippi.* Cambridge, MA: Belknap Press, 2019.

Lewis, Mel Michelle. *Biomythography Bayou.* Lewisburg, PA: Bucknell University Press, 2025.

Long, Alecia P. *The Great Southern Babylon: Race, Sex, and Respectability in New Orleans, 1865–1920.* Baton Rouge: Louisiana State University Press, 2005.

Luxenberg, Steve. *Separate: The Story of* Plessy v. Ferguson, *and America's Journey from Slavery to Segregation.* New York: W. W. Norton, 2020.

McKelvey, Robert S. *The Dust of Life: America's Children Abandoned in Vietnam.* Seattle: University of Washington Press, 1999.

Miller, Marilyn Grace. *Rise and Fall of the Cosmic Race: The Cult of Mestizaje in Latin America.* Austin: University of Texas Press, 2009.

Murphy, Tessa. *The Creole Archipelago: Race and Borders in the Colonial Caribbean.* Philadelphia: University of Pennsylvania Press, 2021.

Nguyễn, Eric. *Things We Lost to the Water.* New York: Knopf, 2021.

Nguyễn, Phan Quế Mai. *Dust Child: A Novel.* Chapel Hill, NC: Algonquin Books, 2023.

Nguyen, Viet Thanh. *A Man of Two Faces: A Memoir, a History, a Memorial.* New York: Grove Press, 2023.

———. *The Refugees.* New York: Grove Press, 2017.

O'Hearn, Claudine Chiawei. *Half and Half: Writers on Growing up Biracial and Bicultural.* New York: Pantheon, 1998.

Owens, Emily A. *Consent in the Presence of Force: Sexual Violence and Black Women's Survival in Antebellum New Orleans.* Chapel Hill: University of North Carolina Press, 2023.

Painter, Nell Irvin, *The History of White People.* New York: W. W. Norton, 2011.

Parham, Angel Adams. *American Routes: Racial Palimpsests and the Transformation of Race*. Oxford: Oxford University Press, 2017.

Perata, David D. *Those Pullman Blues: An Oral History of the African American Railroad Attendant*. Woodbridge, CT: Twayne Publishers, 1996.

Perry, Imani. *South to America: A Journey below the Mason-Dixon to Understand the Soul of a Nation*. New York: HarperCollins, 2022.

Phan, Aimee. *We Should Never Meet: Stories*. New York: St. Martin's Press, 2005.

Powell, Lawrence N. *The Accidental City: Improvising New Orleans*. Cambridge, MA: Harvard University Press, 2013.

Rice, Anne. *The Feast of All Saints*. New York: Ballantine Books, 1979.

Rogers, Kim Lacy. *Righteous Lives: Narratives of the New Orleans Civil Rights Movement*. New York: NYU Press, 1995.

Root, Maria P. P. *Racially Mixed People in America*. New York: Sage, 1992.

Shaik, Fatima. *Economy Hall: The Hidden History of a Free Black Brotherhood*. New Orleans: Historic New Orleans Collection, 2021.

Sharpe, Christina. *In the Wake: On Blackness and Being*. Durham, NC: Duke University Press, 2016.

Shigematsu, Stephen Murphy. *When Half Is Whole: Multiethnic Asian American Identities*. Redwood City, CA: Stanford University Press, 2012.

Smith, Clint. *How the Word Is Passed: A Reckoning with the History of Slavery across America*. New York: Little, Brown, and Co., 2021.

Strom, Dao. *You Will Always Be Someone from Somewhere Else*. Hanoi: AJAR Press, 2018.

Sussman, Robert Wald. The Myth of Race: The Troubling Persistence of an Unscientific Idea. Cambridge, MA: Harvard University Press, 2016.

Thompson, Shirley Elizabeth. *Exiles at Home: The Struggle to Become American in Creole New Orleans*. Cambridge, MA: Harvard University Press, 2009.

Tisserand, Michael. *Krazy: George Herriman, A Life in Black and White*. New York: Harper, 2016.

Trethewey, Natasha. *Bellocq's Ophelia*. Minneapolis: Graywolf Press, 2002.

———. *Beyond Katrina: A Meditation on the Mississippi Gulf Coast*. Athens: University of Georgia Press, 2012.

———. *The House of Being*. New Haven, CT: Yale University Press, 2024.

———. *Thrall: Poems*. New York: HarperCollins, 2015.

Truong, Marcelino. *Such a Lovely Little War: Saigon, 1961–1963*. Vancouver: Arsenal Pulp Press, 2016.

Tye, Larry. *Rising From the Rails: Pullman Porters and the Making of the Black Middle Class*. New York: Holt s, 2005.

Upholt, Boyce. The Great River: The Making and Unmaking of the Mississippi. New York:W.W. Norton, 2024.

VanHuss, Laura Kilcer. *Charting the Plantation Landscape from Natchez to New Orleans.* Baton Rouge: Louisiana State University Press, 2021.

Verdin, Monique. *Return to Yakni Chitto: Houma Migrations.* New Orleans: University of New Orleans Press, 2019.

Vidal, Cécile. *Caribbean New Orleans: Empire, Race, and the Making of a Slave Society.* Chapel Hill: University of North Carolina Press, 2019.

White, Sophie. *Wild Frenchmen and Frenchified Indians: Material Culture and Race in Colonial Louisiana.* Philadelphia: University of Pennsylvania Press, 2012.

———. *Voices of the Enslaved: Love, Labor, and Longing in French Louisiana.* Chapel Hill: University of North Carolina Press, 2019.

Williams, Danielle Terrazas. *The Capital of Free Women: Race, Legitimacy, and Liberty in Colonial Mexico.* New Haven, CT: Yale University Press, 2022.